Ethics That Matters

Ethics That Matters

African, Caribbean, and African American Sources

Marcia Y. Riggs and James Samuel Logan, Editors

Fortress Press
Minneapolis

ETHICS THAT MATTERS
African, Caribbean, and African American Sources

Cover design: Laurie Ingram
Cover image: *Angel with Guitar* by Anthony Armstrong, copyright © Anthony Armstrong (www.armstrongart.net). Used by permission.
Book design: PerfecType, Nashville, TN

Library of Congress Cataloging-in-Publication Data
Ethics that matters : African, Caribbean, and African American sources / Marcia Y. Riggs and James Samuel Logan, editors.
    p. cm.
 Includes bibliographical references and indexes.
 ISBN 978-0-8006-1976-3 (alk. paper)
 1. Christian ethics. 2. Social ethics. 3. Blacks. I. Riggs, Marcia. II. Logan, James Samuel.
 BJ1275.E83 2011
 241—dc23
                         2011029715

Manufactured in the U.S.A.
15 14 13 12 1 2 3 4 5 6 7 8 9 10

Contents

Part One: Moral Dilemmas

Part Two: Moral Community

Contributors

Victor Anderson is professor of Christian ethics at Vanderbilt University Divinity School, with a joint appointment as professor of African American studies and religious studies in the College of Arts and Sciences. He is author of *Beyond Ontological Blackness: An Essay in African American Religious and Cultural Criticism* (1995); *Pragmatic Theology: Negotiating the Intersection of an American Philosophy of Religion and Public Theology* (1999); and *Creative Exchange: A Constructive Theology of African American Religious Experience* (Fortress Press, 2008).

Katie Geneva Cannon is the Annie Scales Rogers Professor of Christian Ethics at Union Presbyterian Seminary in Richmond, Va. In 1983 Cannon became the first African American woman to receive a PhD from Union Theological Seminary in New York City and was also the first African American woman to be ordained in the United Presbyterian Church (U.S.A.). She is the author or editor of numerous articles and seven books, including *Katie's Canon: Womanism and the Soul of the Black Community and Black Womanist Ethics* (1998).

James H. Cone is the Charles A. Briggs Distinguished Professor of Systematic Theology at Union Theological Seminary. Dr. Cone is best known for his groundbreaking works, *Black Theology and Black Power* (1969) and *A Black Theology of Liberation* (1970), as well as the highly acclaimed *God of the Oppressed* (1975), *Martin and Malcolm and America: A Dream or a Nightmare?* (1991), and, most recently, *Risks of Faith* (1999). An ordained minister in the African Methodist Episcopal Church, Dr. Cone's current research focuses on the cross and the lynching tree, exploring the relationship between the two theologically.

Lewis V. Baldwin is professor of religious studies at Vanderbilt University. Among his many publications are *There Is a Balm in Gilead: The Cultural Roots of Martin Luther King Jr.* (Fortress Press, 1991); *To Make the Wounded Whole: The Cultural Legacy of Martin Luther King Jr.* (Fortress Press, 1992); and *Toward the Beloved Community: Martin Luther King Jr. and South Africa* (1995). An ordained Baptist preacher, his most recent book is *Never to Leave Us Alone: The Prayer Life of Martin Luther King Jr.* (Fortress Press, 2010).

Riggins R. Earl Jr. is professor of ethics and theology at the Interdenominational Theological Center in Atlanta. His significant publications include *Dark Symbols, Obscure Signs: God, Self and Community in the Slave Mind* (2003); *Dark Salutations: Ritual, God, and Greetings in the African American Community* (2001); and *The Jesus as Lord and Savior Problem: Blacks' Double Consciousness Self-Worth Dilemma* (forthcoming). He is currently researching a book-length manuscript titled *Blacks, the Bible, and the Constitution*.

Noel Leo Erskine is professor of theology and ethics at Emory University's Candler School of Theology and Graduate Division of Religion, specializing in black theology and pedagogy, the history and development of the black church, and theological method in the work of James Cone, Karl Barth, Dietrich Bonhoeffer, and Martin Luther King Jr. His publications include *From Garvey to Marley: Rastafari Theology* (2005); *King Among the Theologians* (1994); *Decolonizing Theology: A Caribbean Perspective* (1981, 1998); and *Black People and the Reformed Church in America* (1978).

Melanie L. Harris is associate professor of religion at Texas Christian University in Ft. Worth. An ordained minister in the African Methodist Episcopal Church, she holds degrees from Union Theological Seminary, Iliff School of Theology, and Spelman College. As a former broadcast journalist, Dr. Harris worked as a television news producer and news writer for ABC, CBS, and NBC news affiliates in Atlanta and Denver. She is the author of *Gifts of Virtue: Alice Walker and Womanist Ethics* (2010).

Barbara A. Holmes is professor of ethics and African American studies at Memphis Theological Seminary, where she was formerly vice president of academic affairs and dean of the seminary. Ordained in the Latter Rain Apostolic Holiness Church in Dallas, she has privilege of call in the United Church of Christ and recognition of ministerial standing in the Christian Church (Disciples of Christ). Her most recent publications include *Liberation and the Cosmos: Conversations with the Elders* (Fortress Press, 2008) and *Joy Unspeakable: Contemplative Practices of the Black Church* (Fortress Press, 2004).

Dwight N. Hopkins is professor of theology in the University of Chicago Divinity School and senior editor of the Henry McNeil Turner/ Sojourner Truth Series in Black Religion. Among his many works are *Being Human: Race, Culture, and Religion* (Fortress Press, 2005); *Heart and Head: Black Theology—Past, Present, and Future* (2002); *Introducing Black Theology of Liberation* (1999); *Down, Up, and Over: Slave Religion and Black Theology* (Fortress Press, 1999); and *Shoes That Fit Our Feet: Sources for a Constructive Black Theology* (1993); as well as numerous edited and coedited volumes.

James Samuel Logan is associate professor of religion, and associate professor and director of African and African American Studies, at Earlham College. He earned an MA in theology and ethics from Associated Mennonite Biblical Seminary and a PhD in religion and society from Princeton Seminary. His publications include *Good Punishment? Christian Moral Practice and U.S. Imprisonment* (2008); "Liberalism, Race, and Stanley Hauerwas," *CrossCurrents* (Winter 2006); and "Immanuel Kant on Categorical Imperative," in *Beyond the Pale: Reading Christian Ethics From the Margins*, ed. Miguel De La Torre and Stacey Floyd-Thomas (forthcoming fall 2011).

Jacob K. Olupona is professor of African religious traditions at Harvard Divinity School, with a joint appointment as professor of African and African American studies in the Faculty of Arts and Sciences. His books include *Òrìsà Devotion as World Religion: The Globalization of Yorùbá Religious Culture* (coedited with Terry Rey, 2008), and *Kingship,*

Religion and Rituals in a Nigerian Community: A Phenomenological Study of Ondo Yoruba Festivals. A past president of the African Association for the Study of Religion (1991), his forthcoming book is *Ile-Ife: The City of 201 Gods.*

Anthony B. Pinn is the Agnes Cullen Arnold Professor of Humanities, Professor of Religious Studies, and Director of Graduate Studies at Rice University. He is the author of numerous books including *What Is African American Religion?* (Fortress Press, 2011); *Terror and Triumph: The Nature of Black Religion* (Fortress Press, 2003); *Varieties of African American Religious Experience* (Fortress Press, 1998); *The Black Church in the Post–Civil Rights Era* (2002); *Why, Lord? Suffering and Evil in Black Theology* (1999); and *African American Humanist Principles: Living and Thinking Like the Children of Nimrod* (2004).

Marcia Y. Riggs is the J. Erskine Love Professor of Christian Ethics at Columbia Theological Seminary in Decatur, Ga., and director of the ThM program. She is a recognized authority on the black woman's club movement of the nineteenth century, the subject of her first book, *Awake, Arise, and Act! A Womanist Call for Black Liberation* (1994). Her other books include *Can I Get A Witness? Prophetic Religious Voices of African American Women, An Anthology* (1997), and *Plenty Good Room: Black Women Versus Male Power in the Black Church* (2008).

Rosetta E. Ross is professor of religious studies at Spelman College in Atlanta. Her research and writing explore the role of religion in black women's activism and focuses particularly on the civil rights movement. She is author of *Witnessing and Testifying: Black Women, Religion, and Civil Rights* (Fortress Press, 2003), which examines religion as a source that helped engender and sustain activities of seven black women civil rights leaders. Ross's current research explores compassion and common sense in private and public life.

Emilie M. Townes is the associate dean of academic affairs and Andrew W. Mellon Professor of African American Religion and Theology at Yale University Divinity School with joint appointments in Yale University's

African American studies department, religious studies department, and the Women, Gender, and Sexuality program. A past president of the American Academy of Religion, her books include *Womanist Ethics and the Cultural Production of Evil* (2006); *Breaking the Fine Rain of Death: African American Health Issues and a Womanist Ethic of Care* (2006); *Womanist Justice, Womanist Hope* (1993); and *In a Blaze of Glory: Womanist Spirituality as Social Witness* (1995).

Jonathan L. Walton is assistant professor of African American religions at Harvard University Divinity School, specializing in African American religious studies; religion, politics, media, and culture; and Christian social ethics. Walton's scholarly work is grounded in the progressive strand of the African American religious tradition and informed by the creative potentiality and rhythmic sensibility of hip-hop culture. His first book is *Watch This! The Ethics and Aesthetics of African American Religious Broadcasting* (2009).

Traci C. West is professor of ethics and African American studies at Drew University Theological School, Madison, N.J. She is author of *Disruptive Christian Ethics: When Racism and Women's Lives Matter* (2006); *Wounds of the Spirit: Black Women, Violence, and Resistance Ethics* (1999), and editor of *Our Family Values: Same-Sex Marriage and Religion* (2006). An ordained elder in the New York Annual Conference of the United Methodist Church, she has also written several articles on violence against women, racism, clergy ethics, sexuality, and other justice issues in church and society.

Introduction

Marcia Y. Riggs and James Samuel Logan

SOCIAL ETHICS IS DESCRIPTIVE, analytical, and normative reflection upon the complex dimensions of social life. Ethicists are doing social ethics whenever we describe and analyze our human experiences in social groups (race, ethnicity, gender, class) and systems (religious, educational, political, and economic) in order to propose norms that we hope will make our lives together in those groups and systems more just. In the twenty-first century the quest for more just social life is complicated by our ever-expanding acknowledgment of diverse human experiences, plural religious traditions, and global political and economic interdependence. Therefore, ethics that matters in the twenty-first century confronts difficult questions of survival for significant numbers of the earth's peoples, such as hunger, homelessness, poverty, the AIDS pandemic, human trafficking, terrorist violence, and environmental devastation. Religious social ethics in the twenty-first century must urgently propose norms for living life more abundantly and justly in response to such issues of survival.

Given the fact that two-thirds of the world's populations struggling to survive are people of color, the sources for these essays are African, Caribbean, and African American experiences. Thinking of these essays thus as sources for social ethical reflection, this text asserts that social ethics in the twenty-first century is grounded in these presuppositions of liberation ethics:

1. There is no objective or neutral perspective from which to do ethics.

2. The sources for doing ethical reflection are particular, historical, and contextual.
3. Ethical norms have universal relevance (contribute to larger moral meaning), but they cannot be universalized for all time.

In other words, in this volume the particular social, historical, political, and religious experiences of African, Caribbean, and African American peoples are the sources for social ethical reflection upon perennial questions asked by religious social ethicists, such as:

- What does it mean to be human and for humans to flourish in moral communities whose social contract is better understood as a covenant for just relationships?
- Who is our neighbor? What does it mean to love our neighbor next door and across the globe?
- What is the relationship between love and justice?
- How do we understand social sin and our complicity in it?
- What does it mean to be faithful Christians and good citizens?
- What is the relationship between belief in a sovereign God and human responsibility to work for social justice in the society and the world?

This text invites teachers and students to read these essays as sources for a social ethics that complexifies the meaning of and quest for social justice in the twenty-first century. In other words, social justice is not an abstract ethical ideal or philosophical concept; rather, what we *mean* by social justice emerges from the lived experiences—historical and contemporary—of particular peoples engaged in struggles to have meaningful and productive lives. In order for teachers and students of social ethics to use the volume as a textbook that provides resources for thinking about contemporary social issues, each part concludes with a list of key ideas, some resources, and questions that provide avenues from the essays into becoming a constructive religious social ethical thinker and agent in the twenty-first century. The essays are arranged in these four parts: (1) Moral Dilemmas, (2) Moral Community, (3) Moral Discourse, and (4) Moral Vision. Abstracts of the essays follow below.

Part One: Moral Dilemmas. This first part invites the reader to begin the journey toward becoming a constructive religious social ethical thinker by disclosing sources that challenge traditional interpretations of black spirituality, mission history, and indigenous religious sources. In the first essay, "Maps of Meaning: Black Bodies and African Spirituality as African Diaspora Trope," Anthony B. Pinn employs the conceptual tool of mapping to break with the conventional understanding that African spirituality needs to be grounded in divinity-based conceptions of religion. Pinn argues for a more complicated and nuanced understanding of African spirituality and religion that recognizes the nontheistic and mundane resources that have also contributed to the religious and moral ethos of black existence in the face of evil. Next, Katie Geneva Cannon's "Homecoming in the Hinterlands: Ethical Ministries of Mission in Nigeria" is about missions in Nigeria. Cannon presents "a discussion of the intersection of ethics and missions" that exposes the past harms of mission, its accommodation of imperial forms of power, and suggests a reappraisal of Christian mission in the twenty-first century. In "Women in Rastafari," Noel Leo Erskine traces the origins of Rastafari religion to the Great Revival Church of the 1860s in Jamaica so as to expose how a theological break with its own origins produced a religion that is an expression of African patriarchy in the Caribbean. As such, Rastafari religion is premised upon a gender inequality that belies the liberation sought by the Rastafarian transformation of "Babylon." Finally, in "Religious Pluralism in Africa: Insights from Ifa Divination Poetry," Jacob K. Olupona draws ethical insights from Ifa divination poetry by analyzing a series of textual vignettes from Ifa poetry that disclose an Ifa "ethics of tolerance." This ethic characterizes how indigenous religious tradition understands and engages Islam and Christianity in Africa. He suggests that the insights from this ethics of tolerance may shed light on the larger problem of "pluralism, religious interaction, and the role of religion in peaceful transnational coexistence." These four essays provide rich points of departure for discussion of moral dilemmas posed by religious pluralism, missions or global Christianity, the relationship between religious tradition and women's equality, and the quest for spiritual resources to address oppression in the twenty-first century.

Part Two: Moral Community. Riggins R. Earl Jr., in "The American Constitution: Its Troubling Religious and Ethical Paradox for Blacks," reminds readers that the U.S. Constitution has been a source undergirding both the oppression and liberation of blacks. Earl discusses the way in which the constitution as a social contract ensuring justice and equality for all citizens has functioned as a racial contract with respect to African Americans. Next, in "The Challenge of Race: A Theological Reflection," James H. Cone articulates the challenge that race poses for the discipline of theology, the life of Christian churches in U.S. society, and for others committed to lives of faith. Continuing to place race at the center of Christian identity while confronting white supremacy, Cone ultimately views the problem of race as a challenge to human faith in humanity itself. He contends that there are three interrelated challenges with regard to race in U.S. society: (1) the challenge to break our silence, (2) the challenge to listen meaningfully, and (3) the challenge to dismantle white supremacy. Dwight N. Hopkins's concluding essay, "Race, Religion, and the Race for the White House," is an exposé of this country's racist practices during the campaign to elect the nation's first African American president, Barack Obama. Hopkins speaks as a theologian about his experiences as a church member of Trinity United Church of Christ in Chicago. His essay offers insights into the role of media as well as the lack of historical and contemporary knowledge about African American social and religious history, factors which served to vilify the black church and its religious leadership. This part offers opportunities to think about how race in various sociopolitical, ethical, and theological dimensions has ruptured moral community in the United States. Readers will leave this section informed and challenged about the politics of race and religion in the United States and encouraged to break complicity in "the continuing American dilemma"[1] in a quest for authentic moral community.

Part Three: Moral Discourse. The first essay, "'Who is Their God?' A Critique of the Church Based on the Kingian Prophetic Model," by Lewis V. Baldwin, explicates the prophetic ecclesial model embodied in the leadership of Martin Luther King Jr. According to Baldwin, King's prophetic model is precisely what is needed in order to confront the contemporary Christian church's "identity and/or definitional" crisis. Baldwin concludes by offering "a number of steps" whereby the church might reclaim King's "prophetic vision and posture." Next, "Onward, Christian Solders! Race, Religion, and Nationalism in Post–Civil Rights America," by Jonathan L. Walton, is a descriptive and constructive evaluation of the ways in which conservative Christian broadcasters have developed and actively maintained a Christian nationalist worldview. Walton does a comparative analysis of the ministries of the late Reverend Jerry Falwell and Bishop Eddie L. Long as paradigmatic white and African American Christian nationalisms. He concludes by impressing upon us the need to take seriously the rhetoric of Christian nationalists if we as a society desire to have a stable and flourishing liberal democracy. Walton's essay is followed by Rosetta E. Ross's "Overcoming Christianization: Reconciling Spiritual and Intellectual Resources in African American Christianity." Here Ross explores a perennial conflict experienced in African American Christianity and the institutional black churches: the tensions between religion and politics. Ross proposes that reconciling tensions and conflicts around the appropriateness of political engagement by black Christians and churches is critical to the institutional relevance of black churches "to progressive movements that enhance the lives of persons, generally, and dispossessed black people in particular." She makes her case for reconciling the religion/politics tensions by appealing to the legacy of critical thinking and practical reasoning expressed in the civil rights activism of Septima Poinsette Clark and now evident in contemporary young progressives who refer to themselves as the "Joshua Generation." Part 3 concludes with an essay titled "A Moral Epistemology of Gender Violence," by Traci C. West. West gives voice to the conceptual and social breakdown between (1) society's near universal public certainty that gender violence is immoral and (2) an inability to translate that public disapproval into "ongoing social and institutional practices to stop it from taking place." Most significantly, West insists that communities find ways to translate antiviolence moral values into antiviolence public practices. These four essays push us to explore the relationship between moral language and moral practice. Moral language is always a socially constructed product of particular, historical, contextual circumstances. Moral practice reflects moral language. A significant twenty-first-century ethical task is to use moral language that fosters just and nonviolent moral practice in church and society.

Part Four: Moral Vision. This final part opens with the essay "An Eco-womanist Vision" by Melanie L. Harris, who proposes a "new theological inquiry into environmental ethics," ecowomanism. Harris grounds this new inquiry in an articulation of the correspondences between the womanist quest for "the communal survival and wholeness of entire peoples" and the advocacy of "vision and value of community" found in the Christian social ethics of Peter J. Paris. In "An American Public Theology in the Absence of Giants: Creative Conflict and Democratic Longings," Victor Anderson argues for the recovery of an American public theology as the basis of a common public faith that undergirds a truly democratic common life and organization of citizens in the context of our postmodern, fragmented times. Importantly, Anderson is not mired in a lament for the lost giants of the past. Instead, he suggests that it is the "faithful ordinary," local publics, who will now provide the conceptual and lived resources for an American public theology and the vision of a better democracy. Next, in "Walking on the Rimbones of Nothingness: Embodied Scholarship for Those of Us Way Down Under the Sun," Emilie M. Townes draws upon the work of Zora Neal Hurston (1891–1960) to highlight the importance of folklore for theological and ethical reflection. Townes suggests that Hurston's folklore provides a narrative context in which a recovery of the role of vision (or imagination) in black religion may be realized. In addition, Townes extends her argument by inviting scholars of religion and theology to do embodied scholarship, that is, scholarship done in partnership with everyday people. In the final essay, "Still on the Journey: Moral Witness, Imagination, and Improvisation in Public Life," Barbara A. Holmes calls all of us to public lives of care and concern in a post–civil rights, post-9/11, post-Katrina world. Holmes contends that moral witness to justice and truth is preserved in art. She pushes for a trust in human creativity and the regenerative presence and guidance of the Holy Spirit because this will lead to improvisation in public life. In her words: "Improvisation creates opportunities for laughter, community formation, and sharing, even while we continue the work of justice." These final essays bring us full circle to what may be the most critical ethical tasks in the twenty-first century: moral imagination and moral vision. Drawing upon African and African American sources, cognizant of the enduring impact of race, and speaking from the particularity of black faith, religion, literature, and art, these essays move through the descriptive and analytic tasks of doing ethics to the prescriptive task of self-consciously proposing norms. Each essay offers us moral visions and norms for transformation that speak out of and to the "souls of black folk"[2] as a way forward toward a moral community of justice for all peoples and the planet Earth.

PART ONE

Moral Dilemmas

Chapter 1

Maps of Meaning

Black Bodies and African Spirituality as African Diaspora Trope

Anthony B. Pinn

ONE MIGHT THINK OF the African Diaspora as drawn in, on, and through history, and in the process producing life maps.[1] These life maps that constitute the African Diaspora are drawn to various scales—from the personal to the communal, from the national to the transnational. Each, in its own way, speaks to the nature and meaning of human existence within the context of simple and complex interactions and exchanges.

One might also note the manner in which African American religious studies has entailed a particular attention to these life maps and what they say about the religio-theological concerns and commitments of peoples of African descent. While, within African American religious studies, one is more likely to find attention to these mappings as they relate to large-scale developments and communal-based trackings of change, it is important to recognize the connections between personal mappings and collective mappings. In this sense, scholarship related to the nature and meaning of African American life involves a type of layering—of producing greater detail, a richer cartography, through overlapping presentations.

It strikes me that Peter Paris's *The Spirituality of African Peoples* provides an example of this layering process, entailing both the personal and the communal. Paris, in his intellectual and personal geography, represents the reach of the Diaspora. Born in Canada, educated in the United States, and intellectually and emotionally drawn to the Caribbean and Africa, Paris's work marks an effort to recognize the overlapping nature of moral vision and ethical conduct. That is to say, Paris sees through academic concern and personal experience the shared cartography of contact and conquest that marks our world; and, as an ethicist, he seeks to develop a moral vocabulary and grammar for discussing and addressing the messy nature of human life. From his perspective—with which I would agree—discussion of the African Diaspora involves multidirectionality; it involves highlighting both the transnational nature of contact between Africans and Europeans as well as the impact of this contact and conquest on particular communities and individuals.

In what follows, I give attention to the theoretical significance of Paris's notion of "African spirituality" which undergirds his more recent work by arguing that his concept of spirituality serves as a useful trope by which to explore the linkages over time between various African peoples. Unlike other ways in which the African Diaspora is presented as a mode of analysis, Paris's offering foregrounds religion as a primary expression of world making by African peoples. However, I begin with a few questions concerning the shape and content—the particularities— of Paris's notion of religion as a common framework lodged within the larger conceptual arrangement of African spirituality. That is, I would like to say a few words concerning the manner in which Paris "reads" the religious.

Religion and African Peoples

For Paris, the religious message highlighted by the movement and positioning of peoples of Africa is clear and straightforward, and without significant variation from a general cosmic theme: people of African descent have been and continue to be defined by commitment to the idea of supernatural realities (e.g., god[s]). In his words, "One of the most important marks of continuity between Africans on the continent and those in the diaspora is their common belief in a transcendent divine power primordially related to them as the creature and preserver of all that is."[2] Whether defined in theistic, polytheistic, or henotheistic terms, for Paris Africans and African Americans are anything but atheistic in outlook. Why Paris might make this claim—the numerical dominance of divinity-based religious systems—is somewhat apparent; but does this logic really stem from the lived experience and commitments found within the African Diaspora?

"There are no atheists among them," he boldly proclaims.[3] (And, it is safe to believe, based on the blending of past and present in his writing, that Paris means by this a declarative statement covering all recorded time.) Really? How does one support such a claim? In light of Paris's assumption, what does one make for example of the posture of African leaders such as Kwame Nkrumah or Cheikh Anta Diop, who, some scholars argue, is humanistic in orientation? More to the point, what does one make of the humanist, agnostic, and atheistic sensibilities represented in certain examples of popular culture—such as some blues and folktales—found within the African Diaspora?[4] Is it reasonable to exclude from consideration nontheistic, agnostic, and atheistic orientations? And if so, based on what established and transparent criteria?

Paris is rightly concerned with presenting a phenomenology of religion as resistance against modalities of "structural racism"[5] experienced by African peoples; yet, is it reasonable to frame such resistance only within the context of divinity-based systems? Such a theory of unified religious outlook does not involve the "historical retrieval and reinterpretation" Paris deems vital to the promotion of personhood within a context of proper "social development." Rather, it might be said to entail a form of religious imperialism whereby the real thickness and variety of African/ African American religiosity is truncated. His sense of the religiosity of African peoples is based on the use of a particular hermeneutic that one might call the hermeneutic of the problem of evil. That is to say, implicit in Paris's recounting of the dread of structural racism is an assumption that severely oppressed peoples are only able to avoid total destruction, avoid nihilism, through the presence of more powerful forces working on their behalf. His is a narrow, theologically based formulation of the logic of struggle. In short, it suggests selective historical and cultural memory whereby the religious landscape of the African Diaspora is presented in a way that does not challenge Paris's perceptions.

In *The Spirituality of African Peoples*, Paris refers to Toni Morrison, but without noting her rather balanced depiction of historical-cultural memory. From Morrison's perspective, memory is rather fragile—premised on what we seek to retain and what we surrender (either by force or by choice).[6] Hence, what is known about the frames of life meaning(s) developed and embraced within the African Diaspora cannot be stated with lingering certainty. Therefore, Paris's hard-and-fast claims concerning the limited scope of religious (or "secular") commitments should be interrogated and challenged in that he assumes clarity without respect to what, if Morrison is taken seriously, cannot be known with certainty. That is to say, the manner in which divinity-based religious traditions dominate the landscape of African American communities does not suggest the nonexistence of alternative approaches that question, if not reject, divinity-based systems.

I would suggest the mechanisms of oppression resulted in a variety of creative and imaginative responses from people of African descent—some of which were divinity based and others that rejected such allegiances and instead sought life meaning(s) through a clear focus on the mundane. I would not argue for one approach over against another but, rather, that African peoples employed both theistic and nontheistic orientation as a way to make sense of the world. To suggest otherwise, I believe, involves a type of exclusionism—a cartography of life meaning that privileges certain formulations and in this way ignores the overlapping, conflicting, and "messy" religious arrangements that dot the landscape of the African Diaspora.

This is the source of dissonance within *The Spirituality of African Peoples*: Paris seeks a broad and flexible theory of life meaning(s), but limits this possibility through a grammar of religiosity that is rather fixed, and one that takes as paradigmatic a god(s)-centered framework.[7] In this sense, his posture might be read as a type of religious exceptionalist stance—a privileging of a divinity-based orientation to the exclusion of other possibilities.

There are common features of experience for peoples of African descent as they battle structural racism, and some of these linkages involve the "religious and moral ethos,"[8] as Paris puts it, associated with Africa. But that is not to say their quest for meaning (vis-à-vis religion) can be so easily defined as a unified commitment to cosmic forces.

Fortunately, this is not the primary selling point of Paris's project. In other words, the project's fundamental value is not found in his description of religion but in the larger and more abstract notion of African spirituality. And, I believe his notion of African spirituality as he defines it does not require acceptance of his description of religion.

African Diaspora and African Spirituality as Trope

I must note my critique of Paris's phenomenological presentation of religion is not meant to reject the significance of divinity-based orientations. His effort to retrieve the significance of religion within the African Diaspora is to be appreciated. My aim, therefore, is to put those orientations into a context of religious pluralism that recognizes strong difference. The focus of this short essay is not simply a refutation of Paris's rejection of the possibility of an African atheism (or humanism for that matter).

It seems to me "African spirituality" does not function well as a general concept of religiosity due to narrowness of definition. Yet, there is a manner in which it might function as a trope or conceptual arrangement for framing what has been called the African Diaspora. Mindful of this, I am interested in the manner through which his framing of the African Diaspora as African spirituality might provide a corrective to theorizations of the African Diaspora that tend to minimize the religious markings of that shared cartography of African peoples.

For instance, while Paul Gilroy has mapped this Diaspora by offering the "black Atlantic" as a vital "unit of analysis," he has failed to give sufficient attention to the place of Africa in the matrix and he tends to see the significance of cultural production such as African American music devoid of necessary connection to the religious and theological intent of certain musical forms.[9] On the first point, Gilroy focuses on the manner in which a cultural grid marks the American hemisphere (and Europe by extension). In his words,

Artistic expression, expanded beyond recognition from the grudg-
ing gifts offered by the masters as a token substitute for freedom
from bondage, therefore becomes the means towards both individual self-fashioning and communal liberation. Poises and poetics
begin to coexist in novel forms—autobiographical writing, special
and uniquely creative ways of manipulating spoken language, and,
above all, the music. All three have overflowed from the containers
that the modern nation/state provides for them.[10]

What Michelle Wallace notes in support of attention to the visual arts
can be extended: Much study of African American (or one might argue
diasporic) development privileges music and dwarfs the importance of
other cultural markers of meaning and identity.[11] Paris's turn to spirituality as trope does not restrict materials for examination and in that way
is free to interrogate a fuller range of sources for their meaning-making
importance.

While Gilroy's analysis is vital, it fails to consider Africa as anything
more than a place of departure—the starting point for this cultural
matrix but not a vital component of its continuing cultural impact.
Michael Gomez alludes to this oversight when arguing for an alternate
take on the shape and content of the African Diaspora. "Envisioning of
an African Diaspora vitally and inextricably linked to the histories, cultures, and communities of Africa," he writes, "is at least as valid as the
notion of a black Atlantic that effectively excludes the continent (save
as source of a primordial and unrecoverable inception)."[12]

Concerning the second point, I am not arguing that religion within
the African Diaspora has received no attention by scholars, in that there
are numerous volumes discussing the emergence and development of
religious traditions throughout the African Diaspora. Yet, these works
tend to consider religion important cultural material (read historically)
but not the "stuff" out of which a theory of the African Diaspora devel-
ops.[13] Rather, I am suggesting theorizing of the African Diaspora tends
to give little consideration to the manner in which religion might inform
conceptualization, the abstract framing of what we mean by African
Diaspora. That is to say, it is rare for religion to be understood as not
simply the "content" but also as the "form" of the Diaspora.[14] In this
sense, Paris offers a useful heuristic framework.

Paris's notion of spirituality as theory and cartographic framing of the African Diaspora plays on Du Bois's language of "soul" in that it speaks to a general connectedness, self-consciousness—worldview—that connects the individual to a larger reality defined in terms of sociocultural postures, grammars, and symbols. In Paris's words, "Metaphorically, the spirituality of a people is synonymous with the soul of a people: the integrating center of their power and meaning."[15] Put differently, the "soul" in this sense is the "force" that shapes and moves human history. And spirituality codes a general and shared matrix of experience and life meaning(s) in that "the 'spirituality' of a peoples," as Paris remarks, "refers to the animating and integrative power that constitutes the principal frame of meaning for individual and collective experience." Spirituality here conceived entails recognition of the synergy between nature, human history, and the general "push" of life.[16]

The benefit of Paris's framing of transnational developments as spirituality—although his depiction of religion within the Diaspora does not successfully maintain this tension—involves his continuous movement between various points of contact. Paris does not simply appeal to the United States and cultural developments within that context as representative of developments elsewhere. Instead, he maintains a complexity and "thickness," the overlapping spheres that make up diasporic experience(s) and avoids the critique offered by Tiffany Ruby Patterson and Robin D. G. Kelley:

> Diaspora has always been employed (invoked) in such a way as to hide the differences and discontinuities. The very concept of diaspora has been extracted from peoples' lived experiences and then molded into metaphors for alienation, outsiderness, home, and various binary relationships such as alien/native. The metaphor has come to represent those experiences and, in so doing, erases the complexities and contradictions as it seeks to fit all within the metaphor. Indeed, the experiences of those located in the United States, for example, have often come to stand for those not in the US or used as the standard of comparison.[17]

What Paris captures through this theorizing of intrinsic connection is the ebb and flow of cultural formulations, the flexible and porous nature of national boundaries as the yearning for life of peoples push against the logic of distinction that marks modern racism. Or, one might frame this in terms of the similarity between Paris's trope of spirituality as diasporic matrix and Donald Carter's framing of the Diaspora as a matter "of drifting endless on the betwixt and between of the world's boundaries. . . . Diaspora is a way of being 'other' among the established, of keeping live the drama of the voyage of 'otherness' in worlds that seek sameness and homogeneity."[18]

Whether conscious of this or not, Paris provides a response to Carter's sense that much talk of the African Diaspora has privileged displacement, disconnection, and dissonance as the guiding logic. While the spread of African peoples and cultures across various hemispheres has something to do with physical and metaphorical separation, there are ways in which the Diaspora also connotes continuity, connection, and a web of meaning(s). And Paris's trope of spirituality captures some of this.[19] "Spirituality" as trope, although not explicitly wrestling with the possibilities of numerous diasporas, does show flexibility and reach often missing from discussion of the links between African diasporic communities.

Black Bodies and the Mapping of the African Diaspora

The conceptualization Paris offers is all the more useful when one gives attention to the production and meaning of black bodies.[20] That is to say, the transnational and hemispheric cartography as spirituality is given more graphic relief when explicitly viewed through the black body as metaphor and material.

I noted at the start of the essay the manner in which Paris's autobiographical map sheds some light on the importance of the body as diaspora marker; yet, beyond the personal, much of the body's importance must be inferred from the pages of *The Spirituality of African Peoples*. The grammar of embodiment peppers the text, offering by way of gentle description the frequently used reference to the body of material, or the body of evidence. Yet, what if the body is held in frame, continuously marked as the conduit for spirituality, hence as the primary trail of the African Diaspora?

Something akin to the above is suggested very early in Paris's book when he notes that the underlying values that shape the progressive activities (related to identity formation, for example) of people of African descent have a power and that the "energizing and unifying power of those values was and is embodied in the thought and practice of African peoples everywhere."[21] Perhaps is it more than a metaphorical embodiment at work here.

We might consider this embodiment in a different sense: the force of these values is represented in, through, and by the bodies of African peoples—bodies that are both metaphorically constructed and biomedical realities occupying time and space. What I suggest here is an extension, an experiment, by which we maintain the metaphorical and somewhat veiled attention to the body in Paris's work but broaden it to a joint concern with the body as material and the impact of this complex body on notions of the African Diaspora as a cartography of spirituality.

Paris avoids the dominance of the written text, marking the framing of meaning and identity in both text-based materials and nonwritten text-based developments. This provides an opening: one might then suggest that the body became the primary conveyer for (body as material) identity and meaning. The ethos, or framework of life over against injustice, is (re)presented by bodies—in the way in which bodies make possible production of music, creation of written materials, the communication of relationships, and so on.[22]

The body is a complex and multidimensional mapping; it is read and deciphered, and it tells the stories of interconnected worlds. In this way, Paris's scholarship serves to echo the story told by his own body as symbol and as material. He, in both word and body, suggests a certain epistemological geography of life that encourages hemispheric thinking as an approach to African American religion: his body bridges several numerous spaces—Canada, the United States, the Caribbean, and Africa. Hints of this position come across when he claims much of African American religious studies involved and continues to entail "various African American religious ethicists, along with church historians and others" focusing "their scholarly attention on various dimensions of the African American historical experience in search of the basic elements for characterizing the perspective(s) of African Americans."[23] Perhaps this link is closer than we had initially realized, and perhaps it is represented both materially and metaphorically in the bio-autobiographical framing Paris offers. That is to say, the linkage or the commonality is found in all who live in the world through and in a black body.

The Body and the Religion(s) of African Peoples

The above consideration is worth serious attention, if, for instance, Linda Arthur's assertion holds any merit beyond her rubric of "dress" as "expression of identity."[24] In Arthur's words, "we wear our identities on our bodies and our bodies are used by religions to visually communicate world views."[25] If this holds, as it should, Paris's African spirituality as trope surfaces and informs through, by, and in the body. By extension religion, if we broaden Paris's framing beyond a unified supernatural orientation, is related to and expressed not in spite of but, rather, through and because of the body (as both material and metaphor for the social system). That is to say, nothing Paris says (or should say) about religion is possible without the (re)presentation of the body in time and space. And my more layered sense of religion is likewise tied to the body. Thus, our two separate notions of religion share an implied assumption within the African Diaspora: "virtues" are indeed embodied.

Perhaps this is why, for example, Christian conversion involves a reframing of the body: "I looked at my hands and they looked new; I looked at my feet and they did too." These lines and others like them suggest something important about the body within the African Diaspora, or within African spirituality as Paris describes it: religion can offer a refashioning of bodies by changing their relationship to themselves, others, and society at large. Physical bodies are defined in new ways, ways that promote ideally their health and well-being. And bodies as symbols of the social system are recast in ways that challenge the legitimacy of the status quo.

If religion involves a "binding together," it might be the case, then, that religion serves to bind together the various modes of the body and in the process tries to create a cohesive and unified whole—a healthy identity tying the individual to collectives or communities. Religion, one might infer from Paris's work, serves as guide—helping us to know (and develop) in new and more productive ways our bodies by pointing out what is most important to us—a deep(er) sense of life meaning.

Finally, the liberation and "freedom" that Paris wants to highlight as the project of African peoples involves the forcing of black bodies into the world through ways that interrogate, challenge, and change the nature and content of knowledge, the nature and function of relationships, and the promise of self-understanding and community identities. African/African American religion(s), then, might be said to promote disobedient bodies, somewhat unruly in that they buck against the status quo.

This is to suggest the *common notion of life* is firmly lodged in the logic and meaning of our bodies—both as metaphor and material. It is through and by means of these bodies that the shared religious cartography of existence Paris seeks to highlight is framed and shaped. In this sense, the body (as metaphor and material) links the various points of contact that constitute the African Diaspora; it informs and challenges the matrix of life meaning that has marked a history of contact and conquest. The black body, then, becomes plastic. That is to say, it stretches across various nation-states and hemispheres and reaches through time. It becomes the primary vehicle for tracing African spirituality (as a connecting membrane for the African Diaspora) in that the "expressivity of the body is thus the condition for social communication."[26] For Paris this framing of the body helps explain the manner in which, during long periods of injustice, modalities of community and shared concern are communicated and enacted.

Chapter 2

Homecoming in the Hinterlands

Ethical Ministries of Mission in Nigeria

Katie Geneva Cannon

IN FEBRUARY 1982, I had the good fortune of representing the United Presbyterian Church in the United States of America at the service of ordination and installation of the Reverend Mgbeke George Okore, the first woman ordained to the gospel ministry by a mainline denomination in Nigeria. Born in Mkpakpi, a village within the province of Arochukwu/Ohafia, she was a profoundly accomplished and educated woman.[1] On February 20, 1982, when the Presbytery of Aba ordained Okore as Minister of Word and Sacrament, her parishioners at St. Stephen's Presbyterian Church exceeded a membership count of four thousand. Ministries of mission contributed immensely in molding the life of the Reverend Mgbeke Okore.

As part of my preparation for this historic occasion, the Presbyterian Church of Nigeria invited me to embark on a three-week mission tour—a journey through gorgeous rainforests, along magnificent sandy beaches, over creeks and mangrove swamps to Christian communities scattered throughout southeastern Nigeria. Not being a specialist in international

---

This essay represents an expanded and heavily revised version of an earlier attempt at reporting the ethics of Presbyterian missions. See my "Homecoming in the Hinterlands" in the United Presbyterian Women's *Concern* magazine (October 1982): 12–15.

missions, intuition led me to the life and work of Lavinia Johnson, who may have been one of the first African American women missionaries to arrive in West Africa (Liberia) in 1845.[2] Even though I had worked as an Operations Crossroad Africa volunteer in Pleebo, Liberia, during the summer of 1971, with travel junkets to Ghana and Cote d'Ivoire, I lacked a mental grasp of Nigeria. A year later, while matriculating as a seminarian, Dr. Josephus R. Coan, who taught academic missiology at the Interdenominational Theological Center, professed a deep aware-ness of our inescapable Christian duty "to respond in obedience to the mandates of our Lord Jesus Christ as found in the four Gospels (Mat-thew 28:19; Mark 16:15; Luke 24:47; John 20:21) and in the book of Acts (1:8)." This commissioning theme that Christians should go into the world and make disciples of all nations has been improvised into thousands of variations. As a result, expanding my conscientization of imperial power and its painful underside embedded within the Chris-tian missionary agenda in one of the largest, most populous, and—with the increasing revenue from oil—wealthiest countries in Africa became my fundamental quest.

During the month of January, I culled the most reliable data about Nigeria from a wide variety of sources. At the forefront of my investiga-tion I orchestrated hospitable briefings in corridors, on elevators, and on the streets of New York City with everyone that I knew who had ever traveled, worked, or lived in Nigeria. These international travelers were kind enough to provide me with a broad perspective of the cultural dis-position and day-to-day life of Nigerian people. However, the only hint of commonality that proved highly significant was that I should expect the unexpected, allow plenty of time for delays, and drink only boiled water.

Next, I read scholarly journals, United Nations documents, and his-tory books on Nigeria to provide the broader picture of overseas mis-sions that began in 1842, when King Eyamba V of Duke Town, King Eyo Honesty II of Creek Town, and the chiefs of the Efik-Ibibio people (who produced the highly artistic specialized craft of Igbo-Ukwu bronzes and terracotta), invited the Church of Scotland to send educators to Nigeria.[3] In other words, this reflective essay framed around personal observations only partially refers to effective strategies in "the planting of Christianity"[4] in Igboland.

By mid-nineteenth century, there had been more than two centuries of African trade with Europeans. When the Europeans left home on trade expeditions to Africa, a round-trip usually lasted a year or more. Therefore, with the booming trade of palm oil and Eurocentric-exacerbated desire for a constant flow of enslaved African people, ivory, timber (mostly obeche), copra, beeswax, and piassava fiber, it seemed economically wise to build convenient anchorage depots around the coastal villages, near the mouths of the Cross and Calabar Rivers. These depots were located where the Europeans could keep their goods in safe harbors and maintain supplies necessary to refit sailing vessels when their equipment needed repair.

Finally, I acquired an entry visa, completed the required cycle of yellow fever, cholera, and smallpox vaccinations (along with the advisable inoculations against typhoid, tetanus, and poliomyelitis), purchased a mosquito net, packed a suitcase full of summer clothes and, on the fortnight before arriving in Nigeria, began ingesting antimalaria pills.

With hindsight, I admit that none of the preparation for traveling to Nigeria was adequate for my visit to "compound churches, prayer houses, and healing rooms."[5] All of the prearranging of my body, mind, and spirit proved insufficient for the actual experience of living among the largest concentration of black people in the world (more than one hundred million). My three-week sojourn to mission stations located in the Niger River delta was not only a homecoming—a homecoming that is much more than my personal and private kinship reunion, "bone of our bone and flesh of our flesh," people of African descent connecting across hemispheres—but also a critical reawakening of our missionary obligations in twenty-first-century, theologically driven campaigns for social justice.

Therefore, the following pages describe lessons I learned about ethical ministries of mission while living among Igbo Christians. For more than a century and a half, the Church of Scotland Mission, the Presbyterian Church of Canada, the Netherlands Reformed Church, and the United Presbyterian Church, USA, controlled primary schools, secondary boarding schools, teacher training colleges, evangelism training institutes for indigenous church workers, clerical and technical training centers, and hospitals in what is now the Cross River and Imo state.

Missionaries from Scotland, Ireland, Canada, the Netherlands, and the United States offered the most helpful service they could render in a massive multidimensional campaign to eradicate slavery,[6] ignorance, and disease.[7]

An ethical ministry of missions is a wide subject. In this essay I can do no more than lift up as brief illustration the heroic sacrifices of three missionaries in Nigeria, two nineteenth-century exogenous (imported) and one twentieth-century indigenous, whose ethics offer paradigmatic moral possibilities for those who are reappraising Christian missions in the twenty-first century. First, the Reverend Hope Masterton Waddell (1804–1895),[8] an Irishman working as a missionary for the Scots, together with a group of freed slaves from Jamaica, founded the Presbyterian Church of Nigeria on April 10, 1846. Second, Mary Mitchel Slessor (1843–1915), a missionary from Scotland, arrived in Calabar in 1876 and helped the people there to abandon their hostile attitude and murderous customs toward twin children and their mothers.

The last example is Dr. Akanu Ibiam (1906–1995), a famed physician, former president of the University College of Ibadan, and the first civilian governor of Eastern Nigeria in 1960. King George VI of Britain decorated him as Sir Francis in 1951, a Knight of the British Empire (KBE), for his outstanding career as a medical missionary under the auspices of the Church of Scotland Mission in Eastern Nigeria (formerly known as Biafra). Born in a country defined by colonialism, Dr. Ibiam cultivated a liberation consciousness, a genuine response to the ever-crying need to resist the impositions of oppressive systems of terror regulated by globalized force. In 1934, upon graduating in medicine from the University of St. Andrews, Scotland, Ibiam returned to Nigeria and became a missionary medical doctor. His inspiration to pursue this specific form of ministry came from the Scottish missionaries who served in remote places like his home village in Unwano.

This triad of Christian workers was not only a powerful force in proclaiming the gospel message of personal salvation, but the hallmark of their ministries was also the social praxis wherein they effectively applied pressure condemning general persecution, especially pernicious superstitious rituals resulting in death. Therefore, the main concern of this essay is a discussion of the intersection of ethics and missions in the most basic manner. Both are fundamentally concerned with the embodied morality of proclamation, enculturation, and liberation.

Proclamation

The first concept related to an ethical ministry of missions is proclamation. Proclamation is a logical movement from theological ethics to missions because it is the public symbolizing activity that holds in tension the demands of God-in-Christ on one side and the essential life-sustaining needs of the people on the other in our effort to ascertain decision-making norms and their corresponding social practices regarding who we are and what we do as authentic disciples of Jesus Christ. The guiding value in the proclamation ministry of Hope M. Waddell was structurally to combine teaching and preaching as an effective way to propagate the faith while carrying on humanitarian work.

Ever since the British abolished the slave trade in Jamaica in 1807, and with the subsequent emancipation in 1833 of millions of West Indian enslaved women, men, and children, a high priority in the mission planning of Waddell and his Jamaican missionary associates was to discern God's continuing revelation in carrying the gospel back to the continent of Africa. The following persons of Caribbean origin made up the mission team that accompanied Waddell to Calabar: Mr. Edgerley, a catechist and printer; Edward Miller, a teacher; Andreno Chisholm, a carpenter; and George, the aide for Waddell. These men were decidedly enthusiastic about returning to the homeland of foremothers and forefathers who had endured hellish voyages to the Americas in wretched, suffocating, demeaning conditions, shackled and chained as marketable commodities.[9] This group of Christians from the Jamaican Presbyterian Mission took a leading role in transnational abolitionism. As apostles for freedom, they proclaimed, repeatedly, that the call to eradicate slavery was a conviction deeply rooted in Scripture. In turn, Waddell, along with the missionaries from Jamaica, gave substantial weight to teaching as the distinctive form of emancipation proclamation, drawing inspiration from long-lived biblical preaching.

Rosalind Hackett argues persuasively two reasons that missionaries were able to make such significant inroads in propagating the gospel in Nigeria. One is that missionaries were the agents of the transfer of knowledge and not transient traders, who lived on the river in their trading vessels and conducted most of their business from there. Second, she writes, "There was a tendency to view power in religious terms. In other words, many believed that the Bible held the key to European technical (and for some, cultural) superiority and that the missionaries possessed the knowledge to unlock its secrets for the Africans."[10]

Due to the longstanding Presbyterian ideals and practices, educational and medical institutions were built instead of churches. I visited Hope Waddell Training Institution in Calabar, the Duke Town Secondary School (named after its founder, Duke Effiom Okoho), the Ohafia Girls School, the Mary Slessor Memorial School and the Hugh Goldie Training Center in Arochuku, the Women's Training Center in Ikot Obong, the Trinity (Union Theological) College in Umahia, and the Eja Memorial Joint Hospital in Itigidi. The theological charge in the air during my mission tour confirmed that these institutions continue to have strong links with teaching as a key aspect of their Christian witness, wherein members of these believing communities give significant weight to cultivating the mind so that the inner thoughts of the heart can be in tune with the true will of God.

Far from pious preaching full of inflexible rituals, the nineteenth-century Scottish mission concentrated on education as a prerequisite for baptism. Living life trivially and without any significance was not an option. Each mission school was the "nursery of the infant church." Hackett continues, "Full membership in the Mission community was dependent on attaining acceptable minimal literacy levels, as well as the profession of faith."[11] New converts demonstrated a thorough grasp of Christian doctrines based on the revealed teaching of Christ, not only as a duty but the ability to propagate the gospel also served as a guiding light in facing contemporary challenges and responsibilities. The whole program of proclamation ethics advocates educating clergy and laity to be inwardly disciplined as we outwardly witness to the Spirit of God that renews, reforms, and redeems. Christians are only stewards of divinely entrusted material possessions, charged with the sacred responsibility to help the less fortunate. We must never deprive others of their basic human rights. Authentic disciples of Jesus Christ demonstrate by application in the physical world the spiritual values to which we adhere. The emphasis is not on doctrinal purity but freedom to be fully submissive to God. A century later, in *Strength to Love*, Martin Luther King Jr. summed up the ethics of proclamation this way: "To be Christian, one must take up his cross, with all its difficulties and agonizing and tragedy-packed content, and carry it until the very cross leaves its mark upon us and redeems us to that more excellent way which comes through suffering."[12]

In surveying the mission of proclamation in Nigeria, we find that this is a country where ecclesiastical and sociopolitical developments have always been closely intertwined. To their credit, Presbyterian Mission Schools can add some of the leading Nigerian statesmen, medical doctors, marine engineers, electrical technicians, university professors, teachers, bookmakers, agriculturalists, and theologians to their hall of fame. Nigerian Presbyterians, with their mastery of formal training, had great influence in the educational, commercial, social, religious, and political history of the people, not only in their immediate environs, but also in achieving status in the higher grades of media, politics, and the British Colonial Civil Service.[13]

Enculturation

The second concept in an ethical ministry of missions stresses enculturation, the deliberate intervention by which individuals reeducate ourselves about the distinct codification of socially constructed reality, springing forth from deeply held feelings and religious beliefs. Enculturation is the watchword for critical thinking that enables us to change directions, by analyzing the established power relationships, transmitted from generation to generation, that determine cultural, political, and economic presuppositions so that we can abandon harmful, inherited practices breaking into our existential contexts. Differentiating between traditional patterns of social beliefs that are death dealing and embracing those that are life affirming is a moral act.[14] An ethical ministry of missions insists that we stay conscious of legitimating myths that sanction the enforcement of social and political tragedies and violently bizarre cultic behaviors in the name of religion. We must disassociate with things in the human marketplace that betray us, endangering our well-being.

Through a combination of missionary zeal and moral anchors, Mary Slessor (1843–1915) seized every opportunity to rebuke, urgently pleading with Nigerians to reject aspects of indigenous religious practices, laws, and customs that were antithetical to Christianity. Prior to the arrival of Presbyterian missionaries, human sacrifice of wives and slaves upon the death of a chief, the ostracization of orphans and widows, and slave expeditions were rampant throughout southeastern Nigeria. Committed to practicing enculturation within the confined perimeters of British imperialism, they used informed public pressure to eradicate disturbing, distressing, disruptive trials by ordeal with poisonous *esere* beans, sacrificial killings, and perpetual internecine wars.

Giving herself to God's service, Slessor, a twenty-eight-year-old Scotswoman, set foot on African soil on September 11, 1876. She dutifully followed around her teacher and longtime missionary, Euphemia Sutherland, "as she learned the business of being a 'female agent'—teaching, dispensing medications, and making the rounds of the women's yards surrounding Duke Town, mission headquarters in the greater Calabar region."[15] Slessor felt called and sent by God to serve responsibly as an embodied instrument bearing the divine word to the Efik-Ibibio and Igbo people of southeastern Nigeria. Her paramount commitment was to do the work of missions according to God's revealed word and will.

Perhaps the most alarming and difficult challenge that Slessor confronted in her ministry of mission was the persistent custom of killing twins or more children birthed at a time by any mother. This ethical issue is of particular interest to me because my father, Esau, is the identical twin to his brother, Jacob. At one mission station after another I was told that prior to Slessor's arrival, twin babies were murdered and their mothers were killed or treated as outcasts, banished to twin-mothers' villages. Such births were regarded as grave misfortunes. As I traveled throughout the hinterland, clergy and laity alike were surprised to hear that my father and his twin brother were sixty-eight years of age. None of them knew identical twins that old. To them, my father and uncle were an anathema.

John Mbiti contends that the birth of twins is an unusual, abnormal event, an invasion of the ontological harmony, a phenomenon that requires special attention from the community, which may take the form of acts of worship and other religious activity.[16]

Jeanette Hardage reports that as late as 1912, D. Amaury Talbot said that during her time in Calabar with her husband, Percy Amaury Talbot, a district commissioner,

> native men insisted that they only hated and feared twin babies as "something monstrous." But the women believed that "one of the pair, at least, was no merely mortal offspring but that of some wandering demon." . . . Except where the fear of the white man is too strong, twins are not allowed to live even now.[17]

Dr. Laurenti Magesa, one of Africa's best-known Catholic theologians, argues that in some parts of the continent there is an ambiguous paradox regarding the birth of twins. He agrees with Mbiti that in many African societies twin births are not only considered to be abnormalities but also inauspicious occurrences, bad omens.

Magesa goes on to say that in other African countries, however, the birth of twins is a good omen from God, "recalling the fabulous past when all human beings came into existence in twos, symbolizing the balance between the human and divine." Sacrality is bestowed on the mothers of twins because it is believed that they have been touched by a spirit in order to conceive and bear them.

> Twins are seen to have powers not granted to anyone else, and it is hoped that they will use these powers for the good of the community. . . . Twins are born with the mystical powers of sorcery and must be treated with great respect from the beginning.
>
> With the Yoruba the situation is much the same: twins have spiritual powers that influence even siblings born after them. The mother of twins is congratulated profusely for having had them.[18]

Slessor's breadth of ministry, her stubborn drive to present the gospel message in new territories, and "her persistent rescue of twins and orphans, in some cases adopting and raising the children as her own,"[19] made her an object of much honor. While touring mission schools and hospitals named in honor of Slessor, I saw several statures of her holding twin babies, one in each arm. Therefore, when I arrived early one Sunday morning to deliver a sermon at the Duke Town Presbyterian Church, I was not surprised, but found it very interesting, that hundreds of Nigerians, members of the Women's Guild, had large portraits of Mary Slessor printed on the front of their blue and white dresses. The women told me that Slessor was a tireless, energetic, self-sacrificing champion of their everyday common concerns.

Then, as well as now, what stirred Slessor and her successors was a gospel-filled, people-centered ministry and the compelling call to work as messengers from God. Furthering both Christian missions and the gospel message, Presbyterians in Nigeria passionately actualize their faith by spreading the message of God's love and in services that speak directly to the specific needs of congregations and surrounding communities.

Liberation

The third and final concept related to an ethical ministry of mission is an appeal for liberation of the oppressed. In the order of divine providence, God sends liberators. In this instance, it was Sir Francis Akanu Ibiam (1906–1995), "the second son of Chief Ibiam Aka, a well known and highly respected traditional ruler in the village clan of Unwana."[20] Imbued with the spirit of Christ, Dr. Ibiam was given the name Francis when he was baptized in 1919. Ordained a ruling elder in the Presbyterian Church, he was one of the foremost Christian leaders in Nigeria. In 1961 he was elected as one of the six presidents of the Third Assembly of the World Council of Churches in New Delhi, India (1961–1970). He received the Knight Commander (of the Order) of St. Michael and St. George from Queen Elizabeth II in 1962. He repudiated the title during the Biafran War due to Britain's lack of support.

On February 21, 1982, I was filled with profound gratitude when the Very Reverends Akanu A. Otu, E. A. Onuk, O. Mbila, and other executives from the Presbyterian Church of Nigeria in Imo State arranged for me to have a face-to-face conversation with Ezeogu Dr. Akanu Ibiam. As we sat on his front porch talking about his biotext, he shared his ethic of liberation. Throughout his medical ministry, from February 1, 1936, to January 31, 1967, he never wavered in his insistence that oppression interferes with God's justice. The core principle in his basic religious conviction was the inseparability of Christian faith and freedom. As the founder and honorary president of the Student Christian Movement of Nigeria, Ibiam professed that as members of the Christian church, a community composed of committed disciples, united in a bond of love to God and to each other, we are responsible for a just social order and not merely the salvation of individual souls. As the only Nigerian among a group of some seventy European missionaries for twenty-five years, he repudiated the notion that the world could not exist without inequality of persons, some free, others enslaved, some lords, others servants.

Serving as a missionary medical doctor and surgeon, it was incomprehensible to Ibiam that spirituality should have no bearing on the dailiness of life. Christians must constantly minister to others as Christ has done. True believers should imitate Christ in concrete expressions that alleviate unjust conditions. Nigerian researchers capture in a vivid snapshot how Ibiam connected faith and praxis.

> He opened the first missionary hospital in Abriba which also served the people of Ohafia, Item and suburb. He later moved to Itu hospital now in Akwa Ibom where he established a school of Nursing. From Itu he went to Uburu where he promoted maternity and child welfare.[21]

In other words, faith in Christ provides the oppressed, and those who cast their lot with them, the moral impetus to change conditions.

In talking about his medical ministry, Dr. Ibiam shared how God's grace, an unmerited gift, enabled him to receive and experience the benefit of Christ's atoning work. Ibiam emphasized that a God-pleasing faith must find expression in every aspect of our being. Authentic faith should never be divorced from practical life:

> As an African and a member of the Igbo culture, Dr. Ibiam understood the impact of superstition and witchcraft beliefs on his people. These beliefs caused the people to attribute all their problems—be it barrenness, the birth of twins, malaria, miscarriages, fever, stroke—to

demonic attacks. Dr. Ibiam was bold and fearless but sympathetic in dispelling these fears from the minds of his patients. He gave them physical healing through western medicine and spiritual and emotional healing through the dynamic preaching of the gospel.[22]

Ibiam looked to the New Testament messages for biblical warrant and for active and transparent models of humanitarian service to neighbors. Setting at liberty those who are oppressed was one of his core Christian values. In 1958, he was appointed as the first Nigerian Principal of the Hope Waddell Training Institute (HWTI) in Calabar, one of Nigeria's prestigious, international, academic institutions. Attacking a plethora of abominable societal practices, Ibiam, as principal, maintained that the elementary necessities in this earthly life are that we should protect the good, punish the wicked, maintain public peace, educate youth, care for the poor, and provide protection for all.

Ibiam believed wholeheartedly that it is wrong to submit to incompetent and corrupt civil authorities that act unjustly, especially when obedience to such government ordinances and crooked bureaucracy leads to the continuation of injustice. He insisted that if we are serious about carrying out God's commandments, then Christians must resist the government if citizenship requires disobedience to the word of God and thwarting the gospel. His convictions are brought to life in these words.

> One of the distressing issues that bothered Dr. Ibiam was that of "tribalism." He consistently condemned national appointments that were based on tribal affiliation and not on merit. He publicly lamented the enthronement of "mediocrity" in the place of "meritocracy" in the nation's civil service and government appointments.[23]

In 1968, Ibiam journeyed to the Fourth Assembly of the World Council of Churches so that he could share stories about the organized killing and destructive atrocities in Biafra (formerly Eastern Nigeria) during the Nigerian Civil War. Speaking to Christian organizations in Europe, Ibiam requested food, clothing, medical supplies, and war relief for thousands upon thousands of starving, displaced refugees, civilian victims whose property, worth millions of pound sterling, was seized.

Dr. Ibiam concluded our conversation by sharing with me the content of his 1967 protest letter to Queen Elizabeth II. His opposition to the Queen of England has been summed up this way.

> In view of the British government's open hostility to Biafra, Dr. Ibiam dropped his English name Francis and returned the insignia of his knighthood as a Knight of the British Empire (KBE), with these words: "I consider it illogical and immoral to wear the insignia of your knighthood in view of the most dangerous weapons you give to the Federal troops to eliminate me and my people. Henceforth I wish to be addressed as Dr. Akanu Ibiam."[24]

As a parting gift, Dr. Ibiam presented me with a book, *Why We Struck: The Story of the First Nigerian Coup* by Adewale Ademoyega,[25] and a sending-forth blessing, affirming how faith in God gives Christians the confidence to live boldly, to risk all, and to stand by the truth, no matter what the cost.

Conclusion

When I arrived at the Presbyterian Church in Abakaliki, the last stop of my mission tour, the Nigerian sisters and brothers consummated my homecoming. As we drove into the churchyard, the congregation surrounded the car and reprimanded the Reverend Richard Fee, the Canadian missionary who was serving as their pastor, because he had promised to bring the woman minister from the USA to their church, and yet there was no stranger with him. Some of the parishioners of this thirty-point parish had walked more than twenty miles to welcome this long-awaited, international clergy guest. Again and again they asked, "Rev. Fee, where is she?" "Where is the lady priest from the United States?" "You promised, Rev. Fee, you promised that you would bring her to our church."

As the commotion died down, we entered the sanctuary, and Fee introduced me to the congregation as the woman minister from the United Presbyterian Church (USA). Spontaneously, cheers and hallelujahs were shouted throughout the church and folks of all ages started dancing. Through a translator, I learned that the Nigerian congregants had been scolding the pastor because they were completely surprised that I was the guest minister from the USA. Our color pigmentation, hair texture, embodied physicality, and mannerisms were all the same. The parishioners, women and men, youth and adults alike, had simply taken for granted that I was an Igbo woman. They said to me, "Welcome home!" "Africa to Africa, strength to strength."

Chapter 3

Women in Rastafari

Noel Leo Erskine

THE ROOTS OF RASTAFARI religion date back to the Great Revival Church of the 1860s in Jamaica. The Great Revival was a logical outgrowth of the Native Baptist Church, due to the preaching of African Americans, who started the Ethiopian Baptist Church in Kingston, Jamaica, in 1784. In fact, the first Christian preaching that most enslaved persons in Jamaica heard was by the original Native Baptists, George Liele, George Gibb, Moses Baker, George Lewis, and Nicholas Swiegle, even though the Moravian Church in Jamaica preceded the Baptists as early as 1754. Because the Moravians were invited to the island by the planters and the Moravians themselves owned slaves, however, their impact on the enslaved population was minimal. Another reason for the limited success Moravians had among enslaved Afro-Jamaicans was their failure to adopt the class-leader system as practiced by the Baptists, which empowered enslaved people to provide leadership as "Mammies" and "Daddies." It also provided an organizational basis that allowed newly converted Afro-Jamaicans to be in charge of a class, a group of converts, for which they were responsible. The class leader, a Mammy or Daddy, had real power to interpret what the preacher said, and in many cases the power to refuse applications for baptism and, at times, even expel members. Needless to say, it was not long before the class became the basis for the founding of new churches, which were under the control of the class leader.

It is important to note that from 1783 to 1814, when George Liele and his fellow African Americans arrived in Jamaica and started to interpret Christianity from an African perspective, Jamaicans were unhindered by European theological traditions. Later the missionaries were forced to deal with cultural issues along with the reality that there were not enough missionaries to cope with the vast number of enslaved persons on the island at this time. The important fact to remember is that for twenty-eight years the Native Baptists were unhindered by European orthodoxy as they constructed a theology that would speak with cogency to the enslaved situation.

The primary theological position of the Native Baptists was that of elevating the Spirit above the written word. The overarching theological position was that of possession by the Spirit. It is quite understandable that there would be less emphasis on the written word, as many of the class leaders were unable to read. "The followers of Baker and Gibb were required to be possessed 'of the spirit' before baptism was administered. This meant that the spirit had to descend on the applicant in a dream, which was then described to the leader. If the dream were satisfactory, the applicant could enter the class. There evolved a regular technique and ceremonial for bringing on spirit-possession, which included a fast according to a set canon, followed by a trip to the bush alone at night to wait for the spirit to descend."[1]

It was also important to the adherents of this Africanized version of Christianity that John the Baptist had the priority over Jesus, as he was the one who through baptism transformed Jesus. In this context Jesus was viewed as a prophet, and it was not unusual for leaders of the faith to see themselves as Jesus. Baptism was a special rite and ritual of this new faith because spirit was associated with water. The central relationship was not between the new convert and God, or with Jesus, but with the Spirit. If Jesus was viewed as prophet, God was regarded as distant, perhaps dwelling in heaven, and was not expected to attend to daily activities or even to attend worship. It is the Spirit that would be present with power and would take charge of the service as well as believers. This was one area in which the Regular Baptists differed from the Africanized interpretation of Christianity. The Caribbean sociologist

Barry Chevannes suggests that Liele himself veered toward the less radical wing among the Native Baptists and perhaps as time went on was closer to the views of the Regular Baptists. The radical wing of the Native Baptists regarded possession of the Spirit as the hallmark of their expression of religion. We should not forget that from 1655 until 1783, when the British took possession of the island from Spain, Afro-Jamaicans were free to practice African religion. When Liele and his colleagues appeared from the United States, this reality changed. The Church of England showed little or no interest in proselytizing Afro-Jamaicans. This means that for over one hundred years Afro-Jamaicans had a great deal of freedom in practicing their religion. Preaching and exhortation was often replaced with possession of the Spirit. As Chevannes writes, "George Liele became so frustrated that he wrote to the Baptist Missionary Society in London, asking for help. When the Baptist missionaries arrived . . . they could scarcely recognize a trace of Christian orthodoxy. Much to their embarrassment, the name 'Native Baptist' was being widely used to refer to the more Christianized forms of Myal [African-based religion]."[2]

In 1860 most of the established churches in Jamaica participated in what was labeled as a revival of Christianity throughout the island. The mission churches launched a united assault against Afro-Jamaicans' approach to Christianity through the Great Revival, which aimed to convert Afro-Jamaicans from their "heathen" ways to "pure" Christianity. The revival was a great success in terms of the number of Afro-Jamaicans who attended. There was fasting and praying, and the high point came when the Baptists set aside the last Sunday of April 1860 for God's arrival in Jamaica. There is no mistaking what had happened—the revival had turned African. The new convert was usually struck prostrate on the floor, and as the revival progressed African converts were given to oral confessions, trances, dreams, "prophesying," spirit seizure, wild dancing, and mysterious sexual doings. The revival became increasingly a mixture of Myalism and Christianity, ending in a permanent addition to the Afro-Christian groups—Rastafari religion, thus leaving the missionary churches at their lowest numbers.[3]

Revivalists and Rastafari

The missionaries discovered that there was no Christianity among Afro-Jamaicans to be revived. What was revived was an interpretation of Christianity from an African frame of reference. Building on Revivalist beliefs, Rastafari is able to make the leap of faith and speak of Haile Selassie I, the emperor of Ethiopia, as Christ. There is a shift of emphasis and perspective. The Rastas represent a move from the Revivalist focus on Spirit possession to actually encountering the Christ figure. For the Revivalists, the presence of Christ at their worship service is not crucial for authenticating their faith. The change for Rastafari is this: the divinity of the man-God Haile Selassie I ensures the divinity of African people. The emphasis here is on the "uplift of the race."

For the Revivalists, it is the Spirit that is the locus of divinity. The ideal life is life in the Spirit. The goal of the Revivalists is that all who come within the purview of the Revivalist faith may be possessed with the Spirit. A practical consequence of living in the Spirit is that one does not sin. The main sin against which the Revivalist counsels is stealing from one's family or one's community; also counseled against are lying, hatred, criticism, thinking evil, deceitfulness, fornication, being unjust, coveting a neighbor's goods, and placing an evil spirit or spell on a member of the community. Other sins include cruelty to human beings, starving when one has money, and destroying the garden of another person. But it seems that the primary virtue of life in the spirit is that the Revivalists discover that the Spirit does not discriminate between male and female leadership in the Revival Church. Although in practice the spirit often chooses women over men, it is deemed that it has to do with the openness and availability of women to the Spirit. In many of the Revival churches, especially in the parish of St. Thomas, in Jamaica, where I was reared as a young man, men were often seen assisting Spirit-filled women by carrying and playing drums at meetings.

The mood changes in Rastafari. When one looks at the contributions of the early pioneers of Rastafari, it becomes clear that for most of them the emphasis and organizing principle of faith was belief in the divinity of Haile Selassie I and the repatriation to Ethiopia, often referred to as Zion. The notion of Spirit possession and leadership by the Spirit, which we find in Revival churches, does not have the same currency in Rastafari except in the case of Robert Hinds, who was one of the early leaders of the faith. It can be inferred that in the theology and ministry of Hinds, there is inclusion of the Spirit and therefore a linkage to the Revival Church.

It should not surprise us that because of the openness to the spirit, Hinds's community, the "King of Kings Mission" (a reference to Haile Selassie I), numbered over eight hundred persons. Hinds, who was closely connected with Marcus Garvey and Leonard Howell, the founder of Rastafari, organized his mission along the lines of a Revival Church and yet, at the same time, never deviated in terms of his fidelity to Haile Selassie I. Taking his cue from Revivalists, "Leader" or "Shepherd" was a title Hinds claimed for himself. This was also true of Leonard Howell, the foremost founder of Rastafari, who chose "Shepherd of the King of Kings Missions" as one of his titles. The hierarchy represented here was this: Shepherd Hinds at the helm, secretaries (all women), two chaplains, an armor bearer, twelve male officers, and twelve water mothers. The secretaries were recording officers; literate, they read lessons at meetings and were responsible for correspondence, such as asking police for permission to hold a march. The chaplains, water mothers, and officers were indispensable at baptism rituals, which took place twice a year to mark the reception of members into full membership.[4] At the King of Kings Missions there were fasts, feasts, and baptisms—all a carryover from Revivalism.

A key feature at the King of Kings Mission was the preponderance of women as members. It seems as if in the early years of Rastafari, when the influence of Revivalism was still strong, the place of women was not an issue. However, we must never lose sight that in Rastafari, unlike the Revival Church, women were never in charge. The difference in the role of women in both Rastafari and in Revival churches was theological. In Revival churches, the emphasis was on spirit possession as well as receiving direction from the Spirit. There was more openness for women to providing leadership because one could not decide ahead of time how the Spirit would lead or whom the spirit would choose to lead. Even in the case of Hind's King of Kings Mission, which seemed, at best, to provide a combining of Spirit emphasis with that of the Christ figure Haile Selassie I, women were not in charge. There were always subordinate roles for women. The further Rastafari moved from an emphasis on the Spirit as guide, to the embrace of a Christ figure in Ethiopia, the more patriarchal it became. As Rastafari became full blown, with reliance on the Christ figure and the Bible, the role of women became even more circumscribed.

Now, it must be kept in mind that Hinds did not see a conflict between holding a Spirit theology and the affirmation of Haile Selassie I as messiah. Hinds was unflinching in his belief that the people of Jamaica needed deliverance from the shackles of poverty and colonial harassment. He was convinced that the answer was in the messianic figure Haile Selassie I, who would provide deliverance through repatriation to Ethiopia, Zion. Christology provided the main key for his understanding of God and the world.

This was not the case with Archibald Dunkley, another of the early founders of Rastafari. While Dunkley embraced Revivalist practices such as chanting and drumming, and occasionally quoting from the Bible, he was opposed to dancing in the Spirit. A report states:

> We went to Highholborn Street and the meeting was so powerful that I find myself couldn't stand up. All I try to keep down myself I was just wheeling and spinning. And I hear him say him don't want that in here, and continue talking. I feel that I want to stop to steady myself, but I couldn't control, and him say that him don't want that there. I didn't say anything, but I never go back. Because if you living clean, the Spirit of Almighty God lives in you and if him find a clean body him will move in you.[5]

The central theme for the Revivalist faith was the power and the presence of Spirit. The rhetorical question for the emergent Rastafari faith was, Where do you stand in relation to Africa as this is interpreted in the light of His Imperial Highness, Haile Selassie I?

Rastafari and Mainline Churches

There is a related factor that I believe influences the place of women in Rastafari, which many scholars do not take into account, and it has to do with the place of women in mainline churches. Although Rastas criticize the church for being in collusion with the state and contend that they focus too much on life after death, there is a not-so-audible conversation with the church. Rastas co-opt church language and make pivotal use of the church's book, the Bible. Indeed, I assert that the subordination of women in Rastafari is due not only to Rastas' preference for Christology rather than life in the Spirit but also because of their preoccupation with the Bible. Rasta's faith is steeped in doctrinal statements and is often the outcome of reasoning, primarily among males, and does not have the openness to the surprise of the new that we find in Revival churches led by women. This is one area in which Rasta theology and ideology more closely approximates the European pole rather than the African.

Moreover, Rastas use the Bible selectively to facilitate their own ends. They do not regard it as coincidental that Eve, the first woman the Bible mentions, was portrayed as weak and an instrument of evil. Rastas contend that on the basis of their reading of the Bible, Eve was a "temptress" who led Adam astray, hence men in Rastafari must be careful not to allow women to lead them astray. Rasta reasoning about women as portrayed in the Bible is as follows.

> The first female character is Eve. She it was who, tempted by the devil, in turn became Adam's temptress. Next is Sarai, when asked by her husband to pose as his sister in order to safeguard his life, did so unquestioningly. Following Sarai is Rebekai who schemes against her husband to ensure that her favorite son would receive his blind father's blessing. Rachael and Leah, both sisters, vied with each other for their husband's affection, each relying on her fertility to win favor in his eyes. Potiphar's wife attempts to seduce Joseph then, thwarted in her attempts to do so, reported that he had attempted to rape her.[6]

This is a classic case of Rastas' selective use of the Bible. Here no mention is made of Queen Esther, after whom a book in the Bible is named, or even the important role of Miriam in safeguarding Moses. Again, it must be observed that the selective use of Scripture to serve their own ends and to keep women in their place in Rastafai is not unique to Rastas. I do not believe we can say with a clear conscience that

Rastas took this proof-texting of Scripture to a new level. The Christian church in Jamaica during this period also used Scripture as a weapon against oppressed people. Unlike the Rastas, who turned to the Old Testament, the mainline churches would turn to Paul's letters and through their interpretation construe that Paul ordered women to be quiet in the church and to take a secondary role to men in the home, society, and church.

Liberation or Subordination

Rastas also used issues of "purity" to subordinate women to men. They supported their argument on the Levitical code; Rastas contend that during the menstrual cycle women are impure and should not participate in worship and their roles in the home should be limited. In 1996, when I visited the Bobo community outside Kingston with scholars from the Society for the Study of Black Religion, women were not allowed to enter the tabernacle for worship unless they first had a conversation with the empresses of the faith to determine if they were clean. The women later explained that this depended on the time passed since their last menstrual cycle. Several women were not allowed to enter the tabernacle but had to hear the preaching and drumming through windows. After worship, the Rastas invited only the men among us to enter the upper room for reasonings.

While it may be true that the Bobo community is careful in its insistence on differentiating roles between men and women in such a way that women are subordinate to men, the bottom line is that it is true of all Rastas that women are subordinate to men regardless of age or economic status. The male is the "King-man" or the "God-man" and as such is naturally superior to women, even though women are often referred to as "empresses."

Obiagele Lake, who did a study of Rastafari, explains that a woman will be ceremonially unclean for seven days after giving birth to a son. After circumcision she must wait an additional thirty-three days to be purified from her bleeding. When she gives birth to a daughter, she will be unclean for two weeks, as is the case during her period. She has to wait for sixty-six days to be purified from her bleeding (Lev. 4:12).[7]

According to Leviticus 4:15, a male's discharge is also considered unclean, and the days of atonement are considerably fewer than those of the woman. When a woman has a female child, her period before acceptance back in the community is much longer than that of the birth of a male child. This is an indication of the female inferior status. The Jamaican society as a whole accepts the notion that a woman's inferiority is based on Christian dogma. This is in agreement with Rasta culture and practice. For example, in the Bobo community, women may serve guests but may never serve Bobo males. In Jamaican society, women usually cook and serve, but in the Bobo community the males cook and serve. If women choose, they may cook for themselves, but never for the males.

Velma Grant, a former member of the Bobo community, supports these claims of inequality between men and women. She points out that male and female housing is located on separate sides. The female's menstrual status is made evident by a flag displayed at the entrance of her quarters. A white flag indicates that the female is "free" and is not on her menstrual cycle. During that period, she is allowed to have female or male visitors. A red flag means she is not "free" and is menstruating. During this time, she is confined to her residence and off-limits to visitors. According to Grant, the focus on the menstrual cycle enforces a separation that carries over into the tabernacle. The female is allowed to enter the house of worship only if she is "free." The men are seated in one area and women on the opposite side if they are "free." And there is no interaction between the genders except in the culmination of a fast, in which a male priest will administer a ceremonial piece of bread and a cup of water to a female to "break" the fast.[8]

In fact, as Lake writes, "many Rastas believe that a woman can only enter into Rastafari faith through Rasta men. Rastafarian women are said to receive guidance from Rasta men and are sometimes dependent on them to gain access to the organization. Rasta men are also considered the spiritual leaders of the movement and the heads of households."[9] Lake points out that the majority of Rasta women live by these principles and guidelines and that at its core Rastafari is a patriarchal movement that looks to the Bible, especially the Old Testament, for its structure and philosophy. Lake makes another observation about why women are not treated as equals in Rastafari: because this faith was founded and organized by men. This argument parallels the argument given by some Christian churches for the exclusion of women from leadership roles. The claim is that Jesus, who is the Son of God incarnate and founder of Christianity, exercised his divine prerogative when he chose twelve men to be his disciples, and if it were God's will that women should exercise leadership within the church, then Jesus would not have chosen all male disciples. Of course, this argument becomes controversial when it is acknowledged that at his resurrection Jesus sent Mary to tell the disciples that he had risen, thus making her the first apostle. In Christian hierarchy, the apostle has as much power as the disciple.

From Babylon to Zion

While Maureen Rowe, herself a Rasta woman, agrees with Lake that Rastafari is essentially a patriarchal religion, she is able to nuance her assessment with a historical profile of women's relationship to the movement and their impact on the movement. Because Rastafari emerged from a long line of African religious experiences, Rowe argues that to understand the role and place of women in Rastafari one needs to pay attention to how African patriarchy functions in the Caribbean. Over and against African patriarchy, European patriarchy is based on wealth. In this setting, male authority has a direct connection to wealth. In the European construct of male authority, the male is the chief breadwinner; if the female works, she does so in order to support the male. In instances where the male does not work or makes less than the female, the male is emasculated. Maleness and authority are related to wealth.

Rowe highlights, however, that in African patriarchy, authority is intrinsic to maleness and is not dependent on an extrinsic source such as wealth or title. The African male is expected to wield power in the family by virtue of being male. Rowe continues:

> I have often thought that the African women place such a high value on procreation that they allocate a value to the male based on their own valuing of children. The male in this context would have a value assigned to him by the female. The African male, therefore, expects to exercise power and authority in the family by virtue of being male. The male role in relation to the female seems to be one

of empowerment. The woman is facilitated by the male, who also supports the family in a manner similar to that of the male in a traditional polygamous household. He will often facilitate her income, generating activities by providing critical support in some areas of domestic life.[10]

To get a meaningful grasp of the role of women in the movement, Rowe suggests the division of Rasta history into three moments: 1930–50, the formative years; 1951–72, the early years; and 1972 to the present. During the formative period, the coronation of Haile Selassie I was celebrated as Jamaica witnessed the crossing of the island by several itinerant preachers extolling the divinity of the emperor. The majority of the membership during this period was drawn from the Jamaican underclass, which shaped the Rastafari belief system. There was an explosion of the membership in the period between 1951 and 1971. During this period, Rastafari became an urban movement and developed a powerful following. In the third period, Rastafari received both national and international recognition through the efforts of musicians who incorporated Rasta beliefs in their music. The most notable among these musicians was the honorable Robert Nesta Marley. But this was also a time of severe challenges, as Rastafari had to deal with the deaths of His Imperial Highness, Haile Selassie I, and of Marley, the foremost evangelist of Rastafari.

Rowe indicates that while it s true that in the chronicling of the movement little mention is given to the role of women, George Simpson, one of the early researchers of the movement, counters this view when he says that as early as 1948 he saw both women and men who identified themselves as Rastafari dressed in red, gold, and green scarves and caps. Interviews with women, who attended meetings and sided with the Rastas against police brutality, make it quite clear, according to Rowe, that there was not much difference between how women and male adherents in the movement were treated between 1950 and 1960. But after making allowance for the role of women in the movement during the formative years, sharing and participating in the rituals and even in one case receiving a vision from Jah (God) to go out on the street and testify (which would be quite significant, because in this case women would be the receiver and bearer of divine revelation), the bottom line is that they belonged to a movement organized and directed by men. Women's participation was limited in the area of doctrine. In this regard, women would not have equal status with men.

A breakthrough for women began in the late 1950s, with the emergence of "dreadness" as a way of life for Rastafari. Rowe points out that while it is difficult to date the emergence of "dreadlocks" within the movement, history records that by the early 1950s they were present. Prior to the emergence of dreadlocks within the movement, combed hair and beard identified the male Rastafarian and head-ties and scarves the female Rastafarian. In addition, Rastas were identified by their dressing in red, green, and gold. By the 1970s, dreadlocks became a way of identifying Rasta and differentiating them from the people of Babylon. It is fair to say that during this period the two defining realities of Rastafari were the wearing of dreadlocks and smoking ganja (marijuana). My recollection of the beginning of the movement in St. Thomas, Kingston, and Westmoreland, where I served as pastor in the church founded by George Liele, is that Rastas always felt they had a right to the holy herb ganja. I cannot recall a period in the 1950s or 1960s when Rastas were not associated with the holy herb. On the other hand, my recall of the preponderance of dreadlocks dates to the late 1950s and early 1960s. I do not recall women wearing dreadlocks in the 1950s. I suspect part of the reason why this was not common among women in the 1950s was because dreadlocks and the smoking of marijuana were associated with the criminal element in Jamaica, and during this period there were several confrontations between the police and the Rastafari community. To wear dreadlocks in the 1950s in Jamaica, especially in urban centers, was to encourage police harassment. The position began to change in the 1960s, when Rasta families including women and children began wearing dreadlocks. Needless to say, the general public saw them as outsiders. No one outside the Rasta faith would consider wearing dreadlocks during this period. To wear the locks was a badge of membership.

The dilemma for women in Rastafari is that membership does not mean equality. Although women have important roles and may be referred to as empresses or queens, they continue to be subordinate to the "king-man," a title reserved for the male in Rastafari. This posture reflects life in Babylon, a place that Rastas claim Jah will destroy because of its oppression of the poor as Jah takes them to Ethiopia, Zion. The challenge for Rastas is not to flee Babylon or merely to interpret Jah's displeasure with Babylon but to work for transformation in Babylon. This would include releasing women from the shackles of subjugation and second-class citizenship within Rastafari. Rastas must begin to understand that their dignity and freedom is tied up with that of women. As they allow the wind of Jah's spirit to blow freely in the community, women will once again be empowered as in the Revival Church to take their rightful place in Rastafari and in the wider community. Rastas will begin to view the world from a new place, Zion, not Babylon. In Babylon it is fashionable for masters to keep slaves and for men to lord authority over women. In Zion, where women are celebrated as daughters of Jah, there is equality and dignity for all Jah's children.

Chapter 4

Religious Pluralism in Africa

Insights from Ifa Divination Poetry

Jacob K. Olupona

IN THIS ESSAY, I problematize the concept of religious pluralism in Africa as a trope for analyzing and interpreting sets of oral tradition called Ifa divination poetry. My objective is to examine Ifa divination poetry so as to uncover the way that this indigenous tradition understands religious pluralism. I argue that the oral narratives of Africa's triple religious heritage present a religious universe in which Islam, Christianity, and indigenous religion share a common space that is the earmark of the complexity of interreligious relations in African society. Whereas we know a good deal about how Christianity and Islam relate to each other, we know very little about how indigenous religious traditions assess these two monotheistic traditions. Therefore, my ultimate goal and objective here is to illuminate how Ifa tradition engages an ethics of tolerance not only within the larger society and culture but also in relation to Islam and Christianity. I will disclose this ethics of tolerance through the commentary on Islam and Christianity that is expressed in Ifa divination poetry. This essay is based on almost two years of field research among the Yoruba of Western Nigeria, where I conducted extensive field work among Ifa diviners, several of whom have converted to either Islam or Christianity and some who retain their indigenous religious tradition.

What Is Ifa Divination?

Ifa is a form of geomancy—a process of divination—and the name of a deity of divination; it is regarded as the highest religious tradition in Yoruba culture and society. The Ifa tradition of Nigeria also extends to the neighboring countries of Benin and Togo and the African Diaspora in Brazil, Cuba, and the United States. Most practitioners are born into a lineage of diviners, but the practice can also be learned and transmitted from generation to generation. The divination process begins when a client consults a diviner on a particular problem or issue, such as a future marriage, to explain a bad dream, or to determine what the gods have in store for the client. While holding the divination chain, which consists of about sixteen cowries, the diviner recites a prayer formula appealing to the gods to provide an ultimate answer to the client's question. The client takes a coin or a currency, whispers his or her problem to it, and places it on his or her forehead, joining the *ori* (inner head) and his or her destiny to determine the answer to the queries. The money is placed on the divination chain, and the diviner, reciting some prayerful incantations, begs Ifa to provide and reveal the true answers to the client. He throws the divination chain on the divination mat, and suddenly a form of message or text appears, which the diviner will then read or recite and interpret for the client. Because the divination chain is in binary form and contains sixteen cowries, in principle, it is capable of producing 256 different signatures and chapters of oral recitation. Each signature produces hundreds of verses of oral poetry. The poetry consists of narratives, myths, folklore, songs, prayers, and so forth that contain powerful images and metaphors of archetypal figures of past and great diviners who are seen as models of human character. The client believes that the message relayed is related to his or her problem because Ifa is the spokesperson for the gods, and it is through his divinatory process that the gods reveal themselves to humans. Through further divination, the diviner will pinpoint to the client the exact nature of his or her problem and prescribe the proper sacrifice.

Because Ifa poetry, in principle, is the Yoruba encyclopedia of knowledge, it is assumed that the poems deal with all kinds of topics—that there is no topic that is not reflected in Ifa divination poetry. Since the end of the nineteenth century, scholars have begun to collect this poetry for the purpose of understanding not only the Yoruba religious universe and secular life but also for interpreting the messages that these texts carry. The poems are sources of epistemological, metaphysical, existential, and pragmatic events and meanings that pertain to the totality of Yoruba life; it is assumed there is no problem under the universe that is not addressed by Ifa. In the past two years, I have collected huge amounts of this oral tradition. This essay will discuss issues related to Ifa's discourse on pluralism, religious interaction, and the role of religion in peaceful transnational coexistence.

A final observation: consultation with Ifa is often a metaphorical reference to finding answers to troubling questions. As a Yoruba proverb says, "*Imoran ni nda ki a to da ifa,*" that is, "We seek advice or counseling first before performing divination." Ifa is a great historian and storyteller (*Baba Opitan*). He is a counselor. The Yoruba proverb also says, "*Adani imoran bi iyekan eni,*" that is, "The one who gives counsel or advice is like one's own relations." This means that one can rely on Ifa's suggestions, advice, and counsel at any given time.

We must also make a distinction between pluralism and plurality. Here I will invoke Diana Eck, who defines pluralism as the intrinsic understanding of multiple religious traditions coexisting with one another and plurality as the existence of traditions that may or may not be on good terms with others.[1] In this essay, I am concerned both with religious pluralism and how it relates to religious plurality, that is, how Ifa relates to Islam and Christianity and vice versa. What lessons about peaceful religious coexistence can we learn from Ifa's exposé? I am not fully interested in the theological enterprise, as significant as that approach may be. Rather, I am doing social ethical reflection about how the religions are addressing questions that I consider to be of interreligious importance or influence.

Examples from Ifa Texts
ÒTÚRÚPÒN'DI

According to an early text, Orunmila (the grand priest or grand/supreme prophet of Ifa) developed a relationship with Alu, whom he purchased as a slave. The two worked together and shared ideas. In Òtúrúpòn'dì, a babalawo (a priest or faithful follower) tells Orunmila not to put all his trust in Alu. The text alludes that Alu was Muslim because he spoke Arabic and he came from Mecca. At first, the encounter between Orunmila and Alu seemed friendly. Alu requested hospitality from Orunmila and was warmly received into the divinity's home. The two developed a healthy rapport with one another because, in Orunmila's eyes, they spoke the same language. "Though [Alu] was speaking Arabic language, he was using the language to say the words of Ifa and as well using Ifa tones with Arabic language." In other words, the Ifa text teaches that Islam and Yoruba share principles, knowledge, and spiritual concepts in common. Furthermore, the two religions can fruitfully coexist.

Difficulties emerge in the story, however, after Orunmila departed on a twenty-year journey and left his house to Alu. Over time, Alu conspired against his host and defiled his divination paraphernalia. He and his children planned war against Orunmila as well. When the god of divination returned to his house, he pummeled Alu as punishment for his deeds. Alu's children instigated a war against Orunmila but quickly realized they could not defeat him—spiritually or physically. At this point, they repented of their actions. Orunmila forgave them but renegotiated his relationship with Alu's children. Ifa concludes, "[Orunmila] should continue to use them to fend for himself but that under no circumstance should they have anything to do together neither should they ever relate in any way." Reading this story as a comment on interreligious conflict between Yoruba and Islam reveals intriguing insights. It is important to note that problems ensued when Orunmila left his house in Alu's hands. One could interpret this to mean that ill fate befalls the Yoruba when/ if they leave their culture, communities, politics, and economy to be monopolized by Islam. At the same time, the babalawo's forewarning to Orunmila suggests that Islam's arrival would bring limited benefits to Yoruba religion and society. The amity between the two traditions had its limitations from the start. In other words, Ifa clearly makes an allowance for plurality but not necessarily for pluralism.

Moreover, this narrative portrays Islam in mixed light. On one hand, Ifa points to common denominators between Muslim and Yoruba religious thought. On the other hand, the text depicts Islam as untrustworthy, a tradition whose aims will dismantle indigenous spirituality and culture. It is unclear how the two religions are to live peaceably together if they are not supposed to "have anything to do with one another." Perhaps this is an unresolved tension in the text that manifests as sociopolitical conflict.

ÒFÚN ÒKÀNRÀN

This text recounts Òyígí and the immaculate conception of her son's birth. The story is almost exactly as the one told in the Christian testament. Significant features in this story include a divine apparition that communicates to Òyígí that a special event will happen to her, similar to Mary's annunciation. She sought out a diviner who consulted Ifa and informed her of her divine pregnancy. Like Mary's Jesus, Òyígí's son, Ela, was born wiser than his years. His arrival was marked by the presence of three people bearing precious gifts, a reference to the magi from the East bringing gold, frankincense, and myrrh. Whereas the biblical text attributes Jesus' power to God, Ifa portrays Ela as Orunmila's mentee, a capable and intelligent student who impressed his mentor. Ifa says, "Orunmila loved him so much" and that Ela "was obedient to Orunmila." In other words, Ela's miraculous abilities to heal sick people through touch, spoken word, or herbal remedy had much to do with his being intertwined with the god of divination. Alas, like Jesus, Ela's contemporaries persecuted him because of his power. When he died, the whole community suffered catastrophe. Upon divination, it is revealed that his absence caused the destruction. In contrast to the biblical texts, Ifa says Ela cannot return but that one must invoke his name "during worship, preparation of medicine and the sayings of incantations," a reference to the origin and establishment of the Christian religious tradition.

This narrative's presence among Ifa texts suggests the Yoruba had a context for Christian doctrine when it arrived on the African continent. Perhaps Yoruba communities were able to receive the concept of an immaculate conception and miraculous savior because such a teaching already existed in the Yoruba canon. On a more subtle note, the story advocates for religious pluralism. It illumines what Christianity and Yoruba have in common and seems to provide talking points for amiable interreligious dialogue. In some sense, if a savior exists in both traditions, what reason is there for one tradition to expunge the other?

OTURUPON'FU

In this Ifa passage, one finds another rendition of Orunmila's first encounters with Alu, a slave who became the diviner's student. The text explains that Alu became proud and failed to pay deference to his teacher, a probable reference to the habit of Muslim proselytizers intimidating others with their faith. For this reason, Orunmila cursed him and thereby caused Alu to "do much work with little gain." The work included the rigorous five daily prayers, the bowing and fasting that Muslims perform in their religious practice. Unlike the previous text, Alu's Muslim identity emerged only from the curse placed upon him.

To some degree, this passage explains the origins of Islam, claiming that the tradition's roots lie in Yoruba sacred knowledge. Yoruba Muslims generally refer to themselves as *Eru Olorun*, "the slaves of God." It is Orunmila, god of divination, and Ifa who educate Alu in the art of incantation, ritual administration, and herbal preparation, emphasizing the symbolic relationship between the two. If that appears too bold a claim, one could read the relationship between Orunmila and Alu as a testament to the similarities between the two traditions. Ifa suggests that conflict emerges between Islam and Yoruba when the former religion begins to espouse its supremacy. While the narrative does not explicitly elevate Yoruba over the exogenous faith, it makes clear that Ifa possesses greater power and held that power prior to Islam's arrival. So much so, it is Orunmila who becomes the cause of Muslim devotional habits (i.e., bowing, fasting, etc.). Nevertheless, the curse on Alu creates a sharp critique of Islam and its tendency to assert its supremacy in the world. Intolerance, in other words, is not a virtue.

OTURA MEJI

Otura Meji presents a similar moral to that in *Oturupon'fu*. In this account, Baba Mole ("The Elderly Muslim"), the progenitor of Islam, became engrossed in Orunmila's teachings. The god of divination revealed all his secrets to Baba Mole. After mastering the teachings, the first Muslim purported himself as superior to his instructor. He developed his own methods and, according to Ifa, began to do the opposite of Orunmila. His techniques included using sound instead of Ifa powder, a rosary in place of an opele, and speaking Arabic instead of Yoruba. Nevertheless, Ifa makes it clear that Baba Mole still consulted Orunmila "to seek authority for the potency of his medicine," a reference to forms of Islamic medicine that combine Yoruba cultural practices with Islamic "magic." Patrick J. Ryan, in his book *Imale: Yoruba Participation in the Muslim Tradition*, refers to this phenomenon as *mixing*.[2]

This text furthers an argument present in *Oturupon'fu*. It explains more of Islam's traditions and makes sense of them from a Yoruba worldview. Examining this through an anthropological lens, one could claim this passage evinces the Yoruba response to the Muslim encounter. It demonstrates an indigenous ethnic group reacting to and reflecting upon the presence of a foreign tradition. Ifa's explanation points to plurality but not necessarily pluralism. It allows for both traditions to exist but attests to tensions between the two faiths. Ifa is clear on a key point: there is a difference between competition and conflict. Unlike in previous stories, this narrative permits Yoruba and Muslims to interact. Baba Mole's continuous consultation with Orunmila suggests that the two traditions continue to inform each other.

OTURA MEJI (DIFFERENT SEGMENT)

Another section of *Otura Meji* yields a profound revelation about Islam. The Ifa text claims the first Muslim, Olomo a sun gbangba, was a warrior. He fought with everyone, including his own people. For this reason, he lacked community and became lonely. After consulting with Orunmila, he offered a sacrifice in order to ensure he would maintain companions despite the unavoidable battles he waged. The prescription proved effective, and now, according to Ifa, Islam wages wars but maintains many followers. The text certainly predicates our current social and world order that is troubled by radical Islam with threats of war, battles, and violence in the name of God. But Ifa predicts that incessant war only leads to isolation and militates against building communities and civil societies.

A central Yoruba concept emerges in this narrative. The text explains Islam's *iwa pele*, or "character." *Iwa pele* is an individual person's best way of being in the world, and it is unique to each person. *Otura Meji* states the warrior is restless without war; it is in his nature to fight. Being a warrior is not necessarily evil but can lead to being ostracized, especially when traditions manifest indiscriminate and unprovoked violence, such as intrareligious wrangling between Protestants and Catholics, Shiites and Sunnis. This does not mean, however, that the warrior should be lonely because of his character. Therefore, it comes as no surprise that the warrior, through divination and sacrifice, is able to obtain companions. In terms of religious dialogue, *Otura Meji* reveals Yoruba's approach to Islam, one that differs drastically from the means taken by Western Christians. Yoruba makes space for the aggression displayed by jihad. Jihad is recognized as an intrinsic part of Islam, and some would argue it is the fifth pillar of Islam. However, Yoruba abhors forms of jihad that make one lose a sense of communal well-being and peaceful coexistence, especially with one's relations and neighbors. Upon close analysis, it becomes clear that this Ifa text may be a response to Muslim militancy in West Africa. Interestingly, though, the text encourages neither violence toward nor rejection of Islam. Rather, it seeks to make sense of the behavior demonstrated by Islam's proponents.

Conclusion

In our current world fraught with religiously motivated conflict and violence, indigenous religious and cultural traditions may be one of our most important resources. The challenge for the Western religious and educational elite is to learn how to respect (and often seek forgiveness from) the peoples from whom these traditions emanate. If mutual respect for one another can authentically develop, then dialogue for the sake of our common good may indeed occur.

For Reflection and Study

Key Ideas

- Africanized Christianity
- African spirituality
- body as metaphor and material
- conscientization of imperial power
- ethics of tolerance
- historical-cultural memory
- intersection of ethics and mission
- proclamation, enculturation, liberation
- religious pluralism
- religious plurality
- Revivalist Church
- Rastafari religion

Resources for Further Study

The Pluralism Project at Harvard—http://www.pluralism.org; http://pluralism.org/pages/pluralism/what_is_pluralism; and http://pluralism.org/pages/pluralism/essays/from_diversity_to_pluralism.

Cardoza-Orlandi, Carlos F. *Mission: An Essential Guide.* Nashville: Abingdon, 2002.

Hill, Jack A. *Ethics in the Global Village: Moral Insights for the Post 9-11 USA.* Santa Rosa, Calif.: Polebridge, 2008.

Sullivan, William M., and Will Kymlicka. *The Globalization of Ethics: Religious and Secular Perspectives.* Cambridge: Cambridge University Press, 2007.

Wilmore, Gayraud S. *Black Religion and Black Radicalism: An Interpretation of the Religious History of Afro-American People.* Maryknoll, N.Y.: Orbis, 1998.

Thinking Critically and Constructively

1. What do you think are pressing social justice moral dilemmas of the twenty-first century?
2. What religious traditions would you draw upon to construct an ethic that addresses religious pluralism and plurality?
3. What is the church's mission in the twenty-first century?

PART TWO

Moral Community

Chapter 5

The American Constitution

Its Troubling Religious
and Ethical Paradox for Blacks

Riggins R. Earl Jr.

FOR AMERICANS, THE U.S. Constitution symbolizes America's social contract, but for black Americans it has been used paradoxically both to disempower and to empower them individually and collectively.[1] The Constitution's negative and positive references to blacks has produced in them despair on the one hand and hope on the other. By examining the different phases of the historical development of the Constitution, it is possible to see how the white framers and amenders of the document crafted it to speak in troubling exclusionary/inclusionary terms regarding black Americans' worth. Originally, the white framers of the Constitution produced the *three-fifths compromise clause* for the purpose of excluding blacks from the political process as their equals. Later, with the Thirteenth, Fourteenth, and Fifteenth Amendments, whites sought to amend the Constitution in ways that blacks, at least marginally, could be included in America's social contract and its promises of justice and equality. Between the clause and the amendments resides the primary source of a troubling ethical and theological paradox for blacks regarding their religious, moral, and political worth, a paradox that has shaped the social and political being of black Americans.

Importantly, the Constitution's contradictory evolutionary history as it relates to blacks exposes the commitment of its framers, interpreters, and amenders to making what Charles Mills calls their "racial contract."[2] Mills's central argument is that there exists a racial contract that is even more fundamental to Western society than the social contract. This racial contract determines who counts as full moral and political persons, and it therefore sets the parameters of who can "contract in" to the freedom and equality that the social contract promises. White men are full persons according to the racial contract, thus deserving of equality and freedom. Their status as full persons accords them the social, political, and legal power to make contracts as well as to be the subjects of contracts, whereas other persons are denied such privilege and are relegated to the status of objects of contracts.

Except for the Bible, the Constitution is for blacks the paramount symbol of authority. The faith of blacks in the authority of the Constitution has prevailed despite unwillingness of whites to "contract them into" its sacred promises of equality and justice for all. A significant example of this faith in the Constitution is the great passion of blacks to prove themselves worthy recipients of America's social contract by serving in the nation's military during major wars.

Furthermore, blacks have never lost hope in the promissory ideals of equality and justice expressed in such documents as the Preamble to the Declaration of Independence and Abraham Lincoln's Emancipation Proclamation. Blacks have employed the ideals of equality and justice expressed in these documents as an antidote to the exclusionary ideology of the racial contract symbolized in the Constitution's three-fifths compromise clause.[3]

The Preamble to the Declaration of Independence and Lincoln's Emancipation Proclamation

The Declaration of Independence and Lincoln's Emancipation Proclamation highlight a religious tension between the belief that freedom and equality are gifts from God and the political belief that the nation bestows these gifts to black Americans. The Preamble to the Declaration asserts divine equality for all men (*sic*), and the Emancipation

Proclamation has been recognized as the nation's symbolic granting of citizenship rights to blacks.[4]

With a belief in the natural rights of equality bestowed by God as set forth in the Declaration of Independence as well as the symbolic granting of the rights of citizenship through the Emancipation Proclamation, blacks have rightly taken offense at the Constitution's reduction of them to less-than-full-human status. Blacks have understood this official form of reductionism as challenging their inherent worthiness for citizenship, and this challenge produces in the black consciousness a religious and ethical paradox. At the heart of this paradox are two presuppositions. The religious presupposition of the white framers, interpreters, and enforcers of the Constitution is that God originally endowed only their racial group with the natural rights of freedom and equality. The ethical presupposition of the white framers, interpreters, and enforcers of the Constitution is that it is their right to decide *whether* and *when* blacks are worthy of full citizenship rights. In sum, the religious and ethical paradox is about the social, ontological, and epistemological capacity of blacks for citizenship.

Three questions are at the heart of this religious and ethical paradox. First, must blacks have their citizenship rights conferred upon them (a question about the human bestowal of rights)? Second, are blacks endowed by their Creator with certain inalienable rights (a question about the divine inheritance of rights)? Third, are blacks expected to achieve their rights by meritoriously proving themselves worthy of citizenship (a question about the achievement of rights)? Discussion of each of the positions represented by the questions will be provided below.

The Human Bestowal of Rights

President Lincoln's Emancipation Proclamation is the document that symbolizes the human-bestowal-of-rights argument. The question is whether Lincoln's act, the human bestowal of rights, is to be interpreted politically and/or theologically—a point that will be explored more fully throughout the remainder of this essay.[5]

From the perspective of the human bestowal of rights, millions of blacks and whites have believed that President Lincoln's signing of the

Emancipation Proclamation gave blacks their freedom as well as the rights of American citizenship that the Constitution had denied them. This belief was obviously most pervasive in the minds of blacks immediately following the Civil War. According to this belief, freedom for black people in America is the result of the effort and grace of white people. Nowhere is this dramatized more than following the Civil War, when some Union Army officers issued what they called a certificate of freedom to slaves who had served in the U.S. military. Here is an example of a certificate of freedom:

> An "American Citizen of African descent" bearer of this Declaration by me issued at Helena in the State of Arkansas in the Federal Union, formerly held as a slave within a District in rebellion against the United States, has been by a Proclamation of his Excellency Abraham Lincoln President of the United States declared to be henceforward and forever free.
>
> The freedom of Daniel *Webster* will be *recognized* and *maintained* by the forces under my command and he is commended to the *kindness* and *protection* of other military or naval authorities and to the respect and esteem of civilians as he journey northward to the state of Ohio.[6]

According to black leaders who had initially celebrated the Proclamation, the limitations of the document were evident by the end of Reconstruction. Frederick Douglass, one of those leaders who had celebrated it, became very critical of its failure to protect the rights of blacks. Following Reconstruction, in 1888, Douglass denounced Lincoln's Emancipation Proclamation "as a stupendous fraud . . . a fraud upon him, a fraud upon the world."[7] Douglass's rationale for this denunciation was that "the national government had abandoned the African American, ignored his rights as an American citizen," thus leaving the black person "a deserted, a defrauded, a swindled and an outcast man—in law, free, in fact, a slave."[8]

Importantly, the celebration of Lincoln's signing of the Emancipation Proclamation as an act of divine intervention[9] was now understood as the means by which the white nation became the dispenser of rights to blacks. Indeed, Lincoln's Emancipation Proclamation positioned white America in the role of being the *sovereign giver* of rights to black people.

The brutality of slavery and the failure of the Emancipation Proclamation clearly demarcate why blacks inevitably see the whole rights issue in America through a different lens than do whites. White Americans born in this country have never had to speak of their rights as having been given to them by an earthly source, persons, or nation. It is for this reason that white people perceive the nation as the *sovereign protector* of the rights given them by nature's God. Ironically, these are the people who believed, as colonialists, that it was their sacred duty to take up arms to defend their God-given rights against mother England. Contrary to their own history of fighting for and attaining their rights from an oppressive government, white America has in respect to blacks betrayed the seminal idea that was the driving force of the American Revolution and the birthing of the United States of America.

Nevertheless, both before and after the Civil War and through today, black leaders have posited great faith and hope in these words found in the Preamble to the Declaration of Independence: "All men are endowed by nature's God with certain inalienable rights." Accordingly, from Frederick Douglass and Sojourner Truth to Fannie Lou Hamer and Martin Luther King Jr., black leaders have held firm to the belief that the Constitution fully affirms blacks' humanity because of their hope in its "We the people . . ." declaration. These leaders have therefore faithfully believed that the Thirteenth Amendment assures blacks of their rights and promises the protective legal space for blacks to become full citizens.

In this argument, Lincoln's Emancipation Proclamation is thus the precursor (so to speak) to the amending of the Constitution following the Civil War. The Thirteenth Amendment symbolized the nation's collective promise to protect the rights of black people that the Proclamation had conferred symbolically. This amendment's promissory of protection was the wounded nation's effort to make null and void Chief Supreme Court Justice Judge Taney's infamous ruling that the black man had no rights that the white man was bound to respect.[10] Recent black scholars of the American Constitution, such as Leon Higginbotham (a scholar of constitutional law), have consequently noted that the Thirteenth Amendment's promise of protection of blacks' rights was in theory rather than in practice. Higginbotham and others draw their conclusion from the fact that the federal government literally withdrew its protection of blacks when the troops were withdrawn from the South following Reconstruction; the Thirteenth Amendment was to guarantee equality under the law for freed persons, but it did not eliminate the belief in the inferiority of blacks.

Higginbotham doubted the original inclusiveness and protection for blacks of the Thirteenth Amendment, and he was even less hopeful about it at the end of the civil rights era of the 1960s. A look at Higginbotham's position and that of minister and abolitionist Henry Highland Garnet almost one hundred years earlier is instructive at this point. Higginbotham asserted that the Thirteenth Amendment merely states that slavery and involuntary servitude shall not exist within the United States. It does not state explicitly whether African Americans can "become citizens and enjoy equal rights."[11] Conversely, Garnet, in his 1865 address before the U.S. House of Representatives, declared that the Thirteenth Amendment abolished slavery and thus entitled black Americans to citizenship. From the vantage point of history, Higginbotham could make the counterclaim to Garnet as to the impact of the Thirteenth Amendment because he knew that a contemporary civil rights movement was necessary to continue the struggle for equal rights for black Americans. Indeed, the masses of black Americans are still struggling for *full access* to America's house of democracy.

Finally, for blacks Lincoln's Emancipation Proclamation was interpreted as a human bestowal of rights precipitated by divine intervention. This notion of divine intervention in the human-bestowal argument opens up theological questions behind the religious and ethical paradox of black citizenship rights. Do blacks interpret the bestowal of their rights through the lens of deism? Or do they see it through the lens of theism? Or do blacks see it through the lens of christocentrism? Historical leaders such as Frederick Douglass were more inclined to employ both deistic and theistic ideas when describing God's relationship to the bestowal of rights. The rhetoric of more contemporary black protest and civil rights leaders uses deistic, theistic, and sometimes christocentric ideas about God interchangeably. Overall, a perusal of the rhetoric of blacks before and since the Emancipation Proclamation tends to indicate that because of their evangelical heritage blacks move back and forth between theocentric and christocentric views or a fusion of the two.

The relevance of how God is related to humanly bestowed rights leads to interesting assumptions about God and human responsibility. Such assumptions provoke religious and ethical questions that are inextricably tied up with the theory of the divine inheritance of rights. To this we now turn.

The Divine Inheritance of Rights

It seems that Thomas Jefferson's deistic perspective of nature's God as the one who grants rights was perhaps too impersonal for the masses of oppressed black people. This is probably the case because blacks were deeply influenced by evangelical Christianity and its emphasis on the personal salvation of each individual's soul. Blacks obviously found this belief highly appealing because it allowed each individual to affirm God as his/her personal creator and redeemer through Jesus. It was this belief that gave each individual a sense of "I am somebody" in the sight of God. Furthermore, the biblical story of Jesus portrays a special relationship between Jesus and downtrodden people. In the end, black people delight in the fact that they are individually and collectively the handiwork of the Christian God both in creation and redemption. This emphasis on creation (being made in the image of God by the hands of God and redemption (being saved by that same God through Jesus Christ) has led blacks to conclude, often uncritically, that they are equal with *any* and *everybody*. In short, blacks have concluded that, because the Bible's God has *created* them in God's image, they inherit the rights of freedom and equality.

Having been told by whites that their race descended from apes and monkeys, it is not surprising that blacks chose to affirm that they were created in the image of a personal God. Henry Highland Garnet asserted that "the black man" was created in God's image as normative. Following the ratification of the U.S. Constitution, Garnet addressed the issue of the black man being created in the image of God in the House of Representatives in 1865:

Our poor and forlorn brother whom thou hast labeled a slave, is also a man. He may be unfortunate, weak, helpless and despised and hated; nevertheless he is a man. His God and thine has stamped on his forehead his title to inalienable rights in characters that can be read by every intelligent being. Pitiless storms of outrage may have beaten upon his defenseless head, and he may have descended through ages of oppression; yet he is a man. God made him such and his brother cannot unmake him. Woe, woe to him who attempts to commit the accursed crime.[12]

In the above quote, a highly educated black minister assimilates the language of the Bible with that of the promissory ideals of the Preamble to the Declaration of Independence. Garnet portrays God as the "stamper" of God's qualification for inalienable rights upon the black man's forehead. The image of God as stamper of these rights complements the image of God in Genesis as "the *maker* of man in God's own image." He thinks that these stamped characters of inalienable rights upon the black man's forehead reflect God's image. Garnet concludes that the black man by virtue of this fact has inherited from God innately the right to be free. The ideas of black leaders about freedom and equality based upon the inheritance of God-given rights have been fairly consistent with Garnet's position.

Black church leadership has drawn heavily upon this tradition. A careful reading of black Christian ministers' rhetoric of the civil rights struggle throughout the twentieth century points to the question of blacks' rights as a matter of divine inheritance. Black ministers have been convinced that Jesus' adoption of black people into his universal plan of salvation makes them bona fide candidates for the Constitution's rights. These ministers' belief is consistent with the idea that the God of personal salvation also influenced the framers of the Constitution and the writers of the Declaration of Independence. The oppressed individual out of his/her biblical faith believes that Jesus has personally saved him/her from sin. It is this sense of personal salvation that gives blacks a sense of having inherited rights to the common good of America.

Civil rights leaders' speeches and sermons all suggest that blacks believed that the biblical God created them with equal rights. Martin

Luther King Jr. drew upon this embedded sentiment in the consciousness of black people as he led the civil rights movement.[13] He and other
leaders celebrated oppressed black peoples' idea that somebodiness is
a gift from Jesus and God. It is this possession of somebodiness from
Jesus and God that has emboldened oppressed black people with the
conviction that they "have a right to" what their slave ancestors called
"the tree of life," that is, to Jesus Christ, who died upon the cross. On
the one hand, blacks have believed in the biblical notion of rights that
derive from their being created in the image of God. This belief leads
them to assert that they are qualified holistically (that is, body, mind, and
soul) for equal inclusion under the Constitution. For many evangelical
black leaders, God's act of creation transcends the Constitution and this
truly makes blacks entitled their rights. On the other hand, blacks have
believed that their *adoption rights* from Jesus qualify them for membership in the family of God and humanity. Adoption rights are a gift from
Jesus, a consequence of having been washed in (redeemed by) his blood.
These two understandings of how blacks have inherited their rights,
derivative of being created in the image of God or derived from being
redeemed in the blood of Jesus Christ, represent two different theological perspectives, thus nuancing the inheritance-of-rights argument for
blacks. Now, it is time to turn to the third argument regarding the rights
of blacks: the struggle of blacks to achieve their rights by satisfying the
expectations of the white meritocracy.

The Achievement of Rights

The achievement-of-rights argument operates from the presupposition
that blacks must achieve their own rights. This argument asserts that
freedom is acquired through human effort. For some, the acquisition of
these rights stresses that blacks must be willing to fight violently with
whites for their freedom. Long before the Civil War, Henry Highland
Garnet supported this position; he made his convictions unequivocally
clear in a speech delivered before the National Convention of Colored
Citizens in Buffalo, New York, on August 16, 1843. Countering the white
abolitionist William Lloyd Garrison, Garnet told blacks, "However much

you may . . . desire it there is not much hope of Redemption without the shedding of blood."[14] Garnet believed that the colored citizens of this convention should fight to free their brothers and sisters in slavery for two reasons: (1) "they were, by birth, just as much American citizens as anybody"; and (2) "they were bearers of a Christian conscience." Garnet argued: "Brethren the time has come when you must act for yourselves. It is an old and true saying, that 'if hereditary bondsmen would be free, they must themselves strike the first blow.' You can plead your own cause, and do the work of emancipation better than any other."[15] The achievement argument makes human struggle the mantra of the oppressed, and both abolitionists in the nineteenth century and integrationists in the twentieth century have espoused this argument.

The idea of the unworthiness of blacks was institutionalized in slavery, and it is conceivable that the very nature of the slave society perpetuated an individual and group sense of unworthiness among blacks. One of the most visible ways of creating a consciousness of unworthiness among slaves occurred at the auctioning of slaves. The auctioning of slaves demanded a capitalistic way of valuing the slaves in terms of their market value. On the auction block, the slave was valued according to his/her work skills, physical size, and breeding capacity. Institutionalized slavery was thus premised upon a system wherein slaves were valued in terms of their extrinsic rather than intrinsic worth. The slave's work skills established extrinsic worth. However, when some slave masters allowed some slaves a half-day off on Saturdays to work for pay, those slaves took full advantage of the opportunity to make money, and sometimes they were able to buy their freedom. This practice undoubtedly created in some slaves a rare sense of somebodiness, a precondition for a sense of intrinsic worth. The response of blacks to being assigned by whites extrinsic and intrinsic worth was to engage constructively to achieve their rights to the satisfaction of white people. These constructive efforts are referred to as the *self-help ethic of uplift*.

At least three constructive approaches have dominated black Christians' *self-help* ethical efforts to achieve their rights in America. First, *the acquisition of literacy skills*. Because slavery made it illegal for blacks to read and write, generations of black preachers and educators admonished their people to acquire literacy skills. Leaders such as Booker T.

Washington[16] and W. E. B. Du Bois[17] thought that the acquisition of literacy skills was one of the premier means of proving themselves worthy for inclusion under the protection of the Constitution. This notion of the virtue of literacy has been transmitted generationally. It is consistent with the classical Greek philosophical belief that education is foundational to democracy and prerequisite for a free citizenry.

The clarion call for education has been at the heart of the civil rights struggle since the end of slavery. The civil rights movement under the leadership of Martin Luther King Jr. was clearly an experiment in democracy premised upon the importance of education to freedom. Every mass meeting was a lesson in making choices individually and collectively regarding the freedom project. Speeches on the teachings of the Bible and the Constitution regarding blacks were central to mass-meeting presentations. Today zeal for education as a source of power remains a priority of black Americans. With the explosion of computer-based knowledge, educators face a greater challenge than ever of convincing this generation of the value of highly developed literacy skills. This is particularly important when the intelligence of poor children in public schools is often compared to the intelligence of the computer. Meanwhile, the glaring reality is that the country's neglect of public education makes it more difficult for the child in poverty to acquire those literary skills that are fundamental prerequisites to achieving constitutional rights as active citizens. Here again, the worth of black people, in this case black children, is being determined by white standards of worthiness as the educational system creates obstacles to the successful satisfaction of the standards.

Second, *loyal military service for the defense of country*.[18] Blacks have understood loyal military service to America as being another means of proving themselves worthy of full citizenship rights under the Constitution. This has been the case for blacks for generations despite the nation's racist exclusion of them from the reward systems of such service. Malcolm X, Louis Farrakhan, Martin Luther King Jr., and Coretta Scott King have been open critics of the nation's military and their use of black soldiers to fight to free other people in the world while denying blacks access to freedom in America. A historical voice sets this issue in perspective. Minister Francis J. Grimke, following the Civil War, asserted

that blacks had earned their rights through years of unremunerated sacrifices for this country as slaves and soldiers in the nation's wars:

> We are not asking for favors, we are contending only for what justly
> belongs to us; for what we have earned the right to by centuries of
> toil; by the sacrifice of life in defense of the Nation; and by efforts, as
> praiseworthy, as commendable as were ever put forth by any other
> race under similar circumstances, to make something of ourselves.[19]

Every generation of black leaders has thus encouraged their followers to fight in every war—even when it seemed to be antithetical to the
interests of the race. The battlefield itself has been viewed as a theater
for proving and achieving black manhood and womanhood. The sterling
performance of the Tuskegee Airmen during World War II is but one
classic case in point. In every major war, blacks have held on to the belief
that ultimate loyalty and sacrifice to America, against an outside enemy,
takes primacy over the nation's treatment of them. Martin Luther King
Jr. and Malcolm X were the first major contemporary black leaders to
challenge blacks' and whites' blind commitment to the "my nation, right
or wrong" ethic during war. Also, in lieu of economic opportunity, service in the military was viewed as a means for poor black males, who were
denied employment in this society, to achieve employment, a mark of
extrinsic and intrinsic worth in capitalist America.

Third, *acquisition of economic wealth*. This means of achieving worth
in America has been lauded for generations. Both Booker T. Washington[20] and W. E. B. Du Bois[21] deemed economic wealth as a means to
freedom that could bring about a balance of power between black and
white people. This is the case because of the correlation between constitutional rights and the acquisition of wealth in the United States—
political and economic power are inseparable forces in the American
social order. In the twenty-first century, however, holding on to this correlation between political and economic power is being undermined by
a generation of prominent black athletes and entertainers of the hip-hop
culture who are politically conservative.

Finally, the achievement-of-rights argument complicates further the
religious and ethical paradox of the black quest for rights. Central to it
is the idea that blacks have to achieve their rights because they were

created unworthy of them. The need for blacks to show themselves worthy of rights is necessitated by a meritocracy predicated upon race. This meritocracy creates insurmountable odds for blacks as they struggle to achieve rights by changing the rules at every level. In such a system, it is not surprising that blacks are unable to meet the criteria of worthiness set by the whites. This painful reality has often driven many blacks to place all of their energy on the attainment of theological virtues rather than political rights. For this reason, some blacks gravitate toward an expression of Christianity that focuses on the virtues of freedom and equality that God infuses via God's grace in Jesus, thus attaining rights in the other world that had absolutely been denied them because of the color of their skin in this world. Even today, black church leaders seek to help blacks maintain a creative tension between an otherworldly and a this-worldly achievement of their rights.

Conclusion

I have argued here that the history of the framing, amending, and enforcing of the Constitution with respect to the rights of blacks has resulted in a troubling religious and ethical paradox for black Americans. On the one hand, framers of the Constitution refused to acknowledge blacks as having inherited rights. On the other hand, amenders of the Constitution promised to protect the freedom conferred upon blacks by President Lincoln's Emancipation Proclamation. Although Lincoln's Emancipation Proclamation did not actually secure the citizenship rights of blacks, it set forth the legal and moral trajectory for white America to free itself from its own immoral constitutional entanglement that denied the humanity as well as the rights of blacks.

Three arguments about the rights of blacks are presented to grapple with the Constitution's exclusionary/inclusionary history: (1) human bestowal, (2) divine inheritance, and (3) human achievement. These three arguments leave blacks caught between theological and political notions of freedom and equality, thus the crux of the religious and ethical paradox. Finally, there is an inescapable web of paradoxical contradictions spun by the framers, amenders, and enforcers of the Constitution in which black and white America are both caught.

Chapter 6

The Challenge of Race

A Theological Reflection

James H. Cone

The problem of the twentieth century is the problem of the color-line.
—W. E. B. Du Bois (1903)

America must resolve the race problem, or this race problem will doom
America.—Martin Luther King Jr. (July 2, 1967)

W. E. B. Du Bois and Martin Luther King Jr. believed that there is no
greater threat to the future existence of America than the problem of
race. Both spent their lives challenging America to make real the promises of democracy by bridging the gap between what it says about freedom and justice and its practice of racial segregation. Du Bois, author of
the classic *The Souls of Black Folk*, was an *intellectual activist*. He wrote
so profoundly and creatively about white supremacy and black resistance that few who read his books and essays could fail to acknowledge
the brilliance of his analysis and his political determination to destroy
racism in American life and the world. King, a Baptist preacher and civil
rights leader, was an *activist intellectual*. His reflections on the problem of
race emerged not from academic research but primarily out of his faith
in God, who empowered him to stand up to white bigots in the South
and liberals in the North, knowing that it would cost him his life.

I am a *theological activist*. I have spent my life trying to understand the challenge that race poses for faith—for theology and the church in society. What is it about the nature of the Christian faith that makes it necessary for theology and the church to engage the problem of race in America and the world? Since the publication of my first book, *Black Theology and Black Power* (1969), I have challenged white and black theologians, preachers, and Christians to rethink faith so that the problem of race is not ignored or marginalized but placed at the center of Christian identity. There can be no true understanding of the Christian faith in America without confronting head-on white supremacy.

Race challenges not only the Christian faith but also our faith in humanity. One does not have to be a Christian, as I am, to see the great contradiction white supremacy poses for humankind. Race was not only the great problem of the twentieth century, as Du Bois said; but it also continues to challenge us today. If America does not solve the race problem, as King said, it will doom America.

As I explore the problem of race in this essay, there are three challenges that I want to examine. The first challenge is to break our silence; that is, to speak openly and often about how to engage each other across our racial and cultural communities; the second is to learn how to listen to one another in a meaningful way; and the third is to work together to dismantle white supremacy.

Breaking Silence

There is no way to solve the race problem if we do not talk to one another about it. Yet I do not know any subject that silences white and black people more than race. People get nervous and start to look away from one another when race enters the conversation. Race is such an explosive and sensitive topic that whites hardly know what they can say that will not inflame black people. And black people hardly know what they can say that will encourage whites to talk freely and honestly, but in an informed manner that reflects a deep awareness of why many blacks *still* feel homeless in the land of their birth, *still* feel like they are "rolling through an unfriendly world." The depth of this profound agony is found in an old slave song still sung in black churches today:

"Sometimes I feel like a motherless child, a long ways from home." It is not easy for whites to enter into this experience and move into the depths of black existence, because whites often know so little intellectually—and even less existentially—about the history of the black experience in America.

African Americans know a lot existentially about what it means to be black but often not much intellectually about the history of racism and the black struggle against it. We tend to take ourselves for granted without examining deeply and critically the paradoxical nature of blackness. Our artists—the poets and musicians, grassroots preachers and teachers, and other cultural workers—transport us to a transcendent realm of existence, an otherworldly experience that makes rational discourse unnecessary and even out of place. What did I do to be so black and blue? is not a rational question but an existential query about blackness and the blues and why these realities are so inseparable in African American life. But this existential knowledge cannot be used as a substitute for historical knowledge—knowledge of "the ways of white folks"[1] and of black survival and resistance in a world of trouble. It is impossible to have a meaningful dialogue about race if the participants do not have an informed knowledge—existential *and* intellectual—about the history of race in America and the world.

Lack of knowledge can cause whites to make insulting comments about black people. For example, whites sometimes talk as if there is little or no difference between the life chances and opportunities of blacks and whites. They contend that the civil rights movement corrected past injustices and thereby created a level playing field for all Americans. With a black president of the United States, this shows that everyone now has an equal chance for "life, liberty, and the pursuit of happiness," they say. Some whites will acknowledge that there are still economic and educational gaps between whites and blacks, but they argue that it is due largely to the cultural and family values and choices in black communities. It is necessary, the argument goes, to teach black women not to have too many babies and black men to become responsible fathers, and they too will succeed, just like whites. Whites work and take responsibility for their lives; blacks expect the government to take care of them.

Of course, not all whites share this view, but many do, and too often whites who disagree remain silent. It is hard to know how to talk to people with that skewed perspective. When we consider that whites enslaved blacks for 246 years and then segregated and lynched them for another one hundred—accumulating wealth as blacks were excluded from acquiring it—we can see that fifteen years of civil rights activity, marching and sitting in, were not enough to erase the tremendous inequities of three and a half centuries of legalized slavery and segregation. The most important results of the civil rights movement were the passage of the Civil Rights Bill (1964) and the Voting Rights Act (1965). Both achievements transformed the social and political life of America. Without those victories, Barack Obama and many other blacks would not be holding political office today. As one who lived his childhood and teens during the reign of Jim Crow, I can testify to the far-reaching changes that have taken place in this country, especially in the South. We can now travel with much less fear of violence and racial insult, and with the comforts our economic resources can afford.

Yet despite the great achievement of the civil rights movement, it did not succeed in getting rid of white supremacy. White supremacy is still deeply embedded in the social fabric of the nation. The most obvious instance is the huge difference between the net worths of blacks and whites. The legacy of slavery and segregation is the main reason why blacks are so much poorer than whites, so much less likely to go to college, and so much more likely to be unemployed, underemployed, incarcerated, or homeless. Just as wealth is inherited, so is poverty. While young whites are positioned to replace their parents in prestigious colleges and universities, young blacks are positioned to end up in prisons. That is why nearly one million black people are in prisons today—almost one-half of the more than two million people residing there. Blacks represent only 12 percent of the general population but nearly 50 percent of the prison population. Blacks receive more than double their share of everything bad about America and far less than their due of everything good. The exploitation of blacks is so widespread and accepted that whites often wonder why blacks are still griping and complaining. "What do they want now?" whites still frequently ask.

Blacks do not know what to say to whites that will help them to understand that all we want is justice—simple justice, no more and no less. Justice is fair play, dealing justly. In most instances there is nothing complicated about its meaning between individuals and communities. We learn about it early as children at home, school, church, and play. I remember my parents insisting that we play fair with each other. And we knew when we were fair and when we were not. We did not need our parents to tell us what was fair, and the one who was unfair did not want our parents or an unbiased adult to decide who was and who was not being fair.

Whites do not seem to know what justice means when dealing with African Americans. They knew what it meant for the white South after the Civil War but not for black slaves. They knew how to talk about justice for their war enemies in Germany and even Japan following World War II, but not for blacks who fought for a freedom in Europe and Asia that was denied them when they returned home to America.

Whites have little or no problem reflecting on justice for their racial group. But when blacks make an appeal for justice, that is another story. Talk about justice for blacks seems to puzzle whites, as if they do not understand what we mean. Justice for African Americans is almost always viewed as "special rights," and even as racism in reverse. How can blacks be accused of reverse racism when we have never had the power to oppress whites racially? There is no real racism without *power*, that is, without the ability to implement laws in the society that reflect prejudices toward others. Whites have had special rights ever since there was a United States of America. They accumulated the wealth of this nation on the backs of black slaves, at the expense of the genocide of Indians, through the violent acquisition of Mexico, and the widespread exploitation of Chinese workers. They worked black slaves like animals—backbreaking labor from early morning to late night without pay for two and a half centuries. Whites defined America as a white man's country, and everybody else was regarded as inferior, not worthy of full citizenship. It is, therefore, a little weird to hear whites complain about blacks receiving special rights.

Malcolm X said that whites could make the criminal look like the victim and make the victim look like the criminal. Nowhere is this more clearly illustrated than in the white reaction to affirmative action. White right-wing conservative officials and their political pundits, who vehemently opposed the 1960s' civil rights movement, today use Martin Luther King Jr.'s "I Have A Dream" address to advance their racist agenda. They take King's words about people being judged "not by the color of their skin but by the content of their character" and twist them to undergird the special rights of whites already in place. Whites advocate a color-blind society, as if one can get rid of ingrained racism simply by ignoring it. How can one get rid of white supremacy without naming it and making it visible so all can see the hurt it inflicts on humanity?

There are some conservative whites who make the absurd claim that since African Americans are the most well-off blacks of any in the world, they should be grateful to whites for bringing them to America as slaves. When a Miami radio talk-show host and a call-in listener said that to me, I could hardly contain my rage. I just could not believe that anyone could be so disrespectful and insulting. There can be no dialogue when crimes against humanity are treated as a positive good. And I said so with all the intellectual and spiritual power in my being. I told them that it was like a rapist saying many years later to his victim, who gave birth to a child after she was violated, that she should be grateful that he violated her since the child of the unwelcome intercourse has grown up to be such a nice person. What was so amazing about the radio host and call-in listener was their sincerity. They were not trying to disrespect or insult black people or me. White people know so little about black history and relate to so few blacks who tell them what they really think and feel about race issues. That is why whites end up disrespecting and insulting blacks without even intending to or knowing it. After listening to me respond to their initial insults, they seemed to gain a better understanding of at least one black perspective on race.

I have also heard whites say, "Don't blame us for slavery and racial segregation. We have never owned slaves or segregated blacks. Our arrival was much later." Most blacks do not blame any present-day whites for slavery or segregation. We simply object to their opposition to the U.S. government doing something about correcting its past and present exploitation of black people. When a government sanctions a group's exploitation on the basis of color, it is only just for that government to correct what it did and does wrong. A criminal who robs a bank and is caught cannot just say, "I'm sorry," and let it go at that. He must not only return the money but pay for the harm he caused to individuals and society. When the government is the criminal—as was the case with slavery, segregation, and lynching—it too must rectify the wrong committed. The same is true for other institutions that benefited from injustices in society. If justice means getting one's due—receiving back what was unfairly taken—then every individual and group deserves justice. We must create a society in which the humanity of all is mutually respected and protected. We will never have peace between the races as long as one race dominates others. "No Justice, No Peace!" is not just a slogan for political activists; but it is also a profound truth of human community. Real dialogue will start only when whites first understand that their humanity is tied to blacks, and the route to knowing this is through knowing some of the history.

We have a race problem in America because people of color have a long history of unjust treatment. It is important for all participants to know something about it. Race defines America's identity and distinguishes it from any other country. Of course, the problem of race is global and not limited to black-white issues, but here in the United States the black-white dimension of race has shaped our character, corrupted our religious and educational institutions, and poisoned our economic and political life. There is no place one can go to escape it in America. How can we talk about justice for blacks in the light of America's past and present entrenched structures of racial oppression? Must we ignore the dreadful consequences of slavery and Jim Crow segregation and just start from scratch, as if these evils had never happened or have no bearing on black oppression today? Because whites and blacks view the problem of race from different vantage points, communication between them can get out of hand. That is why most Americans do not talk much about race, at least not across the color line. It is time for us to break our silence and start talking about the America we want to create for the twenty-first century. I can think of no better place to begin than in our educational and religious institutions, and in our social and political life, as well as in our personal and communal life. With Barack Obama as president, we have a powerful symbol that blacks, whites, and others respect, and he could help us to start talking to each other about race.

Lack of knowledge about race is not confined to whites. Blacks also are often ignorant about the history of race in America. Ignorance causes blacks to depend too much on their personal, existential experience, as if they represent the whole black community and the whites they know represent all white people. I have seen blacks get defensive and arrogant about what they know about racism, an attitude that is often a dead giveaway for lack of knowledge. Just because one is black does not mean that one has an informed knowledge about race. Blacks have to read about race just like anybody else if they expect to acquire the much-needed knowledge for multiracial dialogue. Our personal experience is important but not the final or even the most important ingredient for a critical understanding of race.

Like whites, we need to look beyond our personal experience and see to what extent we are representative of blacks in other parts of the country and in history. Not all blacks have the same perspective on race. Abolitionists Martin Delany and Frederick Douglass saw things differently. Delany, the father of black nationalism, advocated a separate territory for black people outside the United States. He did not believe that blacks would ever be accepted as equals with whites. Douglass, an uncompromising integrationist, insisted that blacks can and must be accepted as American citizens equal with whites. He vehemently rejected the idea of a separate land for blacks. The antilynching advocate Ida B. Wells-Barnett and the "Great Accommodator" Booker T. Washington also were contemporaries who found themselves in profound disagreement about the best route to justice for the newly freed black slaves. Wells-Barnett was a journalist freedom fighter who used her pen and risked her life exposing and attacking the daily occurrence of the horrific lynching violence against black men and women throughout the United States in the late nineteenth and early twentieth centuries. Washington, founder of the Tuskegee Institute, was the most powerful Negro leader of his time and perhaps ever in America. He is best known and loved by whites for his infamous "Atlanta Exposition Address" (1895), in which he reassures them that "in all things that are purely social we can be as separate as the fingers, yet one as the hand in all things essential to mutual progress."[2] Martin Luther King Jr. and Malcolm X were Christian and Muslim ministers who have been called the yin and yang of the black freedom movement and of the soul of black America. In the 1960s, they symbolized two roads to freedom, similar to those of Frederick Douglass and Martin Delany—integration and separation. Supreme Court Justice Clarence Thomas and the Reverend Jesse Jackson are radical opposites on most social and political issues today—with the former despising affirmative action, even though he received it, and the latter one of its most fierce advocates, even though he never benefited from it. We need to have a critical knowledge of many black perspectives on race, because they all have something to teach us about the complexity of black resistance in America.

It is also important for blacks to know that not all whites have the same perspective on race. There was the great abolitionist John Brown, who was executed for fighting to end slavery, and Supreme Court Justice Roger B. Taney, who wrote the infamous Dred Scott Decision, saying that blacks had "no rights which the white man was bound to respect"; the brilliant Attorney Clarence Darrow, who used his legal skills to defend blacks, and Senator Strom Thurmond, who used fear and race hatred to organize southern politicians to oppose the integration of blacks in American life (even though he fathered a child with his then-fifteen-year-old black maid). There was the great southern novelist Lillian Smith, who used her literary talent to advance the rights of blacks, and Governor George C. Wallace of Alabama, who used his political position to inflame racist whites to commit violence against civil rights activists. There are KKK racists and "limousine liberals," radical leftists and religious conservatives. To have a meaningful racial dialogue, it is necessary for blacks to have informed knowledge about the wide range of differences in the white community.

Both whites and blacks also need to know about the cultural and political histories of Indians, Latinos, and Asian/Pacific Islanders. They represent racial issues that challenge the black-white monopoly on the meaning of race in America. It is most significant for dialogue that Latinos have replaced blacks as the largest racial minority in the United States. That is why politicians are speaking Spanish and immigration has suddenly become a major political issue. Indians, though the smallest minority, have the largest ethical and legal claim for justice. They are the original Americans, which makes Columbus the first illegal immigrant. Asians are often called the model minority. Though many Asians live above the poverty line, they operate politically below the power line. Latinos, Indians, and Asians add a complexity to the meaning of race in America that renders an exclusive focus on black-white issues problematic. A multiracial dialogue is not easy to navigate, because each group has experienced white supremacy in different ways and thus has developed different ways to cope with and resist it. To think about racial justice means developing a critical understanding of fairness that includes not only just relations with whites for each minority but also just relations among minorities themselves. That is not an easy matter because minorities spend more time talking to whites than they do talking to each other. If America is to survive, we must learn how to get along with all racial groups and not just with whites.

Learning to Listen

The second racial challenge is to learn how to listen to one another. Listening to the other is an indispensable art for creative and critical conversation. It is not an easy accomplishment, especially between racial groups. Groups, as Reinhold Niebuhr persuasively argued, are notoriously selfish and have little capacity to evaluate themselves critically.[3] They identify their interests with the peace and order of the nation and with the eternal values of God. Power blinds the dominant group to the concerns of the powerless. That is why the powerful have the greatest difficulty in listening to the powerless. When a group has been in a dominant position for centuries, its superior status seems natural and right, and to challenge its privileges feels like disorder and injustice to it. While the oppressed are not perfect listeners, they are much better at it than their oppressors, largely because their survival depends upon it. Oppressors do not have to listen since they have an inordinate amount of power, which speaks for them in forceful and violent ways. The great difference in power is the main factor that makes dialogue between the oppressor and oppressed so difficult. Oppressors are not used to listening to views that expose and challenge their special rights.

I am sure the white students who sued the University of Michigan really believed that they were treated unfairly, because blacks, Indians, and Latinos were given twenty points in their application for admission on account of their racial histories of oppression and exclusion. And I am also sure that there are students and perhaps faculty at Union Seminary who think that any form of affirmative action for blacks is injustice to whites. How do we understand different racial perspectives on justice? What is needed is not only knowledge of each racial group in conversation but also openness to listen to the arguments on all sides of the debate. Without an openness to listen to the other, the knowledge we spoke about in the first challenge of race can be used to manipulate the dialogue rather than to deepen it.

Listening means being open to change, open to being transformed through critical knowledge of, and personal encounters with, others. To listen is to acknowledge the limitation of one's perspective and the need to be informed by experiences outside of one's own group history and culture. It requires *empathy*, that is, the capacity to put oneself in the place of another—in the skin of the other—and to feel what she feels. I tell my students at Union that they cannot get a deep understanding of the other view until they share the place of the people who advocate it. Whites cannot understand blacks until they, through profound empathy, become black and experience something of what it means to be rejected and hated. In a series of medical treatments in the 1950s, novelist John Howard Griffin darkened his skin temporarily and traveled in the South because he wanted to experience what it was like to be black. He wrote a book about the experience and called it *Black Like Me* (1960). It was a shocking experience, to say the least. Griffin was black for about five weeks and then returned to being white. A few years later, Grace Halsell, a white woman, underwent a similar treatment and told a similar story in *Soul Sister* (1969).

Many blacks got a chuckle out of whites becoming black for a few weeks and facetiously asked, "Wouldn't it be interesting if they had remained permanently black with no chance of becoming white again? Then they would really learn something from a permanent condition of blackness." Blackness is a strange paradox, an existential dialectic that was born in slavery but also gave us the spirituals and the blues, jazz and rap, soul and gospel. Blackness creates a deep ambivalence—affirmation and rejection, great joy and deep sorrow. Du Bois called this paradox a "double consciousness," a "twoness,—an American, a Negro; two souls, two thoughts, two unreconciled strivings; two warring ideals in one dark body, whose dogged strength alone keeps it from being torn asunder."[4] This experience is not easily understood.

If whites want to know what it is like to be black, I would recommend reading essays and books by and about not just Du Bois, King, and Malcolm X, but also Richard Wright, Ralph Ellison, James Baldwin, Lorraine Hansberry, Toni Morrison, Alice Walker, and a host of other black writers. Whites need to listen not so much to whites who darken their skin temporarily but to *real* blacks who write about blackness not out of a passing curiosity but out of the existential depths of the black struggle for meaning in a society that defines blackness as ugly and evil. Being black in America is not an experience accessible in five weeks. It requires profound empathy and solidarity with the underside of America, the people whom whites labeled "the niggers." To understand blackness means going way back to our African homeland, the infamous slave trade, the terrible Middle Passage, the terror of the auction block and overseer, and the horror of the lynching tree. Being black means fighting against all the things that hinder the development of the black self. Read Wright's *Native Son* and *Black Boy*, Ellison's *Invisible Man*, Baldwin's *The Fire Next Time*, and Malcolm X's *Autobiography*, and then talk to me about blackness. Read Morrison's *Bluest Eye* and *Beloved*, Walker's *The Color Purple*, Audre Lorde's *Sister Outsider* and Patricia Hill Collins's *Black Feminist Thought*, and then talk to me about blackness, gender, sexuality, and racial justice. "Of all our studies," Malcolm X said, "history is best qualified to reward our research."[5] For African American history, John Hope Franklin's *From Slavery to Freedom* is a good place to start for a comprehensive survey of the black story.

In my view, nothing has been more important than religion for understanding the transcendent meaning of blackness in America. As a theologian, I see religion as the most powerful force in our struggle for meaning and community—for belonging and for the affirmation of a spiritual reality more powerful than the forces that seek to destroy our humanity. "It is not easy . . . to believe that our lives have a transcendent meaning or worth when so much that happens seems to negate this. It requires a huge commitment of hope and trust if you're going to claim, against all evidence to the contrary, that the loving human effort is worth making."[6] Religion is that spiritual force that lets blacks know that we are not niggers but rather God's people, called to bear witness in this world to a freedom that will be fully realized in the next. Gayraud S. Wilmore's *Black Religion and Black Radicalism* (1972) is the best historical account of the liberating and accommodating role of religion in black life. Albert J. Raboteau's *Slave Religion* (1978), Peter J. Paris's *The Social Teaching of the Black Churches* (1985), and Allen D. Callahan's *The Talking Book: African Americans and the Bible* (2006) are also fine contributions to the meaning of black religion. My books have focused on the theological meaning of our struggle for justice and hope in the midst of the tragedies of slavery and segregation. *Black Theology and Black Power* (1969) and *A Black Theology of Liberation* (1970) started a conversation that was joined by J. Deotis Roberts, *Liberation and Reconciliation: A Black Theology* (1971), and William Jones, *Is God a White Racist?* (1973). The conversation on race broadened and deepened to include gender, especially with Delores Williams's *Sisters in the Wilderness: A Womanist Theology* (1993), and sexuality, with Kelly B. Douglas's *Sexuality and the Black Church* (1999). There are many blacks writing about race and religion now but not much going on in terms of critical conversation about the controversial issue of race.

Deep listening requires profound empathy, a character trait dominant groups lack when dealing with people not of their status and kind. This is especially true of whites when they deal with blacks. The long history of the cultural degradation of blackness, combined with the sociopolitical exploitation of black people, makes it very difficult for whites to regard blacks as human beings whose lives are just as precious as those of whites. When the U.S. government legalized black slavery, and when, following the Civil War and Reconstruction, it reinstituted black subordination with Jim Crow segregation, it was saying that whites were better than blacks. When the government permitted and sometimes participated in the widespread spectacle of the lynching of black people—announcing to the nation and the world that killing and torturing blacks were acceptable forms of entertainment—whites were saying that black life was a very cheap thing in America. In the past, blacks were lynched by hanging them from trees, but today the lynching takes place in the courts and on the streets, where blacks often find themselves brutalized and executed by the police. When Americans think about criminality, poverty, welfare cheats, drugs, or anything bad, the image that comes to their minds is a black face. How can one empathize or be in solidarity with rapists and killers?

We need to go beyond stereotypes created by the media and other image-makers in society. We need deep dialogue between the races so whites and people of color can together get about the task of making America feel like home for all racial groups.

Eliminating White Supremacy

The third challenge of race is to work together to get rid of white supremacy in America and the world. Talk is cheap and empathy is superficial unless people are empowered to do something that would be effective in exposing and eliminating racism in America. Action deepens faith and bestows hope in the struggle for justice. Without practice, faith loses its credibility. The purpose of action is to show justice and love to the stranger. No person should pass through life in America without working toward bridging community across racial lines and fighting against white supremacy.

It is not easy to create multiracial communities of justice, and it takes a lot of courage to fight white privilege. But that is what our humanity and our faith demand of us. No one can be fully human until people everywhere are treated as human beings. Our humanity is bound together. To enslave another is to enslave oneself. When we internalize this conviction, we will hurt when others hurt and our indignation will empower us to fight just as fiercely for the freedom of the stranger as we do for that of our own group. Seldom do whites express outrage when blacks are treated unjustly, the major exceptions being the nineteenth-century abolitionist movement and the 1960s' civil rights movement. The great abolitionist William Lloyd Garrison expressed his indignation against slavery in the first issue (January 1, 1831) of his *Liberator*:

I will be as harsh as truth, and as uncompromising as justice. On this subject [of slavery] I do not wish to think, or speak, or write, with moderation. . . . I am in earnest—I will not equivocate—I will not excuse—I will not retreat a single inch—AND I WILL BE HEARD.[7]

John Brown got so mad at the injustice of slavery that he took up arms with his sons and a few blacks and was defeated at Harper's Ferry. William Lloyd Garrison was called an extremist and John Brown a lunatic by his contemporaries and most mainstream historians.

White solidarity with blacks in the twentieth century is best revealed among young civil rights activists in the South, especially the ones in the Student Nonviolent Coordinating Committee (SNCC). Radical historian Howard Zinn called young black and white students in SNCC "the new abolitionists."[8] They started the sit-ins and completed the Freedom Rides that challenged legal segregation in restaurants and interstate bus travel. During the "Freedom Summer" of 1964, young whites went to Mississippi in record numbers, and two of them were murdered (along with their young black coworker) during the orientation of new recruits to the dangers they would be facing doing voter registration work. The following year, the Rev. James Reeb, a Unitarian-Universalist minister from Boston, and a white housewife from Detroit, Viola Liuzzo, were murdered for their participation in the Selma March. Like the radical abolitionists of the nineteenth century, their twentieth-century counterparts were not regarded as "normal" by the dominant white society. It seems that when a few whites make radical solidarity with blacks in defense of their humanity, the majority in the white community thinks that those whites have lost their way and are in need of help to get back on course. In the South, such whites were called "nigger lovers."

Both the abolitionist and civil rights movements were great moments of black-white unity. The races came together because slavery and Jim Crow segregation were blatant wrongs that could hardly be accepted by morally decent human beings. Unfortunately, covert racism has not created much black-white solidarity, largely because it would challenge the white privilege that most whites do not even want to acknowledge. "It is so easy . . . to outlaw overt injustice and to sanction a covert form of it."[9] Very few whites want to be overt racists, and they pretend not to see hidden racism. While some whites may acknowledge less visible forms of racism, they are usually not outraged by it, at least not enough to cause them to say or do anything to eliminate it.

For example, if the percentage of whites in prison were the same as that of blacks, this nation would declare a national state of emergency, as it did after the attacks of 9/11. One-fourth of young black men between the ages of sixteen and twenty-nine are involved in the criminal justice system. That is an outrage and whites know it. If the percentage of white unemployment were twice that of blacks, instead of the other way around, whites would be in a state of rage. Whites would not tolerate blacks being more gainfully employed than they, except perhaps as janitors and maids. If whites had to live one week with the injustices that blacks are saddled with daily, there would be no peace in the land. Whites have no problem becoming indignant when they perceive themselves treated unjustly. But they have a tough time even recognizing the extent of the injustice toward blacks, and when they do they take it as a given with little or no indignation.

The demand to do something about the racial divide arises not only from our common humanity but also from the Christian faith. There is no way one can be a Christian and not accept the challenge to fight for racial justice. Racism is America's original sin—the sin that continues to corrupt the Christian faith. If you are a part of a Christian church that does not fight racism in a deliberate and sustained manner, your community is Christian in name only. As the grassroots civil rights activist Fannie Lou Hamer put it:

> It's all too easy to say, "Sure, I'm a Christian" and talk a big game. But if you are not putting the claim to the test, where the rubber meets the road, then it's time to stop talking about being a Christian. You can pray until you faint, but if you're not gonna get up and do something, God is not going to put it in your lap.[10]

People start to change things when they get angry. Anger can be empowering when it is creatively expressed. I can remember when I got angry about racism in American theology, church, and society. What really enraged me was theology's loud silence and the church's laid-back complacency. I just could not take it anymore. I had to speak. I had to write to get the rage all out of my system. It was either write what I saw as the plain truth about the gospel and race, or go crazy. *Black Theology and Black Power* (1969) and *A Black Theology of Liberation* (1970) were the first expressions of my black theological rage. I felt something like the nineteenth-century black editor of the *New York Age*, T. Thomas Fortune, who said, speaking out against lynching: "There is no dodging of the issue. We have got to take hold of this problem ourselves, and make so much noise that all the world shall know the wrongs we suffer and our determination to right these wrongs."[11] Ida B. Wells-Barnett, the great antilynching advocate and contemporary of Fortune, echoed a similar conviction. "Of one thing we may be assured," she told blacks: "so long as we permit ourselves to be trampled on, so long we will have to endure it."[12]

Following the spirit of blacks like Fortune and Wells-Barnett, I was determined to have my say in theology and the church, and to bring both before the judgment bar of faith, reason, and justice for their complicity in the white domination of black people. That is what silence on racism in America is—*complicity*! I knew that white theologians did not want to listen to what I had to say. It has been more than forty years since I began writing, and most white theologians are still silent, still looking the other way, still hoping that I will eventually shut up, as if they do not know what racism is or do not know that it contradicts the gospel of Jesus. But I will not let white theology rest until racial "justice rolls down like waters and righteousness like an ever-flowing stream" (Amos 5:24).

There were, however, a few white theologians who engaged black theology and racism when they first encountered the challenge in the late 1960s and early 1970s. Among them were Rosemary Radford Ruether, then teaching at Howard University School of Religion, the late Fred Herzog of Duke University Divinity School, Paul Lehmann of Union Seminary, and Helmut Gollwitzer at the Free University of Berlin. All engaged race theologically much more deeply than most.[13] Gollwitzer's essay "Why Black Theology?" is one of the most insightful encounters of black theology I have read. But the most informed and creative engagement of black theology by a white theologian was that by Theo Witvliet of Amsterdam University, who wrote a challenging critique in *The Way of the Black Messiah* (1987). It is revealing that the most sustained and insightful analyses of theology and race in the United States are by European theologians.

A few years ago, the Catholic scholar Jon Nilson of Loyola University, Chicago, addressed the silence of white Catholic theologians in his presidential address to the Catholic Theological Society of America, which was titled "Confessions of a White Catholic Racist Theologian" (June 8, 2003).[14] Nilson not only showed that he was informed about the great failure of white theology to engage racism, but he also challenged his colleagues to join him in exposing and fighting racism in theology and society.

James Perkinson is the only white theologian who has critically engaged white supremacy politically and theologically. There is also no white theologian who has engaged black liberation theology, existentially and intellectually, as creatively as Perkinson, especially in his *White Theology: Outing Supremacy in Modernity* (2004). *Disrupting White Supremacy from Within: White People on What We Need to Do* (2004) is another worthy effort by a group of white religion scholars.

What is most revealing is that the most sustained engagement of theology and race to date is by a southern white evangelical whose father had an ambivalent relationship with the civil rights movement. As a child in Mississippi, Charles Marsh could not avoid the problem of race, and as a theologian he has written an award-winning book on the subject, titled *God's Long Summer: Stories of Faith and Civil Rights* (1997). He followed it with *The Beloved Community: How Faith Shapes Social Justice, From the Civil Rights Movement to Today* (2005). Both books are informative, thoughtful, and well written. I have only one serious critique: there is no serious engagement in either of black liberation theology's understanding of the gospel. There is much talk about Martin Luther King Jr. and the civil rights movement, and almost none about the creative contributions of Malcolm X and the black power movement. What is the theological meaning of the two movements—civil rights and black power—when viewed together? When I tried to engage

Charles Marsh on this point at a meeting of the American Academy of Religion in Washington, D.C., he seemed irritated and did not want to discuss the matter.

Mark Noll's recent book, *God and Race in American Politics: A Short History* (2008), is another white evangelical contribution worth mentioning. Like Marsh, Noll avoids a serious theological engagement of black liberation theology. I would like to have a critical discussion about what precisely the Christian gospel *is*. How does one arrive at that understanding? Unless we are able to engage each other about theology across the boundaries of race, there is no way to get a deeper understanding of our differences, and why they matter.

It is really a sad commentary on white theologians that so few have engaged America's greatest moral dilemma. I only wish they could be as honest in confronting their racist theological past as some white historians have been in engaging racist historiography. In their critical look at their telling of the American story, white historians admitted that they had not really told the full truth about the brutality of white racism in America and black resistance against it. Their historical accounts of America were condemned before the moral and intellectual bar they claimed for their discipline: namely, the unbiased, critical pursuit of the historical meaning of America. In their accounts of the American story, white historians told a one-sided racist truth as seen mostly through the eyes of white slaveholders and bigots. The voices of subjugated blacks were silent as if they were not human beings, real agents in history. In the 1950s and '60s, white historians, with the help of radical black historians like John Hope Franklin, and the civil rights and black power movements, repented of their historical sins and proceeded to transform their discipline by listening to the oppressed voices of black slaves and their descendants. The rewriting of American history can be seen in Kenneth Stampp's *The Peculiar Institution* (1956); C. Vann Woodward's *The Strange Career of Jim Crow* (1956); Winthrop Jordan's *White Over Black* (1968); Eugene Genovese's *Roll Jordan Roll* (1974); and Leon Litwack's *Been in the Storm So Long: The Aftermath of Slavery* (1979), as well as in his later work, *Trouble in Mind: Black Southerners in an Age of Jim Crow* (1998). George Frederickson's many texts, especially his recent *Short History of Racism* (2002), established him as an authority on racism in the United States and South Africa. These and many other historical texts transformed how we think about America's past by listening to the voices of blacks. Five additional books that have had an important impact on my thinking are Joel Williamson's *The Crucible of Race* (1984); Eric Foner's *Reconstruction: America's Unfinished Revolution 1863–1877* (1988); David Blight's *Race and Reunion* (2001); Philip Dray's *At The Hands Of Persons Unknown: The Lynching of Black America* (2002); and Stephen Hahn's *A Nation Under Our Feet* (2003). These are only a few of the texts that have reshaped our way of viewing American history. There has been no revolution in theological thinking similar to that in historical thinking about America.

If white secular historians can engage the problem of race in a way that revolutionizes their discipline, why not white theologians and religion scholars, especially since they claim to speak about religious values that demand it? Why can't they foment a similar revolution in the discipline of theology? Why can't subjugated voices be heard in their reflections on God? Of course, I am pleased with the efforts of the few white theologians I mentioned earlier. But when compared with the work of the historians, one wonders whether white theologians' self-understanding of the discipline of theology and religion blinds them to God's truth about race.

Creating Dialogue

Let me conclude this reflection with a challenge to create a dialogue among racial communities in America and the world. We must never be satisfied with the racial divide. Racism is neither human nor Christian. Our humanity and religion call us to be one people. It is time for us to start acting like that.

Dialogue across race and culture may not heal the racial divide. I am not sure what will do that. But we've got to talk, we've got to listen, and we've got to act. Talking, listening, and acting—all three together in a multicultural fashion—is the first step. We may not get beyond this starting point, but it is a beginning. We must never stop trying to mend broken communities. What is the meaning of faith if it cannot break down the barriers of hate? The road to racial healing may be hard and people may not respond to our efforts, but we must not lose hope despite the odds; we must not despair, because we can make a new America, a new world. As the first black president, Barack Obama, has reminded us: "Yes We Can!" We must reject the arrogant, racist, and war-mongering America of George W. Bush, Colin Powell, Condoleezza Rice, and Dick Cheney. We must create an America that loves justice and peace, an America that is a beacon of freedom to all humankind.

When we can make Martin Luther King Jr.'s American Dream a reality, then we can say, as he did more than forty years ago, "Free at last, free at last; thank God Almighty, we are free at last."

Chapter 7

Race, Religion, and the Race for the White House

Dwight N. Hopkins

ONE OF THE FASCINATING developments in the 2008 presidential election was the insertion of black religion and black theology into mainstream political discourse. On February 10, 2007, Senator Barack Obama announced his candidacy for the White House. Shortly thereafter, the *New York Times* published an article that suggested that Mr. Obama was beginning to distance himself from his pastor, the Reverend Jeremiah A. Wright Jr., and that Obama might be linked to a radical form of black Christianity. Also, occasionally throughout 2007, some corporate media attempted to link Rev. Wright with Nation of Islam Minister Louis Farrakhan; and, if Rev. Wright was Obama's pastor, then, in the logic of some corporate media, Obama was tethered to Farrakhan.

Still, the controversy over Senator Obama's religious affiliation did not gain traction until the beginning of 2008. On Thursday, March 13, 2008, America and the world woke up to an amazing media production, when ABC television released to the public a thirty-second video clip consisting of a provocative trio of ten-second sound bites excerpted from three of Rev. Wright's sermons.[1] By the next day, in the United States, and increasingly globally, the lead news story about the American presidential race asked the following questions: How could Senator Obama have such an angry, racist-in-reverse, nonpatriotic black pastor; and was this the form of black religion that Obama believed in?

Not only did some corporate media, Republican candidates, and Senator Hillary Clinton begin to raise questions about Senator Obama, but the very base of his campaign supporters became shocked. On Friday, March 14, in the blog section of Obama's campaign Web site, you could find some of his staunchest supporters responding in confusion, fear, and suspicion. It seemed as if Obama's ground troops were disintegrating. In fact, the contention and the anger on that Web site were so deep that some Obama supporters were accusing other bloggers of being trolls for Senator Clinton. A troll is when one political candidate's supporters post onto an opponent's Web site with the intention of causing disruption and sowing false information among that candidate's core supporters.

On that Friday afternoon, I was in the Fox News studio about to go on live television when one of the reporters called me over and said that he was printing a major news development. We waited for the printer to stop. Then he handed me a statement by Senator Obama. Obama announced in this brief press release that he denounced the sound bites featuring Rev. Wright and that he was not present when they were preached. I went on television; and, of course, the first questions that I was asked were: Do you agree with "God damn America" and that "9/11 meant chickens coming home to roost"?

Over that weekend, a political storm unfolded and the domestic and global media looped the sound bites over and over. The following Tuesday, I was in the NPR (National Public Radio) studio doing a live interview when our program was cut short because candidate Obama was about to begin a live broadcast. Everyone hurried to the back of the studio, where six television monitors hung on the walls. I grabbed a seat on the floor and watched Mr. Obama deliver his "A More Perfect Union Speech."[2] Standing in Philadelphia, draped in American flags, Obama gave his first major speech on race, religion, and the black church.

Still the uproar persisted. Every day for about three weeks I did television, radio, magazine, newspaper, and Web interviews on the topic of black religion, the black church, and black theology of liberation. During one of those weeks, I had to cancel or reschedule classes due to media interview requests. My e-mail, home phone, and cell phone messages filled up. I made media appearances from 9 A.M. to 10 P.M. for seven days straight. The reporters' questions began to repeat themselves: What is black religion? What is the black church? and What is black liberation theology? These requests continued for another several weeks; but, eventually, as the country and the world moved away from the initial sound bites, the media started to ask for a more nuanced explanation.

Then Rev. Wright announced a major press conference at the National Press Club in Washington, D.C.[3] on Monday, April 28, 2008. I sat at a V.I.P. table in front of the podium as Rev. Wright gave his statement and then engaged in the now-famous question-and-answer session. Immediately afterward, Senator Obama held his own press conference where he condemned Wright's remarks and stated that he believed Wright did not represent the black church he knew. Here the leading Democratic presidential candidate and eventual first black American president in U.S. history placed black religion, the black church, and black theology of liberation at the center of American and global political discourse. Clearly, the "Invisible Institution" of the black church had become visible for all to see.[4]

From March 14 until several weeks after the election the following November 4, I continued to do media interviews for the major U.S. corporate media, independent media, local media, and media from Africa, Asia, the Caribbean, Canada, Latin America, and Europe. What became clear to me through this is a need for a nationwide conversation on black religion, the black church, and black liberation theology.

What Is Black Liberation Theology?

In order to understand the discipline of black theology of liberation, or black liberation theology, it is helpful to define each of the three terms in the phrase.[5] The word *theology* in black liberation theology means that it is rooted in the Christian tradition's ongoing study of God and God's relation to the world. That is to say, scholars of Christianity have for the last two thousand years sought to interpret who God is and what God has done in the world, beginning with what is revealed through the historical Jesus, the disciples, and the early church, through to today. The word *liberation* in black theology of liberation denotes that this is a theological framework that asserts that the ministry and orientation of Jesus is liberation. And the word *black* refers to doing theology that interprets the gospel in terms of its relevance to and meaning for the liberation of African Americans in American society. Thus, black liberation theology is focused on three themes: (1) who God is and what God does in the world; (2) an understanding of the historical Jesus' message and ministry as one of liberation; and (3) theological interpretation of how the gospel of liberation is revealed in black life.

Although these three themes can be found in the origin and historical development of black religion and the black church since slavery in the United States, the specific phrase "black theology of liberation" is a recent phenomenon, coined in the 1960s. Specifically, on July 31, 1966, a group of African American pastors and church administrators (the National Committee of Negro Churchmen) published a full-page advertisement in the *New York Times*, called the "Black Power" statement.[6] The ad was a direct response to the cry of black power that Stokely Carmichael had made on June 16, 1966.[7] Black power was a bold move on the part of the youth wing of the civil rights movement that was perceived as a counterpoint to the message espoused by Martin Luther King Jr. and others. The cry for black power spread throughout society and forced various groups to respond.

The black clergy who published the ad were caught in a dilemma that was, in part, made more evident by the challenge of black power. As Christian pastors who were staunch participants in King's nonviolent civil rights movement, they were now confronted with this fundamental question in America: What does blackness have to do with the gospel of Jesus Christ? In short, Is it possible to be both black and Christian? This was the defining question that black theology answered.

At that time, many in America gave a negative response to the question. They believed that a person could not be both black and Christian. Many in the white community associated the black power movement with terrorism, racism-in-reverse, Malcolm X, and law-breaking radicals— unpatriotic militants brandishing guns against the status quo. How could this type of "blackness" be linked to the religion of Jesus? In addition, the black community had its doubters as well. For instance, Malcolm X and the Nation of Islam said people could not be both Christian and black because Christianity was the "white man's religion." After all, Christianity was the religion used by white citizens to enslave Africans; it was used to justify and support slavery for almost three centuries in North America. It was a religion that gave blacks a pacifist Jesus and a hope for heaven in the by and by, while white Christians had their heaven on earth. Christianity, for Malcolm X, was white supremacy tricknology.[8] Black militants and revolutionaries such as the Black Panther Party also said that Christianity was the opium of the black people, suited for Negro "Uncle Toms." These groups characterized Negro preachers as sellouts who fed on the financial insecurity of poor people. The militants thought that power might have to be secured through the barrel of a gun and not from a hocus-pocus Christian Bible. Also, black artists used poetry and fiction to show how Christianity blocked the flourishing of the new African and African American aesthetic with its emphasis on Egypt and African traditional spirituality.

Martin Luther King Jr. and his preacher colleagues also stated that one could not be black and Christian. They believed that Christianity was a nonviolent, love-your-enemy and turn-the-other-cheek religion. In radical contrast, they felt that black power was violence and hatred. Thus, one could not be black and Christian because black power made Christianity a religion of hatred and violence. King therefore believed that one could be *Negro* and Christian, but not *black* and Christian. In fact, King mentioned that perhaps it should have been called "Negro power." And he spoke specifically to Stokely Carmichael about this. Paraphrasing his remarks, King asserted: "You know, Stokely, why do you have to put the word *black* in front of power? Why not Negro or something like that? You know, it's important for Negroes to have power, but why do you have to juxtapose those two words, black and power, so closely together?"

We have to remember that, in the 1960s, a lot of people in the United States, including the black community, were just getting the N capitalized in the word *Negro*. So they were just getting used to even using the word *Negro*, instead of the term "colored people." It was difficult for many people to hear Stokely Carmichael and the youth wing of the civil rights movement put forward their bold self-naming: "We're going to skip all of that 'colored to negro' stuff. We're going to go right to black. And not only are we going to go right to black, we're going to add power to black." Of course, the word *power* surfaced a variety of questions. Does that power mean Malcolm X? Does it mean militant underground movements? Does it mean some alliance with Africa? What is this power and why does it have to be black?

In sum, the origins of black liberation theology were attempts to answer the following: If the black church is being discredited in the North, and if the black church is being discredited in the South, then what is the role of Christianity or religion in social justice for the Negro revolution, as it was first called, and eventually the black power consciousness revolution? In the midst of the national firestorm over race, religion, and the future of blacks in America, a young African American theologian named James H. Cone answered the question about how one could be both black and Christian.

James H. Cone and Black Theology

In March of 1969, James H. Cone published his first book, titled *Black Theology and Black Power*. In this text, Cone asserted that the message of the gospel is liberation. Jesus, in Cone's view, had one purpose: he came to liberate the poor, the oppressed, and those emotionally abused. Similarly, black people were poor, oppressed, and emotionally abused. They, like Jesus, were organizing for liberation. So, if the purpose of Jesus was the liberation of the oppressed, and oppressed black citizens were struggling for liberation, then it followed that Jesus was at work in the struggle of oppressed black communities for liberation. If this was not true, then the struggle of black communities would be contradictory to the message of the Bible.

Cone entered the picture and began to articulate how Christianity was relevant to the new movement of black power and black consciousness. In fact, he asserted that not only is Christianity not anathema to black power but also that black power is the contemporary expression of Jesus Christ for all of America. With that assertion, all hell broke loose. Cone was trashed by many academics and universities and seminaries. Mainstream media came out and attacked his book because they felt that black power plus black theology denoted violence. All of his opponents stridently argued that Cone's black theology was a defiling of the gospel of Jesus. They raised issues about how he could question the authority of not "turning the other cheek." How could he not tell black people to suffer quietly as their oppressor beat them to a bloody pulp? Others screamed out critiques that black theology of liberation was a mixing of politics with religion. Some stated that it was simply an ideological movement on the part of this young radical with a huge Afro hairstyle. For the critics, Cone and his theology stood in stark contrast to the quiet, well-groomed, and law-abiding Martin Luther King Jr. In response to those critics, Cone and those who affirmed black theology argued that poor black people had the right to interpret the Bible for themselves.

Because black theology arose out of the civil rights movement and, even more, out of the black power youth wing, most of the mainstream authorities in the church and civil society described Carmichael's cry for black power as militant madness that was now entering the black church and its theology. Mainstream authorities believed that if black power was against white people, then black theology must be against the white church. In the end, the problem that the mainstream professors in the academy, the mainstream churches, and broader U.S. society had with black theology was that it combined the word *black* with the word *theology*.

But for Cone and the founders of black theology of liberation, Jesus came to save the whole person—that is to say, salvation of both the soul and the body. In other words, salvation happens in both the personal spiritual realm and the public structural realm. In fact, the word *salvation* means liberation from the oppressions of internal spiritual pain and external systematic pain. Thus, the key to black theology of liberation is not primarily the idea of being "black." Rather, it is the interpretation of Jesus and the Bible that is most at stake.

Black Theology and the Bible

The first generation of black theologians offered their own biblical interpretation. They understood clearly how the Bible itself touches on political issues. Because the Bible is the foundation and the substance of black theology of liberation and because the Bible touches on politics, black theology also engages politics. For example, in the Hebrew Scriptures, the so-called Old Testament, there is one plumb line that holds this entire text together. It is a story of how Yahweh, God, made a covenant of liberation and freedom with the ancient Hebrew people, who were physically in slavery, physically in chains. God saw their broken bodies, and God decided to take a political stance by fighting against the political state of Pharaoh.

Yahweh defeated Pharaoh's public policy of slavery and helped the ancient Hebrews to achieve liberation. It was a political liberation where former slaves, with God's leadership, were freed from the power structure of Pharaoh. Then, based on Yahweh's promise, they pursued a political goal—the establishment of their own liberated, free political state. In fact, every year Jewish brothers and sisters celebrate Passover. This ritual reminds them that their ancestors used to be in physical slavery and that Yahweh worked with them to liberate them from Pharaoh's oppression. In addition, the establishment in 1948 of the state of Israel shows that the Hebrew Scriptures, or Old Testament, touch on political liberation.

When we turn to the Christian Scriptures, or New Testament, we see that black theology of liberation is an interpretation of the Gospel accounts of Jesus. In fact, Jesus carries out the liberation tradition of the Old Testament. We must remember that Jesus was not a Christian. He was a Jew. When we focus on Jesus' words as recorded in the Bible, the political aspects of Jesus' message become clear. So these questions come up: Are Jesus' words and life political? What about his relations to political state power? In answering these questions, black liberation theology engages at least two biblical passages that point to political liberation as part of Jesus' ministry and message.

In Luke 3, Jesus is baptized. The baptism accounts symbolize Jesus' preparation to deal with spiritual and systemic evil on earth. This is evident when, after the baptism, the very next passage tells a story of how Jesus was immediately tempted by evil power. Jesus resists all of the negative temptations. Fortified by his baptism and having defeated earthly and spiritual forces, Jesus' next move is to clarify what is his mission on earth. In Luke 4, Jesus gives his inaugural speech or sermon.

AUGSBURG FORTRESS

F.E.I.N 41-1586861

P.O. Box 59304 • Minneapolis, MN 55459-0304
1-800-328-4648 • 612-330-3300 • Fax: 612-330-3455

PACKING NOTE

Page: 1

Bill
To:

THEOLOGY TODAY - NANCY DUFF
PRINCETON THEO SEMINARY
64 MERCER ST
PRINCETON
NJ
US
08540-6819

Ship
To:

THEOLOGY TODAY - NANCY DUFF
PRINCETON THEO SEMINARY
64 MERCER ST
PRINCETON
NJ
US
08540-6819

SHIPMENT NO.	DATE	CUSTOMER NO.	ORDER NO.	Package Information
SS0414637	10/03/11	7100051955	SOF005409	*Package 1*

CUSTOMER PURCHASE ORDER	PAYMENT TERMS	SHIP VIA	Package:
REVIEW COPY	Immediate Payment	Media Mail	Weight: 1.30

Cross-Ref No.	Item	ISBN	Quantity Ordered	Quantity Backordered	Quantity Packed
ED001410	ETHICS THAT MATTERS	9780800619763	1.00	0.00	1.00

AUGSBURG FORTRESS

4001 Gantz Road, Ste E • Grove City, OH 43123-1891

Augsburg Fortress Return

Thank you for your order. If for any reason
you need to return an item, return the item to
our distribution center using the information to
the right as the label. Do not include new
orders or payments with returned

In this first public address to the world, Jesus announces his earthly mission.

Jesus says his primary mission is to bring good news to the poor, to proclaim release to the captives, to give sight to the blind, to give liberty to those who are oppressed. What is striking is the very earthly dimension of his one purpose. There is no reference to a hocus-pocus religion. Rather, the story has Jesus placing spiritual matters within material, earthly concerns. In other words, the purpose of Jesus touches on the whole human purpose—a spirituality inextricably woven into the oppression and liberation of human beings.

In addition, when Jesus pursued his primary mission, he ran into the state apparatus of Rome. Jesus was executed under the political authority of Rome because he would not bow down to false, earthly gods and he would not worship the Roman emperor as God. Rather, he preached that a new and higher authority had power over Rome. Still, some will say that Jesus was not political because he did not engage in politics. Actually, politics is not so much defined by a person who calls him- or herself political as it is about whether or not the state apparatus moves against a person and attacks him or her because he or she is considered an enemy of the state. Therefore, Jesus was political for at least two reasons. First, he tried to liberate poor and working-class people who had been made that way by the Roman colonizers. Second, the Roman colonizers used their political power to eliminate Jesus as a potential power that claimed to be greater than the Roman occupying government.

Another aspect of the political nature of Jesus' mission is found in the words of Jesus in Matthew 25:31-46. In this passage, Jesus gives direct and clear instructions on how to get to heaven. In Christian doctrine, the purpose of Christians is to have hope in a new life, a new reality for themselves and their children and grandchildren. This enduring hope for change is the beauty of Christianity. Here in Matthew's story, Jesus lays out the primary criteria for this hope in a new life. It is the duty of Christians to follow the criteria and mission that Jesus sets forth as the only way Christians can get into heaven. Christians carry out that mission when they do the following: feed the hungry, give drink to the thirsty, welcome the stranger, clothe the naked, take care of the sick, and visit those in prison. It is no accident that the primary mission announced in his first public address in Luke is the same mission for Christians announced in Matthew. The purpose of Jesus and the purpose of Christians is to liberate the oppressed. Likewise, black theology of liberation arose out of a social context that corresponded to the purpose and mission of Jesus. Black theology touches on politics because Jesus touched on politics.

Black Theology and the Historical Black Church

In addition to black theology embodying themes from the Bible, the origin of the African American church in the United States is another source for the development of a contemporary black liberation theology. The birth of the black church in North America was a spiritual and political movement. In fact, the only war ever fought on American domestic soil was because the slave church initiated a political and spiritual opposition to the official state policy of human slavery. Black people in the nineteenth century believed that slavery contradicts the purpose and mission of Jesus.

In the South during slavery, the black church was underground, and that is why it was called the "Invisible Institution." The southern black church began secretly during the slavery period. Late at night, blacks would sneak away to an appointed cabin, or go down in the swamps and ravines, or build brush harbors deep in the woods, or stretch out in the corn rows—all to hope for a better day for their children on earth in the United States. Later, in the North, black churches separated from white churches not only because their religion of liberation differed from whites' interpretation of the gospel, but black people also built their own institutions because they were tired of sitting outside of a white church service or being forced to hover in segregated sections of white churches.[9] Thus, the black church (invisible and visible) was political; it opposed the state's slave politics and the government's later policy of racial segregation. The black church organized against state politics by meeting secretly, breaking the law, and mixing preaching with the politics of liberation. In sum, the black church prayed to God to set them free from both spiritual and structural evil; the church's mission was the redistribution of power, equal rights, and full citizenship. At least these two sources—Jesus in the Bible and the historical African American church—were foundations of the black theology of liberation in the late 1960s.

Black Theology and the Contemporary Black Church

In April of 1968, Martin Luther King Jr. was assassinated. In response, riots raged all across America. Many in the black community were finished with following Christianity and the black church. With King's death, they reasoned that Christianity and the church were not only irrelevant to the freedom of oppressed people but also could possibly be supporting the oppression of African American communities. Many critiqued the church as a Negro institution instead of being a black gathering for freedom. They reasoned that if the way of King, a leader of the black churches and a prophetic Christian witness in society, was killed, then it was time to look for something new. To fill the void, many in the black community, including some churches, began to turn to African political movements and African culture and spirituality. Others took a closer look at the different organizations within the black power movement. Still others sought the possibility of more militant avenues.

In this context, what Cone's book and the new black theology of liberation did was to tell a whole generation of young people that they did not have to leave church and seek other avenues. They could be both black and Christian. The efforts of Cone and other proponents of black theology enabled many to stay with Christianity and stay within the church.

During 1971, one of the churches struggling with how to live out the theological conclusion that a person could be both black and Christian was Trinity United Church of Christ[10] on the south side of Chicago. During that year, the church had only eighty-seven members. Still, they decided to not leave the urban area and move to the suburbs. Rather, Trinity chose to build on their understanding of the *Bible's* message of salvation as a mission of liberation right in the oppressed inner city of Chicago.

When the church concluded that it would cast its lot with the poor and workers of the south side, it hired Jeremiah A. Wright Jr. in March 1972. The congregation instructed him to apply a gospel relevant to black culture to the economic and political plight of black Americans. By focusing on these forgotten citizens of America, the church hoped to redeem the soul of all of America. Under Wright's leadership, members of the surrounding community and others from faraway neighborhoods began to join Trinity. Reverend Wright was successful in bringing in families and also black men back into the church.

By 1981, Trinity had already refined its theological focus. Because it made a conscious decision to relate to the specific conditions of the communities that surrounded it in the Chicago ghettoes, the church had already produced two statements about how it intended to fulfill its mission.[11] In other words, the conditions in which the church found itself had an impact on the specific way the church applied the biblical call for love and liberation in those conditions. The first document is Trinity's statement of self-reflection, which reads:

> We are a congregation which is Unashamedly Black and Unapologetically Christian. . . . Our roots in the Black religious experience and tradition are deep, lasting and permanent. We are an African people, and remain "true to our native land," the mother continent, the cradle of civilization. God has superintended our pilgrimage through the days of slavery, the days of segregation, and the long night of racism. It is God who gives us the strength and courage to continuously address injustice as a people, and as a congregation. We constantly affirm our trust in God through cultural expression of a Black worship service and ministries which address the Black Community.

The second statement is called "The Black Value System." The statement covers eight values: commitment to God, commitment to the black community, commitment to the black family, dedication to the pursuit of education, dedication to the pursuit of excellence, adherence to the black work ethic, commitment to self-discipline and self-respect, and disavowal of the pursuit of "middleclassness." The first value indicates that, like other Christian churches, Trinity has submitted to the leadership of God in the movement for freedom. The second value emphasizes the need to strengthen the black community, which had fallen on hard times. The third value commits the church to strengthen and love the black family. And it also urges all black families to reach out to all those who are less fortunate. Here it is also suggested that black men take more responsibility for their families and black parents take more responsibility for their children.

The fourth value is a dedication to increasing the intellectual and mental potential of all African American people. For Trinity, education has to include elements that produce high school graduates with marketable skills, a trade or qualifications for apprenticeships, or proper preparation for college. Basic education for all blacks should include mathematics, science, logic, general semantics, participative politics, economics and finance, and the care and nurture of black minds.

The fifth value states that the level of excellence of one year must be exceeded by greater efforts in the following year. The sixth value claims that high productivity must be the goal of an African American work force. The seventh value states that even if the African American community is exploited by other forces, the community should have its own self-discipline and self-respect to bring about progress and be positive examples to young people.

The eighth value places quotation marks around the phrase "middleclassness" to indicate a very narrow definition of the middle class. Specifically, the eighth value targets the false goal of focusing only on the "talented tenth" of the black community.[12] That is, rather than only catering to the top 10 percent, progress should also include the poor and working people; in short, all of the African American community has to be the focus of Christian activities.

Once the young pastor Wright was hired, he and the church leaders were able to grow Trinity to 8,500 members. This growth was mainly due to their ability to recognize that the Bible had to speak to the oppressed conditions on the south side of Chicago. A visit to Trinity United Church verifies this analysis. The church does not exist in the suburbs or the wealthy downtown areas. When one drives toward the parking lot of Trinity, it is clear that these Christian believers have made a conscious decision to stay in the inner city, or "ghetto." Going west on 95th Street, one has to cross the railroad tracks. These railroad tracks, which run next to the church's parking lot, often carry a long train of commercial cars over a period that extends from five to sometimes fifteen minutes. A person can be made late for church because of slow-moving, squealing steel cars.

Moreover, a visitor will experience the connection between time, faith, and commercial interests on the south side of Chicago. The south side is the deeply segregated part of Chicago. It is where the city's cross-country businesses route those bleak-looking trains that disrupt parishioners' attempts to carry out their mundane faith by simply crossing tracks to worship. In other words, the appointed time for praising one's God is discounted by economic interests represented by those elongated trains running through the black south side. Being delayed for church indicates that powerful downtown financial brokers see 95th Street as a wasteland.

Similarly, one witnesses few shops sprinkled here and there on 95th Street—such as a small grocery store, a McDonald's, and a hair-care shop. But the low-rent apartments or public housing and the abandoned lots also strike the eye. One gets the sense that hard times have fallen on this part of the world and maybe it is not a place that a parent would necessarily want to raise his or her child.

In contrast, the north side, equally segregated, is where a disproportionate number of wealthy whites own two-million-dollar homes nestled on the lovely Lake Michigan. Some of these houses have private indoor swimming pools. Here, kids attend elite private schools or excellent public schools. Politicians hold their million-dollar fundraisers on the north side. The south side is where politicians come to mobilize black churches to get out the vote. On the north side, police officers ride bicycles and stop and have ice cream with the public. On the south side, cops ride two to a car. They brandish their shotguns and bear the burden of thick bulletproof vests.

Yet, it is because of its physical location enmeshed in the semiblighted, forced-segregated reality of poor and working-class black families that thousands of Christians and voyeurs are attracted to Trinity. In fact, Trinity's 8,500 members and countless occasional seekers jam into the physical building during three regular services each Sunday and every day of the week for social services and spiritual healing. At one time, there was an additional Saturday evening church service for those who planned to go partying later that night. Reverend Wright is a formally trained musician and singer, so he has also built up Trinity's membership by accenting music and sacred dance.

Many people joined Trinity because of the spiritual safety of an extended family and because it preached and practiced a black theology of liberation—a theology interpreting the Bible's concern for the spirit and the material body. As Rev. Wright responded to the instructions of the church committee that hired him, he included a deep reading of the Bible, highly educated leadership, evangelical worship services, dozens of ministries for poor communities, strong labor advocacy, ordination of women, welcoming of diverse sexualities, outreach to Africa and the third world, and a quick wit and humor in one diverse community.

Trinity is made up of an intimate and, at times, contentious group of inner-city South Siders who were primed for an in-depth, educated exposition of the Bible. They yearned for institutions of service to the marginalized communities. They relished the opportunity to create new ways of rebuilding a devastated physical area. And they enjoyed an occasional cutting sermon that spoke truth to power and called out names of those who had done wrong in contradiction to their interpretation of the Bible.

Most of Wright's sermons over thirty-six years centered on standard themes for the black inner-city community and family—self-love, self-respect, black men assuming responsibility, the positive African heritage, service to the poor as a Christian way of life, providing the highest education for children, domestic violence, building black girls' self-esteem, HIV and AIDS awareness, acceptance of a sexually diverse creation, a call for those with more resources to share with the less fortunate, and emphasis on being grounded in the Bible. So occasionally, when Wright chose to explain the wrongdoings of the powerful, he gave an explanation based upon his Christian interpretation of Scripture and the message of the gospel.

At this point in our discussion, let's go back to March 13, 2008, and the bombshell that rocked the presidential election with themes of race, religion, and presidential politics. Remember that ABC television released a thirty-second video clip that included ten-second sound bites from three of Wright's previous sermons. Again, Wright had been preaching at Trinity for thirty-six years during which, each Sunday, it had held three worship services. And each Sunday, Wright had preached three new and different sermons. So that meant that of the 1,872 sermons Wright had preached in all those years, the ABC reporter made a conscious decision to take ten seconds from three specific sermons. In other words, out of 7,500 minutes of Wright's sermons, the reporter lifted up thirty seconds of incomplete preaching.

But still, if one reviews each of the ten seconds in the thirty-second video clips, one might come to a different perspective. For instance, in one sound bite, when Wright mentions "chickens coming home to roost," he is quoting and paraphrasing Edward Peck, who had already expressed these same sentiments about September 11. This statement about chickens coming home to roost is talking about the notion of "blowback violence." That is to say, when a superpower country "perpetrates" violence against a smaller nation, eventually the smaller nations will come back with their own violence. In this sense, that violence blows back to the superpower nation.

Also, we must remember that Peck was not only a former U.S. ambassador to Iraq, but he also had been associate director of a antiterrorist department in the Reagan administration. Peck had given his analysis four days after the 9/11 attacks and the day before Wright delivered his sermon. And Peck is a white man. Ambassador Peck said these words the Saturday after 9/11 and Wright preached similar words the next day, on Sunday. Of course, we do need to note that Ambassador Peck did not say those words with the certain intensity that we heard in the selected sound bite. But that intensity is consistent with the nature of the black church; it's the good and the bad, the up and the down, the joy and the anger, the pain and the resurrection. All of these emotions are mixed in there together.

Now, let's look at the other infamous sermonic sound bite—"God damn America." When Wright says "God damn America," he uses a specific intonation and accent. He says, "GOD damn America." That's different from our popular use of the phrase "Goddammit," which is a sort of vulgar, popular usage of language in America as a curse. But if you listen, Wright is saying, "GOD damn America." When Wright briefly said those words, he believed he was following the Hebrew Scriptures (so-called Old Testament) prophets. In those texts, Yahweh/God made a covenant with ancient Israel. Israel was given resources and abundance. When Israel strayed from the covenant, Yahweh/God raised up prophets as instruments of God's damnation. The deity used human beings to pronounce divine judgment and religious condemnation on a wayward nation.

The second thing we need to observe is this: when Wright says "God damn America," if we listen closely or look closely, he says, "I'm in the *Bible*. It's in the *Bible*." (emphasis added). Well, actually, Wright can make a case that he is preaching from the Bible. "Damn" can mean righteous indignation on the part of Yahweh/God; it can mean divine judgment against the nation and the people of God. So, actually, as Wright says, he is still following the Bible. The problem is that the national and international audiences that watched the thirty-second video clip did not see what Wright preached about before and after the sound bites. Wright did an analysis of the characters and words in the biblical passage to which he referred and then he applied his analysis to the wrong policies of the U.S. government and concluded: God damn America.

In the biblical-passage tradition to which he referred, there is a covenant or relationship between God—Yahweh—and the ancient people of Israel. God calls on them to be a special nation, a blessed nation. But if they break the covenant, then the Old Testament prophets (such as Jeremiah and Amos) will come forth and proclaim, "Thus saith the Lord." The prophets will speak truth to power. God will condemn this nation until it wakes up and turns toward the original path of justice and peace and a positive relationship with all nations in the regions of the Mediterranean Sea. It really is the prophetic task of moving the nation from where it is to the glory that it can be. And a prophet in the Bible gets impatient and can, at times, express some anger.

So basically Wright seems to have been saying the following: "I'm speaking as a prophet for the word of God and its judgment on America because: (1) America has not used its resources to help its own oppressed citizens, like African Americans; (2) America has not helped working-class people; (3) America has not used its foreign policies, strength, and leadership to bring about peace. Instead, America has bombed people." So, on various levels, Wright seems to be stating that the nation needs to be turned away from its wayward path toward a more just and peace-loving path.

Furthermore, Rev. Wright's sermon was an example of classic black preaching. The black-church sermon can contain a range of emotions and practices: from damnation to seduction to cunning wit to theatrical performance. And to that degree, Wright was following the African American sermonic outline of five steps to successful preaching. The first step is where the preacher takes a biblical passage and unpacks that. The preacher looks at word studies, looks at the personality and figures in the story, looks at the context of the narrative.

Step two is when the preacher takes this in-depth study and applies it to personal issues of healing—issues like HIV and AIDS, domestic violence, the loneliness of single adults, low self-esteem, and other things that keep people from feeling good about themselves. After applying the in-depth study of the Bible to personal, emotional concerns, the preacher takes this intensive study of the Bible and applies it to a prophetic message against unjust powers, against structures and systems. This is step three—divine judgment and condemnation. Then the fourth step brings everything together and offers the hope of a new life both for the individual and the nation. Here the preacher tells the congregation the following: "Now that you've gone through the horrendous nights of your personal issues, and the intensity of systems oppressing you, our next question is how we become whole—individually, psychically, emotionally, and systemically as persons, as a people, as a nation, and as a world. And that's because God loves us." At the fifth and final step, the preacher tells the congregation that they can enter a new community of God's love. That is why, in the majority of black churches, the preacher ends with these words: "The doors of the church are open, please enter."

So what we have in the ten-second sound bites of Jeremiah Wright is a jump over steps one and two and the absence of steps four and five. Rather, the sound bites only show step three—the preacher prophet pointing out to the nation its wayward ways. We only see judgment. But the flow of black homiletics is always an openness to the hope of change of the self and change of systems.

Conclusion

Because Barack Obama was not present at Trinity United Church during the sound bites aired by ABC, he condemned what he saw on television.

"white blood." This, however, does not erase the positive and formative experiences he had with Philadelphia whites and Jews.

Wright came to Chicago and there dedicated his ministry to the extremely racially segregated south side. Chicago is "classic" black America with its family history links to the European slave trade on the African West Coast, U.S. slavery, segregation, and the almost superhuman efforts that blacks see themselves exerting to overcome the odds against them. Wright is part of the usual narrative. Here black folk celebrate, worship in, and enjoy the cultural safety of, other black people. At the same time, this black American narrative remembers stories such as the Tuskegee syphilis experiment[14] carried out on black men's bodies by the U.S. government.

Wright emerged out of a specific lineage of black preaching. His father was a very famous Baptist preacher in Philadelphia who was also a son of a Baptist preacher. Thus, Jeremiah Wright Jr. symbolizes three generations of the prophetic wing of the black church, the wing where Christianity is empty rhetoric if not linked to social justice and occasional prophetic denunciation of the powerful. Similarly, Wright actualizes a form of black religious speech that combines the fullness of the body with the intellect. Indeed, black preaching is a verbal and bodily ritual of performance.

Wright and Obama—the preacher and the politician, race and multiculturalism—have different parental, geographic, historical, and personal experiences. Yet both agree that the Bible is partial to the poor. Both agree that a function of the church is organizing for justice. Wright is deeply connected to a segregated black community and the importance of their voice and their obtaining resources for living. From that particularity, he enters into conversation and coalition with all of America. In contrast, Obama begins with a vision for all of America. From that perspective, blacks are simply one strand among many in a larger narrative about whites and blacks (as well as yellows, browns, and reds) being their brothers' and sisters' keepers.

One is a preacher rooted in service to a local church. The other is a politician moved to serve the larger nation. The preacher's prophetic vocation and the politician's universal inclination could have held together in one church building. Race and multiculturalism were wedded in one Christian institution. But with the intense media scrutiny of Trinity United Church of Christ, an experiment of these two differences unified in faith service to the poor could not remain in close proximity in a presidential election year. And so the politician resigned his membership so that neither he nor the church would be distracted. For the sake of the long-term racial and religious health of the nation, however, America needs both at the table of civic engagement on behalf of the citizens' democracy.

For Reflection and Study

Key Ideas

- acquired rights
- black liberation theology
- black-white monopoly on the meaning of race
- imputed rights
- multiracial communities of justice
- multiracial dialogue
- racial contract
- social contract

Resources for Further Study

Fernandez, Eleazar S., and Fernando F. Segovia. *A Dream Unfinished: Theological Reflections from the Margins*. Maryknoll, N.Y.: Orbis, 2001.

Hopkins, Dwight N. *Introducing Black Theology of Liberation*. Maryknoll, N.Y.: Orbis, 1999.

Obama, Barack. *The Audacity of Hope: Thoughts on Reclaiming the American Dream*. New York: Three Rivers, 2006.

Townes, Emilie M. *Womanist Ethics and the Cultural Production of Evil*. New York: Palgrave MacMillan, 2006.

Wilmore, Gayraud. *Pragmatic Spirituality: The Christian Faith Through an Africentric Lens*. New York: New York University Press, 2004.

Thinking Critically and Constructively

Race continues to be one of the barriers to authentic moral community in the United States. However, with the election of President Barack

Obama and his now-famous "A More Perfect Union Speech,"[1] the racial situation in the United States is often described as *postracial*.[2] Some say that being postracial means that race has become less important; others say that it means we have transcended race.

1. What do you think—is *postracial* an appropriate way to describe the state of race in the United States in the twenty-first century?

2. Immigration debates in and around 2010–11 continue the discussion of who is entitled to full citizenship rights in the United States in the twenty-first century. One writer discusses this issue as a "postracial immigration quandary" that revolves around "a nexus of sensitive concerns: security, race and the character of American citizenship."[3] Compare and contrast arguments of immigration debates to those regarding citizenship rights for black Americans.

3. Social justice effects a relationship between corrective, compensatory, and distributive claims of social groups who constitute a moral community. In each of these essays, there is either an explicit or implicit discussion of what social justice is and how to ensure justice for all in U.S. society. How do you define justice, and what is required to establish a just society?

PART THREE

Moral Discourse

Chapter 8

"Who Is Their God?"

A Critique of the Church Based on the Kingian Prophetic Model

Lewis V. Baldwin

Disturbed by the abysmal silence of the Christian church in the face of the screaming mob that confronted James Meredith at the University of Mississippi in the fall of 1962, Martin Luther King Jr. penned these words for an article published in *The Nation*:

> The New Testament admonishes us that the people cannot hear if the trumpet makes an uncertain sound. What is their hope if the trumpet makes no sound at all? I have traveled much of the length and breadth of Mississippi. On lazy afternoons and cold mornings, I've seen tall church spires and sprawling brick monuments dedicated to the glory of God. Often did I wonder, "What kind of people worship there? Who is their God?" When I review the painful memory of the last week at Oxford and cannot recall a single voice "crying in the wilderness," the questions are still the same: "What kind of people worship there? Who is their God?"[1]

The questions King raised are as relevant for the church today as they were almost a half century ago, in part because that institution is going through an identity and/or definitional crisis that is unprecedented in American history. The church is such an illusive phenomenon in the sense that it defies definition, and the churches themselves are deeply divided over what in fact constitutes the true *ekklesia*.[2] Much has been written about the grassroots church, the electronic church, the full gospel church, word of faith churches, the megachurch, the multicultural church, and the dying phenomenon of the neighborhood church; and the mere mention of these and other ecclesial models suggests that the church is somewhat uncomfortable, and perhaps even anxious, about how best to define itself, especially in a culture in which there is a growing distrust of institutions as a whole. This identity and/or definitional crisis is further exacerbated by the loss of a genuine sense of what it means to be prophetic. Thus, there is a need to reclaim and reappropriate Martin Luther King Jr.'s prophetic ecclesial model,[3] for it provides both an astute critique of the church and proposals for effecting the spiritual, theological, and ethical renewal of the church.[4]

Politicizing Christianity

No one has done more than King to restore the public credibility of the church. Indeed, his death, on April 4, 1968, had a kind of redemptive significance for the collective Christian church, especially since his assassination occurred during the Easter season, because he so often challenged the church about transforming undeserved suffering into a creative force, and due to his willingness to die for a higher ethical ideal.[5] Inspired by King and the movement he led, both black and white churches turned to a more politicized interpretation of Christian responsibility in the 1970s, 1980s, and 1990s.[6] Black churches shifted from the mass-social-protest phase of the civil rights movement to establish legitimacy in electoral politics, and they increasingly became arenas for voting clinics and a proving ground for black political leadership, as figures like Jesse Jackson and Al Sharpton worked from those institutions as a base while pursuing the office of president of the United States. White churches, which had previously denounced King for his reformist ethic and activities, turned to a narrow political agenda that included the election of right-wing political leaders, the appointment of conservative judges, and an assault on selective moral issues such as abortion, pornography, and

homosexuality.[7] In time, politicized religious conservatives would dominate not only the ecclesial landscape, but also the faith-and-public-life
debate.

In their efforts to restore what they perceived to be the biblical and
moral foundations of American life and culture, the politically charged
churches claimed to be acting under the inspiration of King. "I feel that
what King was doing," Jerry Falwell, founder of the Moral Majority,
declared in 1981, "is exactly what we are doing."[8] Others in the "pro-life
movement" insisted that "their protests follow in the tradition of Martin
Luther King Jr.'s civil rights movement." "The strength of Martin Luther
King came through his willingness to go to jail," conservative column-
ist Cal Thomas maintained. "Those who regard abortion as infanticide
have got to show that this is not just a bunch of philosophic beliefs
they are holding—that they are prepared to suffer in order to stop the
killing."[9] With the emergence of hard-line pro-life groups, and of anti-
affirmative action voices, anti-gay movements, pro-family coalitions, and
a host of anti-sex education, anti-ERA, proprayer in public schools, and
antipornography constituencies, the image of the church in America
changed radically, thus becoming a serious challenge to what King had
envisioned for that institution. King's model of the prophetic church,
or that body which challenges social evil while struggling for greater
freedoms and civil liberties, was essentially lost in these developments.
Writing in the 1980s, Daniel C. Maguire made the point in terms that
merit extensive quotation:

> There is all the difference imaginable between what Martin Luther
> King, Jr., brought to the political order and what the Falwells bring.
> When King left his pulpit and ceased his political activism, many
> who had lacked rights before had come to possess those rights.
> People were voting who could not vote before, were getting hired
> and educated who would have known only rejection, and were find-
> ing decent housing who could not before. In short, King's interven-
> tions in politics were enabling and empowering. However, when
> the Falwells of the New Right leave their pulpits and end their
> political activism, inasmuch as they are successful, people who had
> rights will have lost them. Their interventions are disabling and
> disempowering.[10]

For Maguire, the contrast between King's prophetic model and that of the politically charged church was reducible to the question: "*How is religion being used?* To disempower and disable or to empower and enable?"[11] Maguire went on to explain how the New Right's attacks on the Equal Rights Amendment contributed to the disabling and disempowering of women, and he concluded that any attempt to "compare that achievement to that of Martin Luther King, Jr., is an obscenity." Clearly, King, unlike those who promoted the politicized, right-wing church type, "took the ideals that were bred in evangelical piety and made them the basis" of a church-centered "movement that yielded" not "support for massive military budgets" and "government cutbacks in aid to the poor" but "civil rights legislation and affirmative action executive orders."[12] Generally speaking, King and representatives of the Religious Right read the Bible differently, and they had different thoughts about how to bring religiously affiliated ideas and convictions into politics and into the larger sphere of public life.

Megachurches and King's Vision

The abandonment of King's legacy and vision for the church continued unabated through the 1990s and beyond, fueled largely, as it were, by politically charged and status-quo-oriented televangelists, the rise and popularity of the megachurch phenomenon, and megachurch gurus. By the beginning of George W. Bush's first term as president, in 2000, even black megachurches, boasting an average weekly attendance of from two thousand to thirty thousand, had capitulated to the values and agenda of the religious and political right wing, as evidenced by some of the public proclamations of Creflo Dollar and Bishops T. D. Jakes, Eddie Long, and Charles Blake.[13] Black and white megachurch pastors spoke increasingly in terms of a contract with America on moral values, expressing opposition to affirmative action, abortion, embryonic stem cell research, women's rights, and same-sex marriage while refusing to address prophetically and constructively racism, classism, economic injustice, poverty, and war. With the rise of the megachurch phenomenon, the conversation about the role of religion in politics, public service, and public-policy making, which had been inspired by King's leadership, gained even more traction in ecclesial circles.[14] When it comes to this and related matters, the mega-churches actually represent an extension of the conservative Christian resurgence witnessed in the 1970s and 1980s.

The mega- or high-profile super-church is really a new church type, and it reflects the changing face of the church and religion in the half century since King's death. The megachurch types cluster in urban centers, and suburbanites, quite unlike the ordinary church folk who marched with King in small towns in the South, flock to them in droves. They hew to a strict biblical line while mirroring the corporate model in their organization, management, and outreach ministries. They have enormous financial resources, ministers functioning as CEOs, dozens of clerical staff, satellite facilities and networks, television airtime, daily talk shows, music studios, publishing houses, graphic-design suites, computer Web sites, and an entrepreneurial approach to matters of an economic and business nature. Also, celebrity-style megachurch pastors obtain great wealth and enjoy lavish lifestyles while reaching millions daily, more than King ever dreamed of in his own time.[15] Although God's call to faithful living is viewed largely in terms of church-sponsored ministries that provide health-care screenings, education, low-income housing, financial advice, and other social services, the manner in which church is redefined is perhaps more important for understanding the megachurches in relation to King's ecclesial vision and legacy.

Some contemporary megachurch pastors see themselves as innovators who are advancing the unfinished agenda of King's holy crusade. Rick Warren of the Saddleback Valley Community Church in Lake Forrest, California, a spokesman for "the purpose-driven church" in "the purpose-driven life," delights in being identified with that long tradition of pastors like King, who were at the forefront of "every major movement" for freedom in the history of this nation.[16] Convinced that Jesus was wealthy, Creflo Dollar, who serves some 25,000 at World Changers in College Park, Georgia, admits to "extending King's ministry by emphasizing issues such as economic empowerment." "Dr. King stood for the freedom of all people," Dollar maintains, "and I believe that deliverance from debt is an integral part of that freedom."[17] While acknowledging that he is not "the next Martin Luther King," and that "mega-ministers are not the civil rights preachers that traditionally populated our pulpits in the past," T. D. Jakes suggests nonetheless that a part of King's mission is being fulfilled by megachurch pastors who devote their resources to a variety of human needs.[18] Despite urging blacks to "'forget racism' because they have already reached the promised land," Eddie Long, whose church has a membership of almost 30,000, has made perhaps a greater claim than anyone else to the mantle of King's leadership, especially since he was supposedly anointed for that purpose by members of the King family in 2004.[19]

By promoting charity ministries and the values of economic self-help, the megachurches are honoring an important dimension of King's vision and ministry. Even so, the high-profile super-churches have little resemblance to the congregations that inspired and nurtured King's crusade for equal rights, social justice, peace, and human dignity. These churches embody a mixture of politics, spirituality, and personal-enrichment themes that King would undoubtedly find quite strange, and perhaps unhealthy. In contrast to King's ecclesial model, one finds, with the megachurch phenomenon, too much of a preoccupation with personal piety, prosperity theology, a gospel of materialism, and the values of individualism. King discouraged an obsession with personal piety to the neglect of radical public piety, decried a materialistic gospel, rejected the values of individualism and selfish ambition, and denounced preachers who "are more concerned about the size of the wheel base on their automobiles and the honorariums that come with their anniversaries" than "about the quality of their service" to the community.[20] Moreover, King lamented the church's tendency to "worship that which is big— big buildings, big cars, big houses, big corporations."[21] Convinced that service at its best has little to do with extending the ranks of the church, he challenged the very premise on which many megachurches and their leadership today claim legitimacy, power, and success:

> This numerical growth should not be overemphasized. We must not be tempted to confuse spiritual power and large numbers. Jumboism, as someone has called it, is an utterly fallacious standard for measuring positive power. An increase in quantity does not automatically bring an increase in quality. A larger membership does not necessarily represent a correspondingly increased commitment

to Christ. Almost always the creative, dedicated minority has made the world better.[22]

Over against the super-church model, King highlighted the significance of the church as creative minority and the church of the least of these. For King, the very nature of the human condition also called for the prophetic church, the sacrificial church, and the church as good Samaritan as ecclesial ideals.[23]

There is every reason to believe that if King were alive today, he would have serious problems with the lack of a social-justice agenda, prophetic witness against social evil, and mass social protest on the part of the megachurches, especially since he denounced the status-quo church while elevating the significance of the maladjusted church or the nonconformist church. King would most likely say to Warren, Jakes, Dollar, Long, and other contemporary megachurch gurus, who take great pride in their charity ministries, what he stated in his challenge to church leaders in 1963: "Philanthropy is commendable, but it must not cause the philanthropist to overlook the circumstances of economic injustice which makes philanthropy necessary." In other words, it is quite all right to provide soup kitchens and bread lines for the poor, but the church also has a responsibility to challenge the unjust structures and the systemic social evils that make and keep people poor in the first place. Here King was suggesting a significant distinction between those who become preoccupied with single individual effects, and those interested in curing "injustice at the causal source."[24]

Also in contrast to King's ecclesial vision, the megachurches have embraced a gospel of intolerance and exclusion that is mirrored at virtually every level of the Christian church. Bigotry, intolerance, and exclusion have become metaphors for virtually all that has gone awry in the church since King's death. This is most evident in the lingering, antiquated thinking about race; in the subtle and not-so-subtle ways in which the churches continue to silence, exclude, and subordinate women and gays; and in the church's refusal to respect and engage worldviews and faith traditions other than their own. King witnessed and protested against personal and institutional racism with a sense of urgency that recalled the ancient Hebrew prophets, and he challenged the Christian church to respect and uplift the dignity and worth of every person while also fulfilling its role as the chief symbol of the beloved community.[25] King also had this in mind when he spoke in terms of "the whosoever will, let him come" church.[26]

King would undoubtedly have problems with Bishop Eddie Long's suggestion that we now live in a postracial America, despite the recent election of Barack Obama as the nation's first African American president. The continuing exclusion, subordination, and disempowering of women and gays in the church would disturb King greatly, and so would the unrelenting assault on gay people's basic right to life, liberty, and the pursuit of happiness. Furthermore, King would lament the church's failure to encounter the challenges of globalization in healthy ways, and also its refusal to seriously promote mutual respect, tolerance, and peaceful coexistence between the various cultures and faith traditions of the world. All forms of bigotry, intolerance, and exclusion conflict with King's idea of the church as a "coalition of conscience,"[27] and also with his conviction that humans live in a globalized and interdependent world in which differences should be celebrated. "All life is interrelated," King declared, and "whatever affects one directly, affects all indirectly." Clearly, King was a precursor of the kind of thinking commonly associated with globalization today, and his concept of "the interrelated structure of all reality"[28] remains a challenge to the church and its enduring failure to become a moral agency of provocation, advocacy, and celebration of difference.[29]

The megachurches have responded to war and human destruction in ways that are equally antithetical to King's vision for the church. In the face of former President George W. Bush's ethic of preemptive war and nation building, the megachurch leaders exemplified what became in effect a conspiracy of silence that involved large segments of the church as a whole. That abysmal silence has also been reflected in the church's response to the invasion and occupation of Iraq, global terrorism, post–cold war ethnic cleansing, and genocide. Small wonder that Jerry Falwell, James Dobson, T. D. Jakes, Eddie Long, Charles Blake, Kirbyjohn Caldwell, and other super-church pastors were always welcome in the Bush White House,[30] a privilege King did not have with President Lyndon B. Johnson, especially after the civil rights leader's prophetic proclamations against the nation's misadventure in Vietnam. Church leaders are commonly seen and heard in the public square, but when it comes to war, military aggression and interventions, and other issues of a controversial nature, they are among the silenced voices of the present age. King's legacy stands as a reminder to the church universal that being prophetic has nothing to do with silence and apolitical neutrality in the face of immoral power, military might, and structural evil and injustice.

King's Model of the Prophetic Church

King's model of prophetic witness and activism, not the prosperity theology and entrepreneurial spirituality of the megapreachers, holds the key to an authentically renewed and revitalized church in the twenty-first century. Clearly, the megachurch phenomenon, which has become the standard and ideal church model for so many Christians today, is capitalistic, elitist, and materialistic; but King offered a powerful alternative model for what constitutes the truly prophetic church. King's model of the prophetic church was designed to enable and empower what he called *the least of these*,[31] while the megachurches have too often led in taking positions that disable and disempower the poor, oppressed, and marginalized in society. King affirmed public expressions of religion, reintroduced themes of freedom, sacrifice, love, redemptive suffering, hope, and deliverance into the nation's public faith and brought the resources of the Christian faith to bear on issues of public policy and the practical problems of daily life in healthy ways, but the megachurches, and other ecclesial bodies that subscribe to a right-wing, conservative agenda, represent a "perversion of public religion."[32] Thus, the contemporary Christian church has much to gain from ethical and theological dialogue with King around the question of what constitutes the true *ekklesia*.

In these times, when many are questioning the relevance and reformability of the church in light of human needs, and some are declaring that the right-wing, conservative agenda has failed, King remains a powerful prophetic voice, a paragon of godly devotion, and a model for theological and ethical reflection.[33] King held that the church must always be subjected to the same levels of critical scrutiny applied to other institutions and structures of power, which means that no ecclesial model, no matter how powerful and popular, should go unexamined and unchallenged. Constructive self-criticism was central to King's understanding of the prophetic role of the church, for he realized that that institution is always under the judgment of what it professes and proclaims.[34] The church's failure to produce constructive critics from within its own ranks, and its refusal to encourage a culture of constructive self-criticism, show that it lacks the collective ecclesial will to be the prophetic church that King envisioned.[35]

But King should not be confined merely to this image of an astute and constructive critic of the Christian church, or to one who simply "raised profound and radical theological questions regarding the presence of Christ and the true nature of the church."[36] One also detects in his ideas and social praxis a blueprint for church-based, prophetic social witness and activism, and proposals for effecting the spiritual, theological, and ethical renewal of the church. As the church explores new paradigms for effective witness as the body of Christ, and as it seeks to be a mission and movement-driven agency, it would do well to reclaim King's model of the prophetic church, because that model can indeed be a vital vehicle in creating and sustaining a consistent ethic and culture of life, a culture of openness and enlargement, a culture of radical democracy, a culture of peace and nonviolence, a culture of sacrificial servanthood, and a culture of constructive self-criticism.[37]

Steps toward Renewing King's Vision

Many questions crowd in upon the Christian church in the early years of this new century and millennium, especially as it considers where it will go from here in terms of fulfilling its moral responsibility toward the world. Can the church lead the way in this new world moment? Can it become a place glistening with new ideas and energy? Can it develop a new identity, vision, and sense of mission and movement? Will the theological shifts it is currently undergoing, due to the challenges of racial minorities, women, and gays, lead to a stronger ethic of openness, enlargement, and inclusion?[38] Will it continue to allow religious and social conservatives to dominate the faith-and-politics debate? How might the church refocus its power, genius, and resources in broader directions in the future? Will it respond appropriately to the current Manichaean division of the world into *us* and *them*? Can it develop a richer vision of its universality?[39] If the Christian church refuses to bring these kinds of questions to the forefront of ecclesiological conversation, and if it fails to answer them in ways that enhance its presence and effectiveness in the world, then the institutional embers that constitute its being and raison d'être will fade in another generation or two.

King modeled a path of ecclesial involvement that the Christian church can follow, but that body must take a number of steps if it is to reclaim his prophetic vision and posture. First, the church must discover new ways of interpreting and practically applying what it affirms and celebrates in its liturgical and/or sacramental life. The entire history of the church reveals an ongoing tension between attempts to preserve traditional teachings, values, and worship styles and the mandate to be Christ in service to the world, or to deal sufficiently and creatively with fresh challenges, shifting cultural realities, and an ever-changing human condition. For the sake of moral consistency, the church must bring its creedal, ritualistic, and celebrational life more in line with mission priorities that meet human needs, hopes, and aspirations. This is what King was thinking when he insisted that the church say and do no more on Sunday morning than it is willing to suffer and die for during the remaining six days of the week.[40]

Second, the church would do well to rethink and redefine its relationship to the state and the body politic, an issue King raised repeatedly in his sermons, speeches, and interviews with various sources in the media. When the state subsidizes the church through faith-based initiatives and other government programs, it becomes virtually impossible for the church to be prophetic in any real sense. King saw this with white churches in his day, and this helps explain the unhealthy alliance between the conservative wing of the church, including the megachurch phenomenon, and parties in the U.S. government over the last decade. Although King cherished the type of partnership between the church and government that benefited the common good, he maintained that church and state are not coextensive, nor are they servants or masters of each other.[41] This point is relevant when considering the public function of the church in any age.

Third, the church should develop better and more practical ways of employing its material power and resources to enable and empower the oppressed, victimized, and outcast. The church remains one of the richest and most influential institutions in the world, but its power is too often misused and abused, an issue King also addressed with prophetic power. Sexism, homophobia, and pedophilia have become metaphors for the general abuse of power in the contemporary Christian church, a problem aggravated by the church's reluctance to be decisively self-critical and self-transforming. The answer, as King so often pointed out in his time, is never in defending the rigidity of present ecclesial patterns and structures but in revolutionizing them and putting them to the service of human liberation and empowerment on the broadest scale possible. The church has much to gain by recovering King's impassioned calls for a church that freely and generously uses its vast power and resources to address human need on life's Jericho road.[42]

A final step on the part of the Christian church must involve a turning toward a more biblical conception of what it means to be prophetic. As King often stated, merely claiming the Bible as an authoritative source and guide in matters of faith, doctrine, morality, and practice is not enough. Scripture, in the Kingian sense, has to be read as a divine command to not only speak truth to power but also to critique and ultimately eliminate evil and unjust structures, laws, and institutions. This was King's understanding of the prophetic church, or that church which becomes maladjusted and nonconformist in its posture.[43] Today there is a need to reclaim the Bible from those Christians who distort it in support of an accommodationist rather than a prophetic ethic and who use it to defend the rich and powerful and to demonize the poor and weak. King's sermons suggest possibilities for constructive thought around the question of how the biblical-prophetic tradition as a whole can be made relevant for the church in this venture.

Conclusion

The ecclesial landscape is shifting, and the Christian church has reached the *kairos*, or moment of truth, in its history, a period during which it is called upon to meet a vast and complex set of challenges that King never really envisioned in his time. A deep restlessness, uncertainty, and insecurity engulf much of contemporary church life, as many pessimists and prophets of doom are reducing that institution to some sad anachronism. Equally disturbing is the fact that few of the faithful are actually talking about breathing new life into the moribund structures of the church. In view of this climate, more and more questions will be raised concerning the church's capacity to remain a living, vigorous organism, and, more specifically, about its ability to spearhead purposeful Christian witness and praxis in a world that changes daily.[44]

There is indeed a need for a new Pentecost to break out in the life of the Christian church, or an experience of discovering God's will anew, and King, a martyr of conscience, has something to say to that institution about these matters.[45] Any attempt to historicize King is not wise, for his constructive reflections on and critique of the church transcend the immediate historical setting in which he spoke, wrote, and struggled. King was unarguably one of the most penetrating and insightful ecclesial minds of his generation, and he reminded the church that its mission is ultimately determined by the norms of Jesus Christ and the needs of society. The Christian church would do itself a great disservice if it ignores King, or if it dismisses him as some meaningless and outdated voice from the distant past. King remains a primary paradigm and a usable resource for the church, even as it seeks to create a new dynamic for ecclesial leadership and activism today and in the years ahead.

Chapter 9

Onward, Christian Soldiers!

Race, Religion, and Nationalism in Post–Civil Rights America

Jonathan L. Walton

AMERICAN CHRISTIAN BROADCASTING IS a primary and productive cause toward the expansion of conservative evangelicalism. The cooling media of radio and television are particularly well suited for the clear-cut though bombastic, and creative though biblically literalist, presentations of the Protestant faith. This is cause for concern. Religious faith is often mounted on the hinges of shared cultural values. Religious broadcasters appeal to their listeners by cloaking particular cultural and political commitments within Christian language so that the two become indistinguishable. This is why within the subculture of evangelical broadcasting, ethnocentric nationalist rhetoric and conservative gender sensibilities have become central tenets of the Christian faith.

The purpose of this essay is to outline and assess the ways that conservative Christian broadcasters both construct and contribute to a Christian nationalist worldview in America. I understand that a comprehensive overview of either Christian broadcasting or Christian nationalism is beyond the prescribed limits of this essay. So in attempts to balance brevity with breadth, I will focus on the ministries of the late Reverend Jerry Falwell and Bishop Eddie L. Long. Differences abound between the two. Jerry Falwell's ministry came of age in opposition to the civil rights and liberation movements of the 1960s as he stood outside the cultural gates as a card-carrying Baptist fundamentalist. Eddie Long is a by-product of the post–civil rights era and interprets his ministry as an extension of Martin Luther King Jr. and the progressive black church tradition. Falwell was a founding member of the principally white Religious Right and Moral Majority movements, while Long is a constitutive cog in the larger charismatic movement that is better known for its emphasis on healing and personal blessings than holiness and political involvement. Yet it is Falwell and Long's shared sense of ethnocentrism and a divinely stratified society framed by their creative use of Christian rhetoric that will serve as my unifying conceptual chord. And I plan to demonstrate that though these ministries may be animated by a different intent, their Christian nationalist rhetoric unites them in a jingoistic and xenophobic effect.

Christian Nationalism and Reconstructionism

By Christian nationalism I am referring to the nostalgic yet neoteric belief that for America to survive, the citizens of the nation must be brought back in line with Christian values upon which this nation was supposedly founded. This belief is nostalgic in regard to the ways conservative Christians overlook America's tragic history of violent conquest, racial and gender exclusion, and religious discrimination by casting America's contemporary story as a narrative of decline, particularly since the civil rights movement. And cultural nationalism is neoteric insofar as it is a newly framed trope of recent decades that erases the anti-Catholic and antisemitic legacies of Protestantism in America toward fostering an alliance between Protestant fundamentalists, Catholic conservatives, and Jewish Zionists.[1]

Christian nationalism is grounded in a larger tradition of U.S. exceptionalism and a particular Christian ideology known as Reconstructionism, also referred to as "dominionism," "dominion theology," and "theonomy." Within this framework, America is cast as a moral exemplar blessed and burdened with the specific task of restructuring American civil society and ultimately the world toward what its proponents understand to be God's natural laws as set forth in the Old Testament. Reconstructionism as an articulated theological system emerged in the 1960s with the writings of Rousas John Rushdoony, a California-based pastor of the Presbyterian Church (U.S.A.). But he was heavily influenced by the presuppositional philosophy of Cornelius Van Til, the Reformed theology professor from Westminster Seminary who interpreted the sixteenth-century ideas of John Calvin literally to mean that all responses to worldly matters must presuppose the authority of God and inerrancy of God's word.[2] For the most part, persons who ascribe to this faith interpret God's laws to include sexuality expressed toward the end of procreation within a heterosexual, monogamous relationship; the nuclear family with women's primary role as mother; and the headship of men in all aspects of society. Civil and criminal codes should be reconstructed to follow Old Testament laws insofar as capital punishment is prescribed for homosexuality, adultery, and even incorrigible children. Moreover, as stipulated in the creation narrative of Genesis 1:28, "God blessed them and said to them, 'Be fruitful and increase in number; fill the earth and subdue it. Have dominion over the fish of the sea and the birds of the air and over every living creature that moves on the ground,'" Reconstructionists believe that God ratified the entire world as an unlimited resource for Christian use. Accordingly, Christian nationalists believe it to be their divinely ordained role and responsibility to institute a theocratic Christian state, which will lead to Christian dominion over the nation and entire world.[3]

To be clear, Christian nationalism neither represents the sentiment of the majority of Americans nor most evangelical Christians. Yet proponents of this ideology are highly organized and disciplined in terms of message dissemination. Beyond the producers of religious broadcasting, prominent megachurches, media publishing houses, politicians, political action groups, and powerful home-schooling initiatives act as conduits to diffuse their beliefs through the dominant society. Rushdoony's Chalcedon Foundation and its publication the *Journal of Christian Reconstruction* (JCR) remains a major player in the conservative Christian world. Contemporary writers such as Gary North (Rushdoony's son-in-law) and Rus Walton continue to promote a two-pronged strategy that includes preparing and pressuring elected officials and raising up a generation of leaders to usher in a postmillennial era. And in the last few decades of the twentieth century, Reconstructionists aligned their core principles to the Republican party in such a way that they have raised their political profile and influence.[4] This is why the recent history of Christian nationalism must include one of the major architects of the Religious Right and founder of the Moral Majority, Reverend Jerry Falwell.

Reverend Jerry Falwell

In the 1970s, as the pastor of the Thomas Road Baptist Church in Lynchburg, Virginia, Jerry Falwell began constructing an ecclesial bridge to unite separatist fundamentalists that eschewed political involvement and more socially engaged evangelicals. The intent was to bring conservative intellectuals like Francis Schaeffer IV and John R. Rice from their fundamentalist islands of isolation into an alliance with evangelicals like Carl F. Henry and members of the National Association of Evangelicals. Falwell embraced the old adage of strength in numbers. And by setting aside doctrinal and dogmatic disputes that meant little outside of the conservative Christian subculture, "Bible-believing" evangelicals could raise both their visibility and credibility in the public sphere.[5] Furthermore, as Randall Balmer notes, infatuated with the ideas of Rushdoony, Falwell began encouraging church members to enter all fields of human endeavor such as public education, law, journalism, and especially politics. Falwell felt fundamentalist Christians could adjust the cultural thermostat toward their particular climate of conservatism over time by increasing their level of cultural and political influence.[6] This was one of the more effective strategies Falwell endeavored to transform his own fundamentalist cultural commitments into a social and political philosophy and vice versa. He created bedfellows out of Christian and social conservatives by discursively fusing their language and sentiment into the standard political tropes. Within a decade, accompanied by the political conservative backlash of the Reagan '80s, he became a major voice in the American political scene.[7]

Throughout the 1970s, Falwell honed his media skills before television cameras inside the sanctuary of Thomas Road Baptist Church.

Falwell's *Old Time Gospel Hour* was a multimillion-dollar media empire that brought his message into the homes of millions of viewers and mass-mailing subscribers each week. There were also the large evangelical audiences his show encouraged as Falwell traveled the country preaching to conservative Christian crowds. Like a politician on the campaign trail, the Virginia-based televangelist had a repertoire of stump addresses at his disposal. With sermon titles like "America Back to God," "I Love America," and "The Spiritual Renaissance in America," Falwell cast his cultural vision for the nation and rallied the faithful by situating listeners within the biblical narrative as God's special elect. Yet upon closer examination of his sermons, one is able to perceive the possible real power of Falwell's core message. It was not Falwell's capacity to pull persons in with his persuasive political rhetoric but, rather, his ability to place those perceived as enemies on the outside of the Christian faith and America's ideals and identity.[8] Falwell's sermons were less about calling "whosoever will" into the kingdom of God and more about constructing walls of demarcation that define the righteous over against a community of evil others that constitute a potential threat to a conservative Christian America. For instance, one particular mass mailing in the design of an official government certificate under the heading "Declaration of War," reads, "The Old-Time Gospel Hour hereby dedicates itself to spearhead the battle and lead an army of Christian soldiers into war against evil."[9] The evils listed include legalized abortion, pornography, homosexuality, socialism, and the deterioration of home and family. And based on Falwell's other sermons and writings dating back to the 1960s, one can add to the list all Communist nations, people of color, and women demanding equal protection under the law, as these groups pose serious challenges to the only three institutions ordained by God, the U.S. government, the family, and the church.

Falwell begins one of his early texts, *Listen America*, with a chapter titled "I Must Listen." In the opening lines, Falwell situates his remarks along the Cambodian border as he narrates his return from a mission trip to the region. Falwell references the "thin, fragile body" of a malnourished Cambodian girl as he departs the war between the "Vietnamese Communists supported by Russia and the Khmer Rouge led by Pol

Pot, supported by Red China." Playing upon cold war anxieties of Communist expansion that characterized the moment, Falwell states:

> There, in the darkness of the cabin of that plane, I looked intently at my son, who was asleep. I could not help but thank God that he has never gone hungry a day in his life. He knows little but what he has read about communism. As I looked at him while he slept, I prayed that God would turn America around so that he would know the America I have known. I vowed that I would never turn my back on the firm decision and sacred commitment I had made to myself and to God that I would preach and work and pray to stop the moral decay that is destroying our freedoms. . . . But that night in that airplane, although I knew that I had to face the grim truth that America, our beloved country, is indeed sick. Our people must be made aware of the fact and be called together to turn this country around before it is too late.[10]

Here we witness Falwell's rhetorical tool of conflating definitions of God, freedom, and prosperity with the United States of America constructed against the backdrop of hunger, famine, pestilence, and war against Communism. There is also a narrative of progression embodied in the plane ride, as Falwell and his son travel from suffering to freedom, from hunger to prosperity, and from war to peace. Falwell answers what he perceives that his divine call is to save his "beloved country" in order to keep at bay the chaos of "moral decay" that seeks to impinge upon the cosmos of America's "freedoms."

A similar ethnocentric theme was evident in Falwell's ministry throughout the 1950s and '60s. He was a part of a larger tradition of southern neo-Confederates that cast civil rights protestors throughout the American South as outsiders rather than American citizens. In a 1964 sermon, "Ministers and Marchers," after attacking Martin Luther King Jr. as a Communist subversive, Falwell affirms the status quo of society by arguing, "Nowhere are we [ministers of the gospel] commissioned to reform the externals. . . . I feel we need to get off the streets and back into the pulpits and into our prayer rooms."[11] And, of course, in the same year that Lyndon B. Johnson required all public schools to follow through on integration plans, Falwell opened his own Christian private school, which only admitted whites for its first few years.[12]

Despite these words and deeds on Falwell's part, some may viscerally protest branding him as a white supremacist. By the end of Falwell's life, he welcomed persons of color inside the Thomas Road Baptist Church, to the campus of his Liberty University, and would publicly disassociate himself with organized hate groups such as the Ku Klux Klan. Yet it remains hard to deny that Falwell continued to employ racialized tropes throughout the course of his ministry that were very much marinated in his divisive segregationist stances early in his career. His repeated revisionist statements aside—such as that he opened his school as a protest against the banning of prayer in schools rather than because of desegregation—Falwell often evoked segregationist codes in appeals to his base as a means of rendering American identity increasingly homogeneous in general, and white and southern in particular.[13]

In a 1986 sermon, "The Spiritual Renaissance in America," Falwell begins with an air of excitement concerning the presumed spiritual rebirth of the nation. His praise is amid Ronald Reagan's backlash against social and economic federal programs that resulted from the mass demonstrations of the civil rights era. Falwell begins, "You and I happen to be living in historic times. There has never been in our history, in modern history, a time when a nation, the great nation of America, that God could make a spiritual turn around such as is occurring in this country." Before moving into further points of affirmation, however, Falwell takes a cautionary tone by injecting, "We've got a long way to go, there is much to be done, but we have bottomed out of those dark ages, the two decades of the sixties and the seventies."[14] One needs little imagination to conceptually flesh out the representative faces of these "dark ages" to which Falwell is referring before his entirely white audience. He is rhetorically framing the quest for full citizenship on behalf of America's subaltern as among the nadir moments of American history even as the dark bodies that courageously challenged the American apartheid are conceptually reduced to evil barbarians at the gate.

Falwell then continues to give an account of a Liberty Seminary graduate and pastor who moved to New York City to start a church. He describes the pastor's daughter as "four-year old, blond, big blue eyes, just a doll," and then proceeds to express how the pastor was warned about never letting that little girl out of his sight. Falwell rhetorically reiterates,

"Blond, blue-eyed, four-year, three-year, four-year-old girls are going at a very high price at the kiddy porn and prostitution market. . . . You hold that child." Such pointed emphasis on her age (read: innocence) and physical characteristics as "blond, blue-eyed" (read: whiteness) places the child in spiritual and racial opposition to her potential captors. One could logically deduce that Falwell was playing on the familiar racialized tropes of nonwhite males preying upon "innocent" white females with the aim of riling the passions of his listeners. Moreover, to describe the pastor as having moved from the South to the North, the dividing line of the Mason-Dixon becomes the line of demarcation in this cultural civil war. Surely Falwell understood the rhetorical race-baiting implicit in his remarks was consistent with a larger neo-Confederate sensibility in general and the new southern strategy of the Republican party at the time in particular. By pitting the century-old obsession of an independent southern way of life where everyone knew their place against an immoral and invasive federal government, both Falwell and Republican strategists effectively turned many white southerners toward their cultural and political agenda.

To be sure, this was consistent with Falwell's rhetorical mastery of framing his interlocutors as negatively as possible before loyal audiences. And by peppering his words with biblical quotations and authoritative allusions such as "God-ordained" and "instituted by God," he was able to both uphold and affirm society's status quo by representing alternative voices as extreme at best and pathological and threatening at worst. He depicted women who supported the Equal Rights Amendment, for instance, as simply those who were "misguided and bored with life." Their claims for equality represented a "spiritual problem" of never having accepted their "God-given roles as housewives, helpmates, and mothers."[15] Falwell even went so far as to connect the feminist movement with the porn industry. Playing upon patriarchal anxieties concerning man's desire to control the female body and dictate women's sexual activity—which ironically but consistently proves to be a shared impulse between men attracted to Falwell's form of divinely sanctioned patriarchy and men attracted to pornographic material and sadomasochism—Falwell suggests, "Many women are saying, 'Why should I be taken advantage of by chauvinists? I will get out and do my own thing. I will stand up for my rights. I will have my own dirty magazines.'"[16]

This sort of shock rhetoric allowed Falwell to call his metaphorical troops to battle by assisting listeners to feel as if they were indeed under siege by American interlopers, citizens who were not authentically "American," which invariably meant Christian. This was particularly the case when it came to the "gay agenda." Members of the GLBTQ community were always depicted as on the prowl seeking innocent prey. Quotes such as, "Homosexuals cannot reproduce themselves so they must recruit," were a common part of Falwell's homiletic arsenal.[17] In 1999, he (in)famously outed a children's cartoon character, Tinky-Winky, as a covert recruiter.[18] And in what may have proved to be among one of Falwell's most hateful and hurtful suggestions in the aftermath of September 11, 2001, he blamed "feminists, abortionists, and homosexuals" as the root cause of the heinous terrorist attacks.[19] Unfortunately, for five decades Falwell circulated the mythology that inclusiveness, tolerance, and a genuinely pluralist public sphere are against the will of God. It was thus not a large leap for Falwell to frame non-Christians, political progressives, feminists, and members of the GLBTQ community as domestic terrorists and enemy combatants.

Though these types of accusations may seem ludicrous to many, an interrogation that challenges simply the historical factualness or coherent logic of Falwell's message is futile for the most part. Rather, it is more productive for ethicists and critics to examine the emotional appeal of this type of discourse as well as the psychological needs it apparently fulfills. In doing so, I find literary theorist Linda Kintz's use of resonance to be both instructive and illumining. For Kintz, the concept of resonance refers to "the intensification of political passion in which people with very different interests are linked together by feelings aroused and organized to saturate the most public, even global issues."[20] This is to say, as in the acoustical sense, feelings and emotions can be prolonged and intensified by tapping into sympathetic vibrations. In terms of conservative religious discourse, the sympathetic vibrations come in the form of cultural familiarity—that which has always been, just is, and should always be. Rhetorical familarity appeals to and fosters cultural resonance by signaling an a priori understanding of what it professes. For example, homosexuality is unnatural because it is! Or, blacks commit violent crimes because blacks are violent people—for God's sake, don't you watch television?! Therefore, in both intent and effect, Falwell was able to promote particular ideological positions, even promoting them to the level of godliness, by appealing to his listeners' mythologized sense of how they already imagined the natural condition of their nation on the one hand, and/or what they desired their nation to become on the other. More often than not, such resonant religious discourse lends itself to the reification and recirculation of base, deep-seated anxieties throughout society that inform the xenophobia that fuels Christian nationalism. Thus, evangelical broadcasters of this ilk both help to foster and then benefit from such a culture of fear and nostalgic longing.

Bishop Eddie L. Long

This Christian nationalist worldview, however, should not be solely identified with the white Christian Right. Similar discursive moves that equate particular "American" values with godliness, profess a commitment to American exceptionalism, and scapegoat the already vulnerable members of society can be readily identified in the rhetoric of prominent Afro-Protestant preachers. Channel-surf from Trinity Broadcast Network (TBN) to the Word Network and Black Entertainment Television, just to name a few, and you will witness impassioned preachers espousing patriarchal family values and using jingoistic rhetoric that conceptually bifurcates "children of God" and those who are "of the world." Like Falwell, many of these preachers profess and promote a sincere yet sophomoric belief that a panacea for black America's problems can be found in men assuming control over their families, women remaining "pure" until marriage, and homosexuals and the poor purging themselves of "demonic spirits."

Bishop Eddie L. Long is the pastor of the 20,000-plus-member New Birth Missionary Baptist Church in metropolitan Atlanta. He is considered among the more influential voices within black religious broadcasting, as his Sunday-morning broadcast *Taking Authority* can be viewed on nineteen national and international television networks. Long is the author of several books and a staple of the megaconvention and evangelical revival circuit. And with his sermonic and writing style, Long embraces much of the Reconstructionist-informed theology and rhetorical tactics of Jerry Falwell. (A few years ago, I purchased Bishop Long's book *Taking Over* through Falwell's online bookstore, wherein Long was the sole African American author whose works were available.) Like Falwell, Long is a devout patriot who interprets his ministerial call as turning America back toward God. Both the dominionist and declensionist dimensions of Bishop Long's conception of American history are evident in the following quote:

> God chose God-fearing men and women to establish this nation. By His sovereignty God established the United States of America; yet because of the failures of the Supreme Court and the executive branch over the last few decades, we have dared to push God away instead of pulling God close. We have rejected truth and refuse to inherit the hearts of our forefathers; therefore we have redrafted this nation into something other than what God ordained it to be. The United States today is a mockery before God and a shadow of what we are ordained to be because we have become a nation in rebellion.[21]

This God-ordained truth to which Long appears to refer involves his understanding of a divine chain of command. In reviewing Bishop Long's sermons and books, no other theme recurs as much as the dominion of Christians over the kingdom of God based upon this military-like hierarchy. He believes that God has ordained a divine chain of command for the family, church, and society, which, if followed, affords Christians dominion over all areas of life. It begins with a Christian man who is under the covering of Jesus Christ and then extends to women and children, who are to submit to men, just as men submit to Christ. Long often appeals to the creation narrative in the Garden of Eden in order to cosmogonically ground his assertions. "God covered man, pulled the woman out of man, and took the child out of the woman. Now He [sic] expects man to cover the woman and the child."[22] The family, then, according to Long, is God's original institution that is intended to be the foremost witness and model for the world, the divine archetype for both the church and larger society.

Long indeed models this divine chain of command within his church. He eschews church governing boards and other systems of ecclesial accountability as "ungodly governmental structures" that are outside of God's order. Rather than being a space of participatory democracy and mutual engagement, church members are called to submit under the covering of the pastor. One might deduce that this is why Bishop Long often refers to God as well as himself as "Daddy." If God is the father or head of the church, his role as senior pastor grants him a claim of paternity over members of the congregation. "I tell the members of my congregation," he explains, "you are the sons and daughters in the church, and I am the father. I don't do this because I'm an egomaniac; I do it because it is biblical."[23]

Moreover, just as the family is the blueprint of the church, the church has been ordained, according to this divine chain of command, to cover society. Long contends that God's functional chain of command is predicated upon respect, submission, and obedience. Male headship respects, submits to, and obeys God, just as women and children are called to do the same unto men. This chain is repeated in the church between pastor and parishioner just as it should be in society among Christians and non-Christians. Only Christians can see God's divine order because, Long argues, it is invisible to the natural eye. Yet, "those who are saved and baptized into this invisible kingdom can see the order and arrangement of God."[24] This is why Long believes that all governmental, civic, and social organizations should submit themselves to the church—because only then will America return to the original divine order that God set forth for this nation.

Here we see just how much Falwell and Long share in common with Rushdoony, though the latter's ideology was most likely siphoned through Falwell and other Christian conservatives into Long's writings and sermons. Both advocate a Christian theocracy, or more literally a fundamentalist ecclesiocracy, wherein the conservative Christian church claims dominion over American society. Reconstructionists do not appear to believe in a separation of church and state insofar as Christians are to render unto Caesar what is Caesar's and unto God what is God's. They believe all things belong to God. Thus, they are well within their divine right to claim dominion over all governmental power, institutions, and resources that are currently in control of Caesar's secular state. As Long responded to critics who accused him of cozying up to President George W. Bush in order to receive federal faith-based funding, "We are not begging for their money. That is our money!"[25] What is more, a cursory glance at the titles associated with Long's ministry reveals how much this concept of dominionism informs his worldview. His television broadcast is titled *Taking Authority*. He has authored *Taking Over, Called to Conquer, Gladiator,* and *It's Your Time: Reclaim Your Territory for the Kingdom*. And if you visit New Birth's local bookstore, named "Conquest," you can purchase sermon DVDs with titles such as "Obedience," "Reign or Maintain," and "Conquer and Subdue."

There is also a strong correlation between Long's theologically informed American exceptionalism framed by militaristic rhetoric and a broader imperialistic impulse. A crusadelike undercurrent animates the Reconstructionist movement, and Bishop Long is quite comfortable extolling the virtues of violent compulsion. The day following the attacks of September 11, 2001, Long told a standing-room-only crowd at New Birth Missionary Baptist Church that America's inevitable retaliation was consistent with God's plan of discipleship. He claimed that great charismatic movements followed both World War I and World War II and suggested that similar would follow America's inevitable military efforts. "Do you realize what is about to happen?" Long rhetorically asked. "The borders are about to explode. . . . It's about God's kingdom, it's about His rulership . . . it's about subduing nations, it's about snatching folk out of the darkness into the marvelous light." Similarly, when President George W. Bush declared war against Iraq, Long justified America's military efforts with an interesting theological claim. Arguing that modern-day Iraq is the original Garden of Eden, Long told a Wednesday-night Bible-study group that America was going to reclaim what is rightfully ours. He went on to say, "Everything about our religion has been confined to the borders of the U.S.A. But God is saying I am bigger than the borders of the U.S.A. So I have to bring you into a worldview. You cannot talk Kingdom and stay in America. . . . You better get ready to fight because it really ain't about Iraq, it is about the Kingdom of God."[26]

But despite Falwell and Long's shared ethnocentric and highly gendered views of God and society, there are possible differences between the animating impulses and self-conceptions that inform charismatic black mainline preachers like Long and those of Falwell and other members of the white Religious Right. I argued above, on the one hand, that Falwell's nationalist rhetoric is hewn out of a neo-Confederate and racially stratified worldview systematized by Rousas John Rushdoony, Gary North, and Rus Walton. His ideal America harkens back to Falwell's southern and segregationist sensibilities of the pre–civil rights era, which is consistent with the Republican party's southern strategy in recent decades. Long, on the other hand, envisages himself as the spiritual successor of Martin Luther King Jr. and civil rights protest. To be clear, this is not solely based on his own delusions of grandeur. Many of Bishop Long's followers, including Bernice King (the youngest daughter of Martin and Coretta), view him as the Joshua to King's Moses, leading African Americans into the promised land of economic prosperity and social inclusion in the post–civil rights era.[27]

The Resonance of Long's Rhetoric

Elsewhere I give a more detailed account for and argue against what I consider to be Long's flawed and fallacious appropriation of Martin Luther King Jr. as well as his consumerist, promised-land metaphors.[28] But here I want to identify possible reasons Bishop Long's postracist, über-patriarchal, and hypernationalist rhetoric resonates with a cross-section of Afro-Protestants who, I dare to suggest, are in no way familiar with Reconstructionist ideology. Unlike Falwell, this rhetoric is grounded in racial inclusion rather than exclusion and builds upon (though fails to move beyond) a tradition of Christian-informed racial politics. Invariably, Long appeals to three longstanding racial strategies in African American history: (1) economic development as a means of racial uplift, (2) the valorization of the traditional family model as a means of racial respectability, and (3) patriotism as a means of racial effacement.

First, economic advancement as a means of racial uplift is one of the most pervasive ideals in African American history, dating back to the antebellum era. It can be traced to the mutual aid societies of the eighteenth century that provided free blacks with unemployment benefits, burial insurance, as well as the institutional roots for the Free African

Church movement. In the post-Reconstruction era, in collaboration with the economic gospel of Booker T. Washington, a decidedly nationalist consciousness developed within black Christian churches insofar as they became an interstitial space in which African Americans could pool their resources toward fostering a counterpublic over against the dominant white supremacist society. African American newspapers, banks, grocery stores, schools, funeral homes, and many other business ventures were bound up with faith communities. According to historian Adele Oltman, a black Christian nationalism developed wherein religious and civic leaders "believed that business had sacred and secular redemptive possibilities" for all African Americans.[29] And since the turn of the twentieth century—from racial accommodationist Booker T. Washington, to black nationalists like Marcus Garvey and Elijah Muhammad, to contemporary televangelists like Bishop T. D. Jakes— a masculinist entrepreneurialism is often heralded as one of the more effective ways to overcome and/or insulate black people from the sting of white supremacy. Like Eddie Long in the contemporary moment, many African Americans believe that the color green disrupts the black/ white binary. Thus, there is a direct relationship between economic growth and racial advancement among many African Americans (even if there is evidence to show somewhat of an institutional shift from a post-Reconstruction cooperative economic model to a post–civil rights personal prosperity ethic within black charismatic and neocharismatic faith communities).[30]

Second, many black churches adhere to Victorian ideals of family and gender roles as a viable means toward social equality and racial respectability. Ironically, this embrace of the traditional family is bound up with a legacy of nontraditional familial practices and gender flexibility. But in order to counter stereotypical images of black life in the dominant cultural imagination, African Americans accept the traditional ideal as a corrective to counter the perception of black social chaos. Historian Julius Bailey writes that African Methodist Episcopal clergymen sought to shape the boundaries of appropriate gender roles and familial values as far back as the early nineteenth century. Prescriptive appeals to domesticity were offered as the panacea for social chaos and the appropriate route to racial progress.[31] Evelyn Brooks Higginbotham writes about Baptist women's movements at the outset of the twentieth century that "emphasized reform of individual behavior and attitudes both as a goal in itself and as a strategy of reform of the entire structural system of American race relations."[32] An image of an African American model family (a providing husband, nurturing wife, and disciplined children) would go a long way, it was believed, toward displacing negative images of African Americans, demonstrating how one could be both "black" and "American."

The final strategy has to do with what social historian and critical race theorist Scott Kurashige refers to as loyalty discourse among African Americans. There is an identifiable legacy of African Americans claiming the mantle of patriotism toward the alleviation of racial discrimination and social inequality. Loyalty discourse was particularly prevalent around World War II and the subsequent cold war era. African American community leaders and preachers sought racial gain by jettisoning racial self-interest and appeals for minority rights in favor of a broad political alliance where African Americans demonstrated themselves as loyal allies against a perceived common enemy.[33] Professions of patriotism and effacing racial distinction thus become a supposed means for African Americans to acquire full social acceptance. For instance, in 1941 Rev. Clayton Russell, pastor of the politically progressive People's Independent Church, organized the Negro Victory Committee (NVC) in Los Angeles. Blending an economic nationalism with a devout American patriotism, the NVC worked alongside the national "Double V campaign" to rally African American support for war efforts while calling on the federal government to dismantle all racial barriers that precluded full African American participation. This was the double victory, victory at home and abroad for African Americans. Those who signed on to this program sought to prove themselves as devout patriots, thereby shaming the dominant society for its own apparent hypocrisies. The ultimate objective was African American employment opportunities in the armed services and inside the booming war industries. By minimizing blackness and emphasizing "Americaness," Russell and the NVC sought for African Americans opportunity and prosperity that could benefit all Americans across racial and class barriers.[34]

The Limitations of Long's Rhetoric

But even if these traditions of racial uplift, respectability, and effacement toward the goal of multiracial democracy have a proven political record of localized success, they come with their own inherent limitations. Black Christian nationalism's concern for economic advancement and racial respectability obscures intraracial class conflicts, ignores racial barriers, and reinforces gender injustice. Consider Eddie Long's commitment to an economic "promised land" for African Americans. (When selected by the King family to offer the keynote address at the annual King federal holiday celebration in 2002, he chastised African Americans for their inability to "forgive and forget racism" in America.) Long suggests that King led blacks out of the bondage of racial discrimination so that African Americans could seize and conquer the economic opportunities that God now provides. "I have an announcement for you," Long declared before members of the historic Ebenezer Baptist Church, "We are already in the Promised Land and if you open up your eyes you will see that a lot of things that we are fighting have gone away and are therefore memories."[35]

This sentiment reveals Long's bourgeois worldview and middle-class commitments, even as it belies the material conditions of a disproportionate number of blacks in America. True, the victories of the civil rights movement quadrupled the black "well-to-do" over the past forty years. But due to concomitant technological innovations and market transformations, the working poor and underclass in the black community grew at the same alarming rate. Computerization replaced human manufacturing, globalization created a cheap inexhaustible labor pool, and, in the process, millions of well-paid blue-collar union jobs were eradicated. These changes had deleterious consequences for black and brown urban communities that no level of entrepreneurial ingenuity could overcome, by and large. Couple this with the growth of the prison industrial complex and draconian drug laws targeting specifically black and brown youth, and one would have to conclude that Long's economic "promised land" remains at the level of allegory. Like Afro-Protestant claims of nationalist destiny dating back to the nineteenth century, the promised land should not be evaluated as a fulfilled prophecy but, rather, interpreted as a prayer of longing.[36]

Moreover, as Higginbotham points out about nationalist discourse within black Baptist churches at the outset of the twentieth century, the rhetoric betrays inherent gender conflicts.[37] Both masculine authority and bias are left unquestioned under the guise of racial uplift and respectability. As a consequence, gender inequality becomes naturalized as the way things have always been and, invariably, should remain. Nationalist emphasis on racial respectability also inevitably reinforces rigid gender proscriptions. I have noted how Long advocates for "God's order" in the black family. Yet, far from encouraging freedom, agency, and individual flourishing among African American women, Long is more concerned with African American men having power and control toward the end of gaining the fidelity and reverence of their female counterparts. A woman can never operate outside of the auspices of male authority. Long is forthright that a woman is under the control of "her father until she is married, her husband after her marriage, and if there is an interim period, her pastor."

And finally, in terms of the tradition of loyalty discourse, there are often conflicting consequences when African Americans seek to minimize blackness in order to affirm their "Americanness." On the one hand, African Americans are able to transcend a truncated racial tribalism toward cross-racial coalition building. This was indeed the goal of the NVC in the 1940s. It was believed that if everyone worked together for the war effort, the rising tide of the American economy would lift all racial boats. On the other hand, it is dangerous for any particular group to efface race within such a hyperracialized context. To do so reinforces the normative cultural conception that reifies America as essentially nonracial (read: white) while placing people of color in opposition to a mythic American ideal. This places racial minorities in a position of racial triangulation where everyone is evaluated according to their proximity to the racial standard and source of cultural power. In the case of black Christian nationalism and loyalty discourse, African Americans are thus impelled to embrace the jingoistic framing of an enemy by the dominant society in such a way that racial and ethnic discrimination get displaced onto other minority groups. This sort of triangulation caused Reverend Clayton Russell and the NVC to turn their support for America into a united front against enemy "Japs," including the very

Japanese Americans that many African Americans lived with along the American Pacific rim.[38] Amid the unjust internment of Japanese Americans during World War II, for the most part, the NVC remained silent. Black Christian nationalists, then, can become so concerned about group acceptance in the larger society that they lose track of the ways they must scapegoat other vulnerable groups to gain that acceptance.

One can witness at least two examples of this sort of triangulation when Eddie Long held his interracial "Stop the Silence" march in 2004. Eddie Long and Bernice King led an estimated ten thousand protestors from the Martin Luther King Center for Non-Violence and Social Change to the Georgia state capitol. When Long aired this video on the Trinity Broadcast Network, the march footage was edited and juxtaposed against the famous 1965 Selma march while omitting all references to the primary purpose of the rally—it is safe to conclude this strategy was a part of Long's continued self-identification with Martin Luther King Jr. But Long called together this multiracial crowd of Christian protestors—some of whom waved American flags and donned military fatigues—in order to promote a state constitutional amendment banning same-sex marriage. Long evoked the American tradition of multiracial civil rights protests in order to rally against gay and lesbian Americans. And if this form of sexual triangulation was not enough, Long's voice was dubbed over a hip-hop track titled "It's Revolution Time," declaring his commitment to "American ideals." "I am not against anyone, I love everybody," Long declares. "But what people must understand that when they come into my house, there are rules in my house. The problem with America is that we have opened our doors to a whole of different people. But if you don't like the rules of the house, you can go back to where you came from."[39]

Conclusion

To those not aware of Christian Reconstructionism, the sorts of theological constructions and hyperbolic claims presented in this essay might easily be dismissed as rhetorical velleity, wishful and imaginative thinking on the part of select Christian communities that will never come to pass. America remains a liberal democracy, and the demands of Christian nationalists contradict principal tenets of the U.S. Constitution. But in the aftermath of September 11, we have all witnessed the eradication of constitutional protections and the intensification of Christian national- ist discourse at the highest levels of government. There are high-ranking officers at America's leading military academies like the Air Force Acad- emy and West Point who condone turning America's military into an evangelical fighting force. Former Secretary of Defense Donald Rums- feld adorned daily intelligence briefings to the White House with war images juxtaposed against biblical quotes in order to sanction the U.S. invasion of Iraq.[40] Several states have passed constitutional amendments in recent years denying gays and lesbians equal protections under the law.[41] And with the rise of the American Tea Party movement, several political leaders like Sharon Angle of Nevada and Rand Paul of Kentucky have amassed followings with their Reconstructionist-inflected libertari- anism, which envisages government only as a source of military protec- tion and criminal punishment, while investing the individual family and ecclesia with all other forms of social responsibility and control.[42] It is within this context that democracy can quickly unravel. In its place, unfortunately, the most politically organized and media savvy are well poised to arise. This is why we should be mindful of the cross-racial Christian nationalist rhetoric that currently inundates millions of faith- ful Christian believers. Though calls for a Christian America strike the right chord among those longing for an Edenic America, it may just prove to be the forbidden fruit of narcissist indulgence.

Chapter 10

Overcoming Christianization

Reconciling Spiritual and Intellectual Resources in African American Christianity

Rosetta E. Ross

IN HER BOOK *Your Spirits Walk Beside Us,* social historian Barbara Dianne Savage says the civil rights movement "with churches, church people, and church culture at its center was a powerful and startling *departure* from" conflicting perspectives about the relationship of religion and politics among black Christians. Within the historical context of "decades of complaints and controversies on the question of how and whether African American churches could be a progressive political force," Savage says, the civil rights movement "changed our notions and expectations about the relationship between African American religion and politics." Because of the magnitude and accomplishments of the civil rights era, many persons today look back through the lens of the civil rights movement and consider the history of black Christianity as having always integrated religion and politics. However, Savage says, there never has been a single perspective among African Americans about the relationship of religion and politics, in spite of the common belief across black Christianity that enslavement was morally wrong. Savage also argues that the civil rights movement contrasts with earlier twentieth-century narratives that "treated African American religion with despair and disdain."[1]

Savage presents an intentional and clear distinction between church people participating in the civil rights movement and the historic posture of black churches. The movement and the people in it pursued (and partially achieved) political ideals embodied in much black church culture. However, within the institutional context of black churches, Savage says, there have been (and continue to be) questions about the relationship of religion to politics and about the religious value of intentionally organizing to achieve political ideals. The reality of some black Christians embodying political and religious ideals apart from churches (sometimes even being seen as conflicting with beliefs and practices of black churches) reflects the tension within black Christian institutions about how to value both the spiritual and intellectual resources that reside there. While some church people, such as those who participated in the civil rights movement, overcame this tension as individuals, the challenge for black Christianity is to determine ways to reconcile this conflict at the institutional level if it is to maintain relevance to progressive movements that enhance the lives of persons in general and dispossessed black people in particular.

Before Savage's observation that some black persons departed from traditional beliefs and practices across African American Christianity and actively engaged political life, Christian social ethicist Peter J. Paris argued that black churches have an institutional dilemma that impedes setting and achieving political goals. Noting considerable ambiguity about affirming the nation while also valuing the race, Paris says black churches lack political realism demonstrated in "a distinct lack of discernment . . . concerning the importance of constructive analytical and critical thought."[2] During the civil rights era, persons like Septima Poinsette Clark used critical thought and practical reasoning to analyze conflicting traditions within black Christianity, to integrate religion and politics, to develop a unified self-concept, and to help pass on critical thinking skills to others. Building on the critical thought and practical reasoning of the civil rights era, young progressives in the Obama movement integrate religion and politics more fluidly by affirming values that sometimes hold together ideas some older religious activists oppose. By exploring analyses of Savage and Paris and the examples of activists like Clark and contemporary young progressives, it is possible to consider some of what is required to reconcile spiritual and intellectual resources in African American Christianity.

Identifying the Conflict: Black Christians and Black Churches Engaging Politics

Embedded in Savage's analysis of the civil rights movement as a departure from the historic posture of black churches is a distinction between the practices of some black Christians who actively engage political issues and the practices and beliefs of black churches. According to Savage, institutional black churches have often wavered on whether there ought to be a relationship between religion and politics. However, some individual black Christians have consistently challenged the idea that religion and politics are incompatible. These persons are intellectually rigorous in considering the relationship of religion and politics and live active lives integrating the two. Savage sees such persons as having made the civil rights movement a reality. By differentiating the practices of black churches as institutions from the practices of some black Christians, Savage suggests a distinction between black churches as institutions and black church norms.

Examining the twentieth-century history of African American Christianity through the lives of politically active black Christian laity—such as Carter G. Woodson, W. E. B. Du Bois, Mary McLeod Bethune, Nannie Helen Burroughs, and Benjamin E. Mays—Savage concludes that African American Christians who combine religion and politics are exceptional. These persons have long called for a "highly educated, politically engaged" clergy that can combine political activism and emotional worship.[3] Moreover, Savage says, they want a religion that engages the intellect, issues of social justice, and the world. Such persons are among a "small remnant of true believers" who hold "that religion belong[s] in politics and that the moral impetus for social change [can] come from within black Christianity, despite its flaws." This "remnant" drove the civil rights movement. "Black churches, their members, and their ministers," Savage writes, "were crucial to what the movement achieved, but it never involved more than a small minority of black religious people."[4] By distinguishing the activity of some black church people from black church institutions, Savage underscores the challenge of realizing the potential of black churches to be politically effective. Moreover, the nature of religion as a private choice of individuals, the decentralized diversity of black religion, and the black Christian community's impulse toward securing black male leadership compound the divide between the black Christian remnant and black churches by straining against the connection of black religion and black politics.

The distinction Savage makes between some black Christians and black churches may be seen in the work of Paris, who identifies "the black Christian tradition" as distinct from black churches. The black Christian tradition, Paris writes, is "the principle of nonracism." The black Christian tradition reflects "a biblical anthropology which . . . strongly affirms the equality of all under God regardless of race or any other natural quality."[5] Paris's distinction of the black Christian tradition from black churches occurs in his assertion that the tradition preceded the establishment of independent black churches even though the churches institutionalized the tradition.[6]

Through an analysis of two black church institutions—the African Methodist Episcopal Church and National Baptist Convention, USA—Paris concludes that black churches express ambiguity in regard to the exercise of political power. There is, Paris says, a "traditional conflict" in moral thought of black churches. Because of dual loyalties to "serving the needs of the race" and "serving the Lord of the church," black churches generally have failed to correlate religion and politics.[7] Black churches have not demonstrated political wisdom, Paris continues, because they tend to subordinate the need for practical political engagement under rhetoric about political ideals.[8] The result has been the development of ideas within black churches that the ideal vision of racial integration contradicts the need for separate racial development. As a consequence, thought and action of black churches have been guided more by the political ideal than by the political reality of the need for separate racial development and the development of critical black theological reflection.

Both Paris and Savage identify a duality in African American Christianity. For Savage, there is a division between what a small number of individual black Christians and the larger black Christian community believe and practice in regard to the relationship of religion and politics. For Paris, the duality is ambiguity arising from the perceived contradiction in African American Christianity of expressing allegiance to both the black race and the Christian deity, and to both the black race and the United States as a nation. Because African American independent churches have embraced white theologies of their parent bodies and followed white models, black churches' conceptions of the Christian deity and of being faithful to the Christian deity means African American Christians must preserve white Christianity. Both Savage and Paris see political practice as important to overcoming the dualities they identify, and both assert that there is a need for more critical thinking ("theoretical rigor" and "constructive analytical" thought).

The legacy of failed critical thought in African American Christianity originates, perhaps, as a result of Christianity being transmitted to African Americans as a tactic of colonization. In spite of the emergence of independent black churches, a prominent element of Africans' encounter with Christianity in the Western Hemisphere was for the purpose of "christianization." Late-nineteenth-century Baptist missionaries who developed schools for newly freed persons, for example, emphasized as "very essential that these colored people shall be Christianized as well as educated." Christianization, the missionaries went on to write, included ensuring that "the Bible is taught daily, and constant attention is paid to morality, truthfulness, and honesty."[9] The colonial distinction between christianizing (inculcating personal morality) and educating (presumably including consciousness-raising and critical thinking) persists as a duality in African American Christianity. Late-nineteenth-century christianization of freed persons by missionary educators continued the U.S. antebellum deployment of christianization as a method of control. Latta Thomas writes that the "catalog of sins" that accompanied christianization "formed another mental chain around the minds of Blacks."[10]

Savage's conclusion that only a "small remnant" of black Christians insist on combining critical thought with religious adherence and Paris's assessment of the conflicted moral agency and deficient political wisdom of black churches point to the need for contemporary black Christian institutions to develop consistent mechanisms seeking to overcome the bifurcation of spirit and intellect that is a legacy of christianization.

Defying Christianization: Septima Clark's Use of Critical Thinking and Practical Reasoning

During a 1976 interview with Jacquelyn Hall, Septima Poinsette Clark said of her father, Peter Poinsette: "they had *Christianized* him."[11] When she made this statement, Clark was a sixty-seven-year-old retired reading teacher and former civil rights activist who had carefully guarded her own identity as an evangelical churchwoman. Clark uses the term *christianized* to characterize her father's attitudes about slavery. During the Civil War a teenaged Peter Poinsette "took water to the [Confederate] soldiers who were fighting to keep him" enslaved. "He really felt that it was perfectly all right," Clark observes, to fight "against the people in the harbor who were coming to free him."[12] In presenting an assessment of her father as having been christianized, Clark expresses both evaluation of what she observed in her father as a form of subjugation and disagreement with the colonial practice of christianization. Clark's statement also demonstrates that she overcame the challenge that has caused moral conflict for some African Americans. Clark did not hold the self-contradictory view that being a faithful Christian requires denial or disaffirmation of one's own identity. Moreover, she distinguished being christianized from being Christian and presented a unified and integrated self-concept as a Christian social activist.

As a civil rights activist, Septima Clark developed and guided implementation of the Citizenship Education Program. During the most intense phase of the civil rights era, the Citizenship Education Program became the primary means of preparing illiterate and semiliterate African Americans to register and to vote. Clark's leadership of the program emerged from her Christian volunteerism as a young elementary schoolteacher at John's Island, South Carolina. During her time off at John's Island, Clark conducted workshops on health issues and provided literacy education. Clark carried out her literacy work by teaching local black farmworkers to read, write, and do math by using objects that were familiar in the world they inhabited. Clark added a political dimension to her literacy work when she consented to focus reading and writing sessions on preparing African Americans to register to vote. As successful John's Island voter-registration efforts were replicated, they easily folded into what was becoming a movement not only to improve the circumstances of rural African American farm workers and sharecroppers but also to change the society. Clark's reputation and circumstances[13] resulted in her coordinating literacy work for voter registration across the South. When she prepared others to lead these small-group citizenship-education sessions, Clark was careful to emphasize that leaders should privilege the everyday lives of those who attended the sessions by teaching at levels accessible to the persons with whom they worked. This provided an opportunity for learners to focus on their own worlds.[14]

Although Clark became known in civil rights circles as the leader of Citizenship Education Programs, she was concerned throughout her life to cultivate an identity as a proper churchwoman. This concern originated with Clark's parents, who taught her a Christianity that involved personal morality and contributing to the welfare of others. Her parents encouraged "being truthful," avoiding "sinful relationships," and giving "service."[15] As a teen and young adult, Clark was active at her mother's congregation, Old Bethel Methodist Church in Charleston, South Carolina, which she joined at age thirteen. When Clark took her first teaching job on John's Island, she attended the circuit of churches on adjacent islands. As an adult in Charleston, Clark regularly engaged local chapters of Church Women United, the Young Women's Christian Association, and Alpha Kappa Alpha Sorority, all women's clubs that accorded with the image of a proper Protestant Christian woman. When she moved away from home, Clark was careful to maintain this image. During her brief stay with in-laws in Hickory, North Carolina, Clark joined their African Methodist Episcopal congregation because she felt failure to join would lower the image her in-laws had of her. When writing or speaking about her civil rights work, Clark consistently used vocabulary from Christianity to do so.[16]

Clark's Christian identity never impeded her civil rights activism and leadership. Neither did it prohibit her ability to make careful distinctions between being Christian as a way that she understood and identified herself and *christianization* as a utilitarian mechanism of social and political subjugation. Septima Clark overcame what may be two dominant cultural views about the relationship of religion and politics. First, Clark did not adopt the politically expedient view that combining religion and politics requires being "a great pretender and dissembler"[17] in order to take advantage of others who profess religious belief. Second, she rejected the view that being religious has meaning only for private, personal relationships. Clark understood being Christian as related to both personal morality and to politics. In fact, her understanding of being Christian stimulated her civil rights activism.

Clark's citizenship-education work derived from her critical thinking and practical reasoning skills and allowed her to cultivate these skills in others. By interpreting literacy education as a form of service, Clark determined a course of action that helped develop her integrated self-conception as a politically engaged black Christian. She combined personal moral piety with community service and developed a relevant method for literacy education that helped persons improve their own lives. Moreover, by teaching how to accurately delineate and recognize written representations of things they regularly spoke about and used, Clark helped change the awareness of persons with whom she worked. Through one-to-one and small-group sessions, she opened the way for persons to see and occupy the world differently. In doing so, Clark passed on the ability to use critical thinking and to engage in practical reasoning as she provided space for persons to think about, develop skills, and determine ways to affirm themselves as African Americans while continuing to be good Christians and good citizens.

Many of Clark's peers and allies in the civil rights movement demonstrated a similar *ability* to use critical thinking and engage in practical reasoning. Some also sought to pass these skills on to others as they took up the work of citizenship education and political education by meeting with persons in small groups at churches; canvassing door to door; and talking with persons in living rooms, barbershops, or beauty salons. Like Clark, these civil rights peers also helped change the awareness of persons with whom they worked.

Critical Thought, Practical Reasoning, and the "Joshua Generation"

Septima Poinsette Clark and other civil rights activists passed on critical thinking and practical reasoning skills to persons whom they engaged directly. They also transmitted these skills to a succeeding generation of persons now carrying on their work. Some supporters of Barack Obama's presidential candidacy present contemporary examples of persons who use critical thinking and practical reasoning in efforts to change the society. These persons also share with their predecessor-movement participants the desire to integrate values and politics generally, and religion and politics specifically. Many of the thoughtful young people who supported the Obama candidacy have or have had connections to churches. Some, like Joshua DuBois (director of the White House Office of Faith-Based and Neighborhood Partnerships) and Acacia Salati (legislative assistant to U.S. Rep. James Clyburn and lead staffer for the Democratic Faith Working Group), continue their relationships with churches. Others connect with churches through their emphasis on values they hope to see enacted in public policy and social practices. Still others have had little or no longstanding relationships with Christian or other religious institutions but share with their peers commitment to specific values that they believe will make the society better.

However, values for persons in the Obama movement are not limited to the one or two ideological issues, such as abortion and gay marriage, that recently have dominated discussions of religion and politics. Young progressive-values voters will more likely speak in broader terms about love, inclusion, and opportunity. With the earlier generation of civil rights activists, they share and articulate the belief "that we can build a society like Dr. King's Beloved Community where we tend to the 'least of these' and everyone has a seat at the table."[18] Specific values about which they speak include overcoming poverty, overcoming environmental degradation, access to health care, as well as commitment to moral integrity.

During the civil rights era, many of the persons who helped transmit Septima Clark's Citizenship Education Program were college students and teenagers who had been nurtured in Christian churches and Christian youth organizations. These black and white youth and young adults took the civil rights movement deep into the rural South, and through their work for the Student Non-violent Coordinating Committee (SNCC) and other civil rights organizations, they helped change the culture of peonage in the areas where they worked. Sometimes young civil rights activists demonstrated their critical thinking and practical reasoning skills by challenging the intellectual integrity of their elders. Pointing out the inconsistency of professing religious ideals of love, justice, and equality while making peace with racial apartheid in the South, student civil rights activists often pushed far beyond the boundaries set for them. Some white students did so through their work with black farmers in the South. Some black students, like Diane Nash, challenged the boundaries by noting the duplicity that inhered within U.S. racial segregation. Segregation, Nash wrote, "makes [white and black] people lie to each other."[19]

Sometimes referring to themselves as the Joshua generation,[20] contemporary young progressives also see themselves pushing beyond ideas and practices of elders, whose beliefs often prove to be irreconcilable with young progressives' commitment to broad values of love, inclusion, and opportunity. Young progressives are less likely to toe ideological lines, and more likely to hold together ideas the generation before them viewed as conflicting or at least as in tension. A recent survey of evangelicals, for example, found that the "majority of younger white evangelicals support some form of legal recognition for civil unions or marriage for same-sex couples." This is a position to which traditional "evangelicals remain strongly opposed. At the same time, young evangelicals are as solidly pro-life on abortion as older evangelicals."[21] Young black progressives such as Jehmu Greene (Democratic political consultant and former executive director of "Rock the Vote") and Yolo Akili (instructor/ trainer at Men Stopping Violence in Atlanta) challenge traditional intrarace ideological perspectives as they call for consistency in critical thinking across the range of African American life. Citing the incongruity of public figures arguing against racism while remaining silent about intrarace crime and wrongdoing, Greene asks, "Why are some African Americans so cowardly when it comes to addressing black-on-black violence?"[22] Akili calls for practical reasoning within African American Christian communities by challenging black clergy to take responsibility for the "damage" they inflict on gay men who "have such self-hatred because of what they hear" repeatedly in churches they attend.[23]

The intensity of Greene and Akili's analyses reflects the impatience many young black progressives have with intellectual compromises of older generations. Thinking young black Christians do not appear willing to countenance the legacy of thought and practice within black Christianity that accommodates and even denies the conflicts of the tradition. The critical intensity of young black progressives, the legacy of Christian activists such as Septima Clark, and the challenging analyses of scholars such as Savage and Paris all point the way to overcoming dualities in black Christianity.

Thinking Black Christians, Black Religious Scholars, and Black Religion

The controversy about black theology and the conflict between Jeremiah Wright and Barack Obama during the 2008 presidential campaign brought substantial public attention to a black pastor and black church *because they reconciled the duality to which Savage and Paris point.* The church's identification of itself as "unashamedly black and unapologetically Christian" with its black value system[24] expressing deep commitment to the well-being of black persons presents a model of critical thought and practice that reconciles spirit and intellect. In spite of Obama's break from Wright, Wright and Trinity United Church of Christ became the congregational home for Obama and undoubtedly for many other young black progressives like him. Obama described Wright's church as a place where "religious commitment did not require me to suspend critical thinking, disengage from the battle for economic and social justice, or otherwise retreat from the world."[25] Quoting this passage written by Obama, Savage notes the significance of this church for Obama as a thinking Christian who, like "reformers such as Du Bois, Woodson, Mays, and Burroughs," she says, "demanded" a critically thinking, "politically engaged" clergyperson and worship context.[26] Determining ways to replicate development of such churches (mosques, temples, and other worship communities) is necessary to ensuring that there are contexts which nurture and affirm religious progressives, young and old, who already possess deep and courageous commitments to sustained critical thought and practical reasoning. Such persons do not, as Savage pointedly notes, constitute the majority in black congregations.

Reconciling spiritual and intellectual resources in African American Christianity will require changes in awareness. This means determining how to overcome the moral conflict in black Christianity that results from christianization and how to overcome the related belief that being a faithful Christian or patriotic citizen requires black self-denial. The challenge of this work is to substantially engage critical thinking and practical reasoning skills of the many Christians who regularly occupy the pews of black churches Sunday after Sunday. Critically thinking black Christians have higher expectations of themselves and others. An important contribution black theologians can make to this work is to determine ways to bring black theological scholarship (their critical thought and practical reasoning) into the lives of these persons and con- gregations. Likewise, thinking black Christians can bring black theology into their churches. Doing this will involve ongoing engagement with churches and church members, perhaps in small-group and one-on-one sessions similar to those undertaken by Septima Clark and by her peers and young progressives during the 2008 presidential campaign. Septima Clark's method of teaching by using objects and issues from the world persons inhabit also would be useful. These practices used in building the civil rights and Obama movements may provide starting points for a new form of black Christian activism, focused internally, seeking to change black religious institutions and black Christianity.

Chapter 11

A Moral Epistemology of Gender Violence

Traci C. West

WE KNOW THAT A man's sexual violence against a woman is wrong. We also know that boyfriends and husbands should not shove, hit, kick, or in any way abuse their girlfriends and wives. But state laws and agencies, as well as religious institutions and nonprofit groups that specifically focus on intimate violence against women, rarely succeed in effectively addressing it. Something goes awry in the process of transforming our certainty about the immorality of gender violence into a constructive communal response. When translating what seems to be nearly universal public disapproval of this violence into social and institutional practices to stop it from taking place, something breaks down.

The consequences of this breakdown are catastrophic for the well-being of many women and girls. Variations on those consequences occur all around the globe. A 2006 United Nations study of seventy-one countries, including the United States, provides a summary of multiple forms and manifestations of gender violence.[1] The summary lists intimate partner violence (most common for women globally), including battering and marital rape; sexual abuse of female children in the household; sexual and physical violence against domestic workers; harmful traditional practices such as forced, early marriage of girl children; femicide perpetrated by strangers, intimate partners, and family members; sexual harassment and sexual violence by nonpartners in community settings; trafficking in women and girls and forcing them into prostitution; state-perpetrated sexual abuse in custodial settings such as police jail cells, prisons, and immigration detention centers; and physical and sexual assaults of noncombatants in armed conflict situations.

Because of its persistence in so many forms in our U.S. society, we apparently know something else about gender violence, besides that it is wrong. We also have preconceptions about gender or about femaleness that fundamentally betray the women and girls who are victimized and that undermine the institutions we rely upon to respond to them effectively. One obvious conclusion inferred from the resilience of gender violence is that the consensus against it must not be as widely shared as it appears to be in most public discourse. Instead of dwelling on that frustrating conclusion, I want to investigate the failure of well-intended moral purposes in responses by trusted community institutions to women victimized by male perpetrators. I concentrate on a few concrete examples of responses to African American women. The violence in these examples includes rape and femicide in one instance and heterosexual intimate partner abuse in the others. I am seeking clues from women's experiences of inadequate responses by government and religious officials. Most importantly, I am concerned with what can be learned from probing the role and content of communal moral knowledge in these selected cases that might aid in a more trustworthy translation of antiviolence moral values into antiviolence community practices.

A creative strategy is needed to identify what kind of communal moral knowledge must be nurtured to uproot gender violence within institutionally based practices. My focus on African American women allows me to explore the role of communal moral knowledge associated with black women's racial identity. In this moment of so-called postracialism, succinctly described by the headline in my local newspaper, "With Obama in the White House, some wonder if Black History Month is still necessary,"[2] how might the particularity of black women's racial identity be relevant for addressing gender violence in the broader U.S. society?

While this essay focuses on contemporary moral life, I assume that it is "still necessary" to understand that black history informs the broader cultural relevance, meanings, and context of contemporary black racial identity. Black women's history during slavery, for instance, is replete with gender violence and reveals broadly based societal relationships. Contemporary racial stereotypes and popular public representations of African American women still bear echoes of this history where their human moral worth was denied through routine sexual violence.[3] It is a history that also illustrates foundational moral and socioeconomic relations woven into the fabric of U.S. culture. During the transatlantic slave trade conducted by Europeans, African women who were sold as chattel could be sexually assaulted while waiting to be loaded onto the slave ships as human cargo or during the long, perilous journey from African ports to the Americas. In the United States, the rape of black women was also a regular part of plantation life in the "breeding" of slaves to work for European American slaveholders in the South. This violence abetted colonialist economic relationships of Europe to Africa and the Americas and anchored the political economy of the United States after the transatlantic slave trade ended.

The global ties forged by this shared history of violence and ruthless greed could be suggestive of the constructive part of my quest for moral knowledge below. In *The Spirituality of African Peoples*, Christian social ethicist Peter Paris argues on behalf of valuable moral and religious linkages between Africans on the continent and African Americans in the North American Diaspora.[4] His work points to a shared destiny for Africans and African Americans "of constantly restructuring our self-understanding in the face of overwhelming negative odds" that resulted from the devastating effects of slavery and related negative propaganda about African humanity.[5] Paris identifies shared African and African American moral resources that help to build virtuous community life. His unifying, Afrocentric emphasis differs from my own woman-centered, liberationist approach here. But his view challenges me to consider whether shared African and African American moral resources could exist that might help in discovering alternative communal moral knowledge that safeguards rather than endangers the well-being of black women victim-survivors of violence. I conclude with speculative, narrative reflections on this possibility related to my visit with African activists working on ending gender violence against black lesbians.

The Moral Knowledge of Community Resources

In the following cases, representatives of vital community resources include the police, state welfare social services staff, and clergy. Their responses to the crises the women face are informed by preconceived moral assumptions and behavioral norms. Sometimes the community representatives defer to these preconceptions in a manner that appears to supersede any awareness of the immorality of the intimate violence or of the need to ensure the safety of women victimized by such violence. Drawn from news accounts and scholarly studies of black women victim-survivors, the details in these examples illustrate how such a life-endangering attenuation of moral responsibility can occur.

In the story of the murder of twenty-one-year-old Guyanese-American Romona Moore in New York City, her parents called the police immediately after she first disappeared. But, according to her mother's statement in a local newspaper, the police investigator seemed to have "'just made up his mind there's nothing wrong' and no matter what he came across, he stuck to that assumption."[6] Romona Moore was repeatedly raped and tortured by two young men. She was kept chained in a basement for days before they killed her and dumped her body. They also kidnapped and raped a fifteen-year-old girl immediately after they killed Moore, but that girl somehow managed to escape.[7]

During the time that the perpetrators, Troy Hendrix and Kayson Pearson, imprisoned and tortured Romona, they proudly displayed her to at least one young male acquaintance, and perhaps to others. Hendrix and Pearson forced Romona to recount to the visitor, Romondo Jack, how she was initially captured.[8] Jack listened to her as she lay on the ground with "the chain around her neck . . . bleeding from a cut near her nose; her face beaten and puffy," the webbing between her fingers cut by her captors, and three cigarette burns in a triangle under one eye.[9] When he left, he told no one about having seen her.

In spite of her mother's pleas to the police, on the second day after Romona failed to return home they marked the case closed. It was later learned that Romona was still alive at that point. Irate after finding out that the case had been closed, the family called local politicians, who then called the police to inquire about the situation, and the police reopened the case a few days later.[10]

Because of the reluctant response from police, Romona's family conducted their own "amateur investigation."[11] They eventually found her before the police did. When the parents called the precinct to report a tip they had received describing the location of Romona's body on the street under an abandoned ice cream truck, the police detective told them "he couldn't leave the office" to investigate.[12] The family followed up by themselves. By the time the police arrived to find Romona's naked body wrapped in a blue blanket with her legs tied together, her mother and other relatives were already there waiting for them.[13]

None of the officials in the New York Police Department (NYPD) who were involved in this case condoned the brutal death of this young black college student. They strongly defended the professionalism of their response to it.[14] But, as press reports suggested, the police who investigated seemed to know that Romona Moore's case should not be treated as a priority in the same way in which the disappearance of Svetlana Arnov had been treated only two months earlier in the city.[15] Svetlana, a white woman who lived in Manhattan, was the wife of a doctor. The second day after it was discovered that she was missing, the police launched an intensive response, including an NYPD press conference; two dozen detectives assigned to it full time; a police van with a loudspeaker driving around the neighborhood giving a contact number for witnesses to call; and even a consultation with a psychic.[16] The police were asked by the press about the differences in their responses to the two cases. In the Svetlana Arnov case, unlike Romona Moore's, the police spokesperson explained, some red flags were "immediately raised that tell detectives that something is wrong."[17] Svetlana was a wife and "mother of a young girl" who had promised to pick up her father from the airport. It seems that the close family ties and reliability of Svetlana described by her family were credible to the police and prompted alarm in a way that Romona's close ties to her parents and reliability that her family described were not.

Romona's mother told police about her dissatisfaction with their investigation of her daughter's disappearance. The mother believed that there were clues indicating Romona had been harmed or was dead. She complained that it did not matter to the police that bank records showed that Romona, who had no credit cards, did not withdraw any money from her bank account for weeks after the day she disappeared.[18] Her mother said that "instead of this raising a red flag" for the police detective, he asked her "if Romona was pregnant."[19]

The police somehow knew that Romona Moore's disappearance should not be treated like a "major" case where they immediately marshal every resource available to make fervent attempts to find her in order to avoid possible harm to her. I cannot definitively identify the role that socioeconomic class and race played in this knowledge, though the fact that Romona was not from a wealthy white Manhattan family probably mattered.[20] I am certain, however, that at least for the few days Romona was kept alive by her rapist-kidnappers, her life depended on what the police assumed they knew about "what was wrong" and about what questions needed to be asked to find out more.

The structuring of collective responsibility in public moral life begins with a discerning interpretation of social realities and contingencies by trusted representatives of the community. The police response in Romona Moore's case illustrates how a tragic failure in public moral life can happen in the initial steps of the movement from conceiving what "is" (what's going on?) to what "ought" to be. A breakdown seems to have occurred when police officials assessed what "is." The public relies on the police to intercede in uncertain and suspicious circumstances such as a person's disappearance. When they intervene, the police make crucial judgments about whether any activities have occurred that violate our communal moral covenant of civility or if there is a possibility of such a breach that warrants further investigation.

In Romona's case, it seems as if too many or too narrowly defined limits were placed on the police view of what was wrong, perhaps based on preconceptions about the worth of Romona's life or about her sexual innocence. I don't know. But the limited assumptions by police about what had gone wrong played a role in their decisions about what ought to be done in response to this young black woman's disappearance. Differing assumptions on their part about her moral worth might have enhanced their recognition of "red flags" and perhaps increased their capacity to intervene in the sexual and physical violence she suffered. At least, they might have recovered her body sooner after she had been killed.

For their responses to even have a chance of effectively preventing or addressing gender violence, full recognition of the equal moral worth of all persons has to be integrated into the initial assessment by institutional representatives such as the police who are called upon for help. However, a specific interrogation of the extent to which racial (and socioeconomic class) biases have an impact on institutional decision making is necessary to test this commitment to full recognition of equal moral worth. The consequences of avoiding this kind of scrutiny of institutional decision making could increase the possibility of femicide for black women who have been victimized.

Fortunately, many women do survive the violence. Those who survive gender violence that takes the form of heterosexual intimate partner abuse sometimes seek help from state social services if they are poor. There is little mystery about what the state assumes it knows about them morally. In her study of battered black women and post-1996 welfare reform policy, Dána-Ain Davis describes the treatment of women in the public assistance bureaucracy as "ceremonies of degradation."[21] Under current welfare-reform rules, the state assumes that it is common for women who come to apply for help to try to perpetrate fraud against the government.[22]

Davis studied the experiences of women who had been battered by husbands or boyfriends and escaped to a battered women's shelter for safety and help in rebuilding their lives. She explains that women in the battered women's shelter who are poor typically "need social services to find an apartment, have the utilities turned on, obtain health care, find child care, and purchase food."[23] Davis charts the encounters with state social services for one group of shelter residents in a small city in New York state. She gives an account of the prescreening process that investigates the women applying for welfare benefits for fraud. Davis witnessed this prescreening when she accompanied Gloria, a black women's shelter resident who had been beaten by her boyfriend and then thrown out of their home by him.

At the government social services office where the prescreening took place, Davis spoke with officials working there about the culture new welfare-reform rules had created. Davis recounts one official's view: "With individuals being watched more closely, a built-in intervention interrupts the tendency to abuse the system . . . [and] the idea that they're 'goin' to Disney World' with this money, he said in a voice that mocked black vernacular."[24] When questioned further, this local government official admitted that the real incidence of fraud did not come close to matching the extent to which it was suspected. He acknowledged that in reality, most clients did not come there to acquire money fraudulently but were actually in "very stressful situations."[25] Davis offers the summary comment that "directors and employees of this bureaucratic institution seem caught up in an ideological trap of what they know to be true and what they think to be true."[26] The problem here is that "what they think to be true" about fraudulent acts guides the policy these government agency directors and employees implement.

The government's refusal to address expeditiously the dire material consequences some applicants face when escaping domestic violence has created a travesty. The government's vigorously imposed rules that reflect its view of the moral deficiency of the applicants instead reflect the government's defective morality. This institutional moral failure differs from the earlier instance involving judgments by police investigating Romona Moore's kidnapping, rape, and murder. When moving from conceiving of what "is" (what's going on?) to the "ought" (what responses to existing circumstances ought to occur to enhance public life?), the moral breakdown does not occur at the level of assessing what "is" wrong. The breakdown occurs at the level of prescribing what the response "ought" to be. The state social service agency charged with distributing federal welfare funding already knows what's wrong. They already know that the applicants are in some kind of crisis related to their material well-being. The whole purpose of the agency under welfare reform is to offer "temporary assistance to needy families" (TANF).

In addition, this agency knows that domestic violence is a contributing factor for many applicants in their desperate need for assistance.[27] In the state of New York, in particular, there is a program, the Family Violence Option, set up to exempt applicants who have been victimized by domestic violence from some of the tedious regulations.[28] Davis documents examples of how black women were unable to access the

Family Violence Option because they were not notified about its existence, even when they utilized the proper forms to make the staff aware of their domestic-violence issues.[29] Based on her concern about the disproportionate occurrence of this failure to offer the Family Violence Option to black women, Davis suggests that "battered women's ability to secure resources if they are on welfare becomes more complex because their status as victims of violence is reined in by race."[30]

Local officials representing the government's current social policies respond to the women with a specific, problematic view of the "ought." The officials have a set formula for how they "ought" to bring about a good society through their agency's services to the applicants. The prescreening process typifies this government institution's assumption that those applying for assistance, such as the homeless black battered women Davis studied, ought to have their supposed proclivity to perpetrate fraud curtailed. This primary goal takes precedence in the women's initial contact with the agency. Any negative moral judgment of the violence or support for the women's attempt to escape it is subordinated to knowledge about the women's supposed moral flaws that require discipline.

To actually reach women victimized by violence who need these programs, there must be an overriding moral imperative within the government institution sponsoring them that considers all women deserving of safety and well-being, *without any conditions* for earning such consideration. But this commitment will be meaningless without an investigation of competing, demeaning moral "truths" attached to poor women's black racial identity. This supposed racial knowledge can coexist even within institutional cultures that adopt unconditional imperatives about all women deserving safety from intimate violence and thus nullify the trustworthiness of those commitments.

Religious institutions are another valued community resource women victim-survivors sometimes turn to for help when trying to escape their violent partners. Too often, the result is just as unresponsive to the crisis as government social services can be. But when religious leaders transmit their misguided preconceptions, their views are uniquely endowed with divine authority. A study of African American women's experiences of domestic violence in heterosexual relationships in Lincoln, Nebraska, included clergy responses.[31] Lead investigator Venita Kelly found that most of the women, not all, received disappointing responses from faith-based community leaders of black churches and mosques.[32] One disappointed woman who sought help from clergy on several different occasions commented that the ministers seem to "have an attitude that implies that God has personally told them how to address the issue of domestic violence" with an expectation that she should "humbly seek" that revelation from the ministers.[33]

Astonishingly, the knowledge that ministers impart about what "ought" to occur in response to situations of abuse can have nothing to do with stopping the violence the women endure. In *Battle Cries: Black Women and Intimate Partner Abuse*, Hillary Potter studies forty African American women who experienced intimate partner abuse in heterosexual relationships.[34] She reports the experiences of several women whose Christian pastors urged them to stay in abusive relationships. In Potter's study, one woman's pastor told her: "He's your husband according to the Bible."[35] Another, Wendy, was asked about her husband's responsible traits by a Christian army chaplain she consulted because her husband was in the military. The chaplain asked: "Was he a good provider?" and "Was he good to the kids?"[36] When she responded affirmatively to these questions, it seemed to Wendy like the chaplain wanted to know "what my freakin' problem was! I was tired of gettin' beat up!"[37] She finally relented to the pressure from the chaplain to go back to the abuser and agreed to do so.

The knowledge problem here encompasses the erroneous preconceptions about women victimized by violence that surfaced in both the police and social service agency staff examples. In these clergy responses, the moral failure includes not only the initial discernment of what "is" wrong but also a faulty, predetermined formula for what "ought" to occur. The clergy start with what "ought" to be and work backward to figure out what "is" wrong or, more accurately, to conclude that nothing significant "is" wrong.

In one of the examples of clergy advice, the pastor cites the Bible as the authoritative source for the prescribed behavior of staying married to your husband. But in the other case, of Wendy, it is not clear that the chaplain made an appeal to Scripture. Nonetheless, the chaplain tried to convince Wendy that she ought to be happy to have a husband who is a good provider and a good father to their children. Beating the children's mother is curiously divorced from the chaplain's definition of what it means to be a good father. In the chaplain's skewed moral logic, she ought to stay with this "good" man.

I am presuming that the clergy in these cases did not regard the beatings by the men as beneficial for the women. More likely, the clergy perspective seems to have been that the violence should be tolerated for the sake of maintaining the marriages and families—because staying married is what heterosexual couples ought to do. What ought to occur to preserve the physical, emotional, and spiritual well-being—the very life of the wife—does not seem to have had an impact on the moral universe of the clergy considerations. The clergy's singular, narrowly constructed concern with what "ought" to be blots out the immorality of what "is." The clergy responses are indifferent to the women's testimonies about their experiences of abuse, and instead reinforce a morally distorted understanding of marital obligation and sex/gender norms. The clergy interpretation of the heterosexual marital covenant is emptied of fundamental moral obligations such as mutual respect, kindness, and tenderness.

Moreover, a woman's racial loyalty is sometimes an underlying factor in the moral pressure she faces in these situations. Venita Kelley's study found that "African American women suffer from or are afraid of accusations of being traitors to the race, to religious communities and faiths, and to African American men when seeking redress from domestic violence."[38] When a black woman is advised to stay with her abusive black husband by black clergy, overriding loyalties to God, church, and husband may jointly seem to be part of the moral meaning of her black racial identity obligating her to stay with him. Said differently, a culturally reinforced notion of a good black woman or good black Christian woman as one who "ought" to privately endure her black husband's abuse may be invoked. Kelley's study provides a reminder that within predominantly black institutional cultures such as black churches, black racial identity may be morally constructed with an understanding of a divinely mandated, self-sacrificial allegiance women victim-survivors owe their black racial group (their men), which trumps their own right to safety and well-being.

Compared to the police and governmental social service agencies, the church is a community-based institution with the most explicitly stated commitment to sustaining the moral and spiritual health of the community. Ironically, its representatives in the specific examples cited above act in the most morally reprehensible and irresponsible manner: advising the women of their obligation to remain in violent, abusive marital relationships.

Searching for a Better Way

These problematic responses by police, state welfare social services staff, and clergy are too costly for the women's lives and dignity. The inadequacies in the responses are related to limitations placed on certain kinds of moral knowledge in each situation. The apparent moral undervaluing of Romona Moore's life seems to have contributed to her case being closed without investigation the day after she was reported missing. Narrow, character-assaulting moral assumptions impede access to critical social services requested by poor women fleeing abusers. For the clergy, a myopic moral concern with women remaining married to men sacrifices the women's entitlement to safety.

Consequently, a radically expansive approach to moral knowledge is needed within these state and church institutional cultures, one that can produce much more generous support for black women who are victimized. This radical expansiveness must include appreciation for the extent to which dehumanizing limitations on black women's personhood (moral worth) furthers ineffective and untrustworthy responses to the crisis of gender violence. We have to generate boundary-breaking moral knowledge about violence, gender, women, black women, and black racial identity that stretches the collective conscience that guides routine institutional decision making in our public moral life. The epistemological shift will require much more than an adjustment to formal policies and procedures. The expansion has to be drastic enough to function as an antidote to the life-endangering constraints on conceptualizing what "is" wrong and what "ought to be" addressed that inhabit these institutional responses to the women.

Finally, I have a speculative, personal reflection on what is required to counter these constraints. I am interested in how a focus on black racial identity might be constructively incorporated in the fundamental expansion of moral imagination that is needed. My fragmentary speculations about this possibility are based, in part, on my own experience of talking with black African activists who are working on a variety of strategies to address gender violence.

I wonder if some aspect of the consistent moral limitations resulting from devaluing attitudes about black racial identity could fuel some sort of boundary-breaking solidarity of resistance. I wonder if consciousness of an intercontinental solidarity of resistance between black Americans and blacks on the continent of Africa might, for instance, break open U.S.-American racially constrained moral definitions of and imaginings about human worth. I hasten to add that I am not suggesting a black nationalist reclaiming of a mythic, idyllic past of gender equality, nor wanting to ignore enormous contemporary cultural and political differences among black peoples of African descent in the United States and in the countries and tribal groups on the continent of Africa. Rather, I want to consider some sort of cognizance of a common black feminist struggle against Western-disseminated negative propaganda about African humanity[39] that does not assume any notion of a uniform, romanticized African history or sameness of sociopolitical identity across divergent cultures. Might this cognizance of such broad interrelatedness in the struggle against identity-based limits on moral worth help to stimulate ideas and inspiration for the broadening of U.S.-American collective conscience needed to create more effective responses to gender violence? I don't know.

I was visiting Johannesburg, for example, talking with a black activist whose work includes strategizing to combat gender violence, specifically the targeting of black lesbians for rape and murder within predominantly black communities. I sat across from Mpumi Mathabela, the media director for an organization called Forum for the Empowerment of Women (FEW). Their work advances and defends the rights of black lesbian, bisexual, and transgender women in South Africa. Their office is housed in the old women's jail section of the Old Fort Prison complex, where many who had been political resisters to the old white suprema-cist apartheid regime had been subjected to terrible conditions over the previous century. Now, the postapartheid government buildings house their constitutional court for human rights cases, offices for various human rights groups, as well as historical exhibits about the prison. In the former women's jail, it was a space that both detailed brutal and sys-tematic racially based degradations of women in the past and concrete, political commitment to their human rights in the present. In that space, as I talked with Mpumi about her organization's strategies to combat sexual violence against lesbians in black communities, I glimpsed vibrant institutionalized moral knowledge about black women's inherent moral worth. That glimpse prompted a sense of hope and inspiration about the potential capacity of shared black feminist solidarity to fuel the kind of boundary-breaking conscientization needed to help uproot U.S. Ameri-can institutional practices and cultural meanings of gender and black-ness that support gender violence against women of African descent.

For Reflection and Study

Key Ideas

- black Christian nationalism
- Christian nationalist worldview
- christianization
- divine chain of command
- fundamentalist ecclesiocracy
- moral knowledge
- moral undervaluing
- racialized tropes
- resonant religious discourse

Resources for Further Study

Davies, Susan E., and Sister Paul Teresa Hennessee, S.A. *Ending Racism in the Church*. Cleveland: United Church Press, 1998.

Lincoln, C. Eric, and Lawrence Maimya. *The Black Church in the African American Experience*. Durham: Duke University Press, 1990.

Pinn, Anthony B. *The Black Church in the Post-Civil Rights Era*. Maryknoll, NY: Orbis, 2002.

Ray, Stephen G., Jr. *Do No Harm: Social Sin and Christian Responsibility*. Minneapolis: Fortress Press, 2003.

Riggs, Marcia Y. *Plenty Good Room: Women versus Male Power in the Black Church*. Cleveland: Pilgrim, 2008.

Smith, R. Drew, ed. *New Day Begun: African American Churches and Civic Culture in Post-Civil Rights America*. Durham: Duke University Press, 1990.

West, Traci C. *Disruptive Christian Ethics: When Racism and Women's Lives Matter*. Louisville: Westminster John Knox, 2006.

Thinking Critically and Constructively

1. Listen to the sermons preached in your church for a month. What is the moral rhetoric of those sermons? Who is morally undervalued? What sources of moral knowledge (in addition to scripture) are drawn upon?
2. What is the resonant religious discourse of the Tea Party movement in the twenty-first century? Is their moral language consistent with a Christian nationalist worldview?
3. What is your ecclesial model for the twenty-first-century church?

PART FOUR

Moral Vision

Chapter 12

An Ecowomanist Vision

Melanie L. Harris

IN *THE SPIRITUALITY OF African Peoples: The Search for a Common Moral Discourse,*[1] Peter J. Paris presents an overarching argument that an African and African American social ethic rests on the primary value of community. In this essay, I use Paris's reflection on the interconnectedness between self and community as well as African cosmology as a point of departure for discussing ecowomanism. Ecowomanism is reflective of the second part of Alice Walker's definition that asserts a womanist quest for "the survival and wholeness of entire people."[2] Moreover, the primacy of community is in keeping with a womanist commitment to establish multiple forms of justice that will promote survival and wholeness in the lives of women and men of African descent in the communities that they call home. Indeed, an ethical imperative to do justice guides the womanist quest for "the survival and wholeness of entire people." Following an explication of Paris's discussion of the interdependence of community and African cosmology, I will present an ecowomanist perspective that celebrates the interconnectedness that humans share with and among creation. This ecowomanist perspective simply enlarges what womanist religious thought already affirms and values: the living presence of ancestors and the earth as part of a cosmic community.

189

The Interdependence of Community

Community, "the preservation and promotion of community," is the primary goal that Paris purports to be central to an African and African American social ethic. Paris describes community as an interdependent group consisting of persons who share cultural and ethnic bonds; this group is linked by the shared values they hold as the basis for common moral discourse. Beyond this broad definition, Paris clearly places the meaning of community within the frame of African cosmology as he states that community reaches beyond these rather obvious connections and bridges connections between living persons, the "living dead" (ancestors), the supreme deity, subdeities, and the realms of nature and history. Explaining the continuous flow of life in the African worldview and the deep understanding that "all is sacred," Paris notes that each of the realms within African cosmology (spirit, nature, history) is interconnected. He points to the ways in which spirit and history are connected by writing about the cyclical process of life that does not end at death; instead, death as a "departure from physical life marks a transition of the human spirit from the state of mortality to that of ancestral immortality."[3] For Paris, the interdependence between the realms of spirit, nature, and history is situated within African and African American cosmological thought. This cosmological thought is thus the basis of African spirituality that undergirds African and African American ethics.

African Cosmology

Of particular note in Paris's writings is the ethical import that he attributes to the natural realm because of its sacredness in African cosmology and the stewardship of the earth that such requires. Paris opens chapter 3, "Community: The Goal of Moral Life," of *The Spirituality of African Peoples* with reference to the important role that ancestral life plays in the cosmological order and how this in turn affects the shaping of African and African American social ethics. Citing African scholar John Mbiti, Paris's point of departure is the African religious worldview that insists that to be human is to be in community; this is the case because community is "a sacred phenomenon created by the supreme

God, protected by the divinities, and governed by ancestral spirits."[4] Indeed, ancestors can be represented in elements of nature that can be used by divinities to create harmony and ethical balance within the cosmological whole. Likewise, in his classic text, *Introduction to African Religion*, Mbiti sheds additional light on the significance of the natural realm within African cosmology and religious beliefs. The locus of the natural realm is the earth, and the earth is viewed as a "living being"[5] in African cosmological thought. This is the case because many natural elements embody the spirit of a divine entity. According to Mbiti, the African cosmology maintains that it is the relationship between the natural and moral order that undergirds harmony in the universe. It is a moral obligation for black peoples to take care of the earth, for ultimate respect for the earth is critical to establishing moral order in the universe.

As both Mbiti and Paris suggest in their writings, there is a vivid moral aspect and direct message to take care of the earth embedded within this African cosmological thought. My contention is that, drawing upon Mbiti, Paris's insights about community push toward an ethical appreciation of the earth. In fact, his work inspires additional inquiry into what ethical imperatives, rituals, values, and virtues will uphold earth justice. In sum, the ethical imperatives to preserve and promote community and to respect the sacredness of the earth in Paris's work open the door for more scholarship on the connections between environmental ethics, black religion, and African cosmology. It is to an example of this emergent scholarship, ecowomanism, that I now turn.

Ecowomanism

Answering the call for new religious and theological inquiry into environmental ethics, ecowomanist perspectives are beginning to surface. Ecowomanism is an approach to environmental ethics that centers on the perspectives, theoethical analysis, and life experiences of woman of color, specifically the voices of African-descended women as they contribute new attitudes, theories, and ideas about how to face ecological crises. This approach applies womanist intersectional analysis to issues of environmental concern in order to engage the complex ways racism, classism, sexism, and heterosexism operate in situations of environmental injustice, including the numerous cases of environmental racism. In addition to investigating cases wherein landfills and other potentially hazardous facilities are deliberately placed in racially identified and lower-income neighborhoods, ecowomanism embodies a religious perspective that highlights the sacred ties that women of color and their communities have with the earth and how this relationship informs their moral action toward earth-justice. As such, ecowomanism addresses religious and theoretical links between women and the earth, particularly the shared identity that women and the earth have as creators (that is, women as creators of human beings, home-spaces, and life and earth as creator of all life). Ecowomanism also examines other connections between women and the earth by doing analyses that carefully scrutinize Western theories that feminize the earth and Christian Platonistic theories that divide the earth from the heavens, thus negating the sacred power associated with the earth. Furthermore, the similar ways in which women of color across the globe and the earth have been oppressed by societal, dualistic, and patriarchal norms are examined.

Ecowomanist perspectives thus help to uncover patterns and parallels between acts of violence against the earth and systemic patterns of violence faced by women of color. From a religious perspective, this reveals the need for a fresh sense of theological justice, one that examines interrelationality and rearticulates the idea of womanist wholeness as a base for an ecowomanist ethic. Some of the ethical principles embedded in this ethic regarding human-to-human and human-to-earth relationships include "genuine love, responsibility, understanding, honesty, trust, compassion, and forgiveness."[6] Other earth-affirming values included in this ethic are equality, economic justice, earth justice, and sustainable community.

Similar to Paris's attention to nature in African and African American religious thought, ecowomanist perspectives affirm the sacred bond between humanity and the earth found in selected African indigenous religions.[7] In fact, the interdependence between the realms of spirit, nature, and history is reinforced by what Paris calls the four "building blocks" of African experience. God, community, family, and person are four spheres of African and African American life that are "fully interdependent . . . manifested in a variety of reciprocal functions, much like the interrelations among the parts of a living organism."[8] Paris's planting of the image of a natural living organism into the mind of the reader, in order to explain the interdependent nature of the four spheres of African life, is not done by accident. In fact, I would argue that his reference to nature is reflective of his attention to the natural realm, explicated as a part of the three realms that guide moral and ethical thought within African and African American religious life. Imagining the intricate motion and interdependence modeled in an organism (such as the system of interdependent parts resembled in a plant or other living thing), Paris's illustration provides insight into the reciprocal function of the four spheres. This illustration is reflective of this discursive theme throughout his work that pushes us to open the boundaries of African American religious thought to engage imaginatively and constructively the relationship between nature, African cosmology, and African American religious experience. While Paris does not, in fact, propose an African and African American ethic regarding nature, or an eco-ethic, I think that his work points us in the right direction.

Chapter 13

An American Public Theology in the Absence of Giants

Creative Conflict and Democratic Longings

Victor Anderson

People in the twenty-first century will need to hear the gospel message. So, what do we do? Well, we reach out, past our own defensiveness, to see where God may lead us. And surely we delight in seeking new ways to speak, not fixed on the past, but on the unfolding future of God. In every age, the gospel is good news.—David Buttrick, A Captive Voice[1]

AT THE END-OF-THE-TWENTIETH-CENTURY U.S. context, David Buttrick describes what he sees as the loss of an American public theology in the absence of its progressive liberal spirit and the categories of its equally supporting theological liberalism. He says:

> Once more we will turn to a preaching of the kingdom of God. Now, talk of the kingdom of God to the twentieth century neo-orthodoxy is a form of heresy; the kingdom of God is regarded as a turn-of-the-century liberal invention, and the word liberal these days is frequently said with a sneer. . . . Through the centuries, like a

This essay is based on the first of two lectures, "Creative Conflict and Creative Exchange: Revising the Public and Its Problems," given as the Clark Horowitz Lectures in Religion Series at Pomona College on March 30–31, 2009. I am grateful to Professor Darryl Smith for allowing me to publish it here.

pendulum swing, the preaching of the church has shifted back and
forth between preaching Jesus and preaching good news of the kingdom, God's new social order. . . . Now at the weary end of the Protestant era, as an epoch that began with the Reformation is ending,
we are called to preach social vision. Prediction: In the twenty-first
century we will recover the gospel of the kingdom, God's new order.
In the future preaching will be eschatological rather than existential, and social rather than solipsistic.[2]

Buttrick's comments and hopes, however, for the recovery of an
American public theology supported by a commitment to a "Kingdom
of God, God's Social Order" are tragically unfulfilled in the twenty-first
century, and its possibility remains impotent in our current climate of
"secularism," on the one hand, and an "incipient nihilism," on the other.
In such a climate, a public theology must now become a political theology based on a "counterecclesiology" that out-narrates claims of such
a vision as Buttrick proposes, but not on Buttrick's terms. Rather, the
terms must be endemic to the life of the church itself, and its actuality
will also be internal to the Christian community. One such thinker is
John Milbank:

> Theology has frequently sought to borrow from elsewhere a funda-
> mental account of society or history, and then to see what theologi-
> cal insights will cohere with it. But it has been shown that no such
> fundamental account, in the sense of something neutral, rational
> and universal, is really available. It is theology itself that will have to
> provide its own account of the final causes at work in human his-
> tory, on the basis of its own particular, and historically specific faith.
> . . . As the Church is already, necessarily, by virtue of its institution,
> a "reading" of other human societies, it becomes possible to consider
> ecclesiology as also a "sociology." But it should be noted that this
> possibility only becomes available if ecclesiology is rigorously con-
> cerned with the actual genesis of real historical churches, not simply
> with the imagination of an ecclesial ideal.[3]

The twenty-first-century reality that Buttrick envisions and hopes for are,
on Milbank's account, part of an ecclesial ideal, which the realities of our
postmodern situation foreclose as any actuality of such a public theology.

This essay is about this state of affairs. What I mean by a public theology is the deliberate use and articulation of religious languages, theological principles, beliefs, and doctrines to critique both the relation of American Christianity to our democratic culture and social forces as well as to critique our society in its exercise of power in relation to the demands of Christian faith. In this essay, I want to move in a rather ironic manner, accenting and privileging the power of speech and voices of usually Protestant preacher-theologians who produced a powerful arsenal of public theologies from the turn of the century to the 1960s. Toward the end of the essay, however, I will shift from speech and voice to the silent, often patient listening of faithful ordinaries within "the local" whose lives and actions may provide new ways of thinking about American public theology.

Whither Public Theology?

We are in an intellectual context in which an increasing number of cultural critics are engaged in discourse on the American empire. In *Democracy Matters*, Cornel West writes:

> A decade ago I wrote Race Matters in order to spark a candid public conversation about America's most explosive issue and most difficult dilemma: the ways in which the vicious legacy of white supremacy contributes to the arrested development of American democracy. This book—the sequel to Race Matters—looks unflinchingly at the waning of democratic energies and practices in our present age of the American empire. There is a deeply troubling deterioration of democratic powers in America today.[4]

His judgment accompanies two decades of similar criticisms of public theology in the United States. Questions arise: What does public theology mean for late-twentieth-century society and culture? More importantly, what does it mean for the future of the twenty-first-century developments, directives, and interventions into late-capitalist formations of global economies? A wide range of theologians and religionists are thinking about these kinds of questions, including Robert Bellah, Robert Wuthnow, José Casanova, James Davidson Hunter, Linell Cady,

Ronald Thiemann, Jean Bethke Elshtain, Stanley Hauerwas, Jeffrey Stout, and Cornel West. The 2008 publication of Stanley Hauerwas and Romand Coles's book *Christianity, Democracy, and the Radical Ordinary* is of great importance to this discussion.

Linking so many thinkers is their theorizing, that is, their imagining, articulating, and socially constructing an American public theology within social and cultural turns in Western civil societies. These social and cultural turns are marked by post–cold war politics, postnuclear formations of power, post–civil rights politics, postindustrial technologies, and a post–Protestant hegemony, sometimes referred to as the "post–Christian." All these social and cultural moves are associated with the deconstruction of our Western technologies of knowledge that Jean-François Lyotard signifies as "the postmodern condition." In our postmodern moment, democracy—not to mention talk of a radical democracy—is contested ground. It is contested not only for its successes insofar as more democratic infusion of the local into public affairs increases more conflict over our agreement on the common good. Democracy is equally contested for the regimes of capitalist powers regulating global economies but which are themselves unregulated in their exertion of market forces that make the world's poor poorer and the most wealthy wealthier, thereby magnifying the poverty gap on a global scale.

Gone are the days when democracy embraced a liberal progressive spirit such as defined the voices of public theology in the past. It was a liberal progressive spirit that provided our democratic experiment with not only a high morality but also a high religion beyond the local faiths of private citizens and regional governments. Indeed, to speak of a high morality and high religion is to evoke a set of universally conceived principles, languages, symbols, and doctrines that work to mitigate apparently interminable conflicts between competing local faiths and morals. The high moralities and high religions of early-twentieth-century American public theology directed Christians (presupposed here as Protestant Christianity) toward creative conflicts that weaved and organized our conflicts into a common life determined by common national concerns and interests. With a high religion and a high morality, the local yields to the common for the sake of what American pragmatist John Dewey once celebrated as "a common faith" (1934).

In Dewey's common faith, the religious elements of our local faiths can be preserved without the external force and constraint of religion, that is, institutional religions, or what sociologist José Casanova calls "public religions."[5] This external organization of religio-ethical sentiments comes to function within our public affairs, operating as a hegemonic public determining the legitimacy of all other publics in forming our common life. At least, that is Dewey's fear as he reflects on the then-contentious "Scopes Monkey Trial" and its ramifications for construing the future of public education.

In his *The Public and Its Problems* (1927), Dewey was very much aware of "The Public," which signifies the common life and organization of citizens around common, national interests. But he was also aware that "The Public" can be jeopardized by local "publics," the tyranny of the few, and that our common life can be put at risk of falling into the failures of past societies determined by oligarchy, monarchy, or, worse, the tyranny of plutocratic regimes. What makes for a common life of the public? Dewey theorized (imagined, articulated, and socially constructed) a high religion and high mortality. His is a social faith in human creative intelligence progressively organizing our local conflicts, conflicts that are rooted in local publics with their local interests, and directing them toward creative conflicts that advance our democratic life, our democratic practices, our democratic longings, and our democratic hopes toward the increase of democracy.

Democracy and creative intelligence stood in subject-positions of conceptual giants. They were operating as moral regulators, guardians of public reasonableness, and referees of claims to universal agreement. Dewey's common faith in democracy and creative intelligence joined with other conceptual giants of liberal progressivism and theological liberalism. Together, they produce an arsenal of American public theologies based on Immanuel Kant's "Kingdom of Ends," Albrecht Ritschl's "Kingdom of God," Walter Rauschenbush's "Social Gospel," Josiah Royce's "Great Community and Great Hope," and Howard Thurman and Martin Luther King Jr.'s "Beloved Community." Each principle stood in the subject-position of our democratic life as a conceptual giant of American public theology. These linguistic giants were called upon to protect our fragile democratic life against false contenders to the absolute, each protecting our common good against conceptual imposters, local publics, local faiths, and private ends masking as universal agreement on the common good and our common life. These theologically informed principles made for an American public theology.

As mapped above, the postmodern condition certainly puts such conceptual giants at risk of decay, disabling their universalizing and secular reason, trivializing their necessary judgments, putting to an end their guardianship over public reasonableness and agreement, and dulling their capability to manage or referee our local conflicts. Now "CONFLICT," "DISAGREEMENT," "IDENTITY," all writ large, step in to fill the void left by the conceptual giants of twentieth-century American public theology. At this juncture between the American empire and the post-Protestant era, and renewed democratic longings inspired by the election of Barack Obama as the first African American U.S. president, we are left asking about and, in some cases, lamenting the loss of the principled giants of American public theology in our postmodern moment. Harvard scholar Ronald Thiemann addresses this concern:

> There has been a great deal of discussion in academic theology about "public theology." Most of that debate has focused on the question of whether theological arguments are available for public examination and whether theological assertions are intelligible beyond the confines of a particular religious community. Although such issues are intellectually interesting and important within a rather small circle of academic theologians, they only begin to help us address what I consider the far more important questions: Will religious convictions and theological analysis have real impact on the way our public lives are structured? Can a truly public theology have a salutary influence on the development of public policy within a pluralistic democratic nation? The real challenge to a North American public theology is to find a way—within the social, cultural, and religious pluralism of American politics—to influence the development of public policy without seeking to construct a new Christendom or lapsing in to a benign relativism.[6]

A new Christendom or a benign relativism? Wow! What options! Neither is lively for an American public theology in the twenty-first century and the public problems we face. The public today sits with an overextension and overtaxing of our armed forces in two active military campaigns while maintaining a policing presence throughout other global economies. Unregulated greed and promiscuity of lending and trading markets and bureaucracies have ushered us into global economic catastrophe. New regimes of racisms and homophobia are determining national policies on immigration and same-sex marriage. Educational violence and massive dropout rates signify the failures of American public schooling. Concomitant wars on drugs and crime have come home to roost in the increasing overincarceration of black and poor youth throughout America.

Now, Thiemann asks us to consider, in the absence of the conceptual giants of American public theology, whether a "new Christendom" is the clue to the revitalization of public theology in twenty-first-century America, or must we content ourselves with the incommensurability of local theologies determining the meaning and content relations of religion to American public life? With a new Christendom, the "church/ecclesiology" gets to check the authority of the "secular" by its power to "out-narrate" all secular contenders, including democracy itself, in an effort to contain the cultural effects of the narratives of the secular, progressive liberal vision of democracy. It does this by determining itself through the production of a larger, more enduring narrative of Christian identity and discipleship that is informed substantively by the politics of Jesus, the peaceable kingdom, or the eschatological community, a neo-Constantinian project.

Our other option leaves us with local knowledges and local publics operating as absolute determinates over our generalized common life. We are left to the contingency of theological or ecclesial city-states, each vying for the loyalty of the other for defense and survival. The state of public theology returns to Thomas Hobbes's "state of nature," which is a state of warring ecclesial interests. Both options for public theology threaten a robust vision of democracy, of our democratic practices, and of our democratic longings in the twenty-first century. In what follows, for purposes of this essay, I want to look more intentionally at just one American public theologian who proves helpful for understanding just what an American public theology looks like in the awareness of giants so that I might later ask questions about the consequences of the absence of our conceptual giants of American public theology in our postmodern moment. Among candidates, I might have called on theologians from Walter Raucshenbush and Reinhold Niebuhr to Paul Tillich, but my illustrative theologian is H. Richard Niebuhr.

H. Richard Niebuhr

In 2009, the academy celebrated the eightieth anniversary of the publication of H. Richard Niebuhr's (hereafter HRN) highly acclaimed and enduring book *The Social Sources of Denominationalism* (1929). Counted as one of the great public theologians in the United States, HRN contended that the crisis of America's public theology and its churches was not so much related to internal conflicts over theology or doctrine. He clearly was speaking in an era of Protestant hegemony over public discourse. Yet, in the United States, this hegemony was jeopardized by the conflict of denominationalism. He proposed quite forcefully that the conflicts of American denominations were the result of the churches' compromise with social change and the malicious effects of America's unresolved and enduring problem of systemic racism. HRN says:

> Christendom has often achieved apparent success by ignoring the precepts of its founder. The church, as an organization interested in self-preservation and in the gain of power, has sometimes found the counsel of the cross quite as inexpedient as have national and economic groups. In dealing with such major social evils as war, slavery, and social inequality, it has discovered convenient ambiguities in the letter of the Gospels which enabled it to violate their spirit and to ally itself with the prestige and power those evils had gained in their corporate organization. In adapting itself to the conditions of a civilization which its founder has bidden it to permeate with the spirit of divine love, it found that it was easier to give to Caesar the things belonging to Caesar if the examination of what might belong to God were not too closely pressed.[7]

HRN's critique of American churches clearly represents the voice of theology in a context deeply rooted in a nonsectarian tendency within the Reformed tradition. So, like his indirect mentor and teacher,

Ernst Troeltsch, he sees compromise as an inevitable consequence of a living organism adapting, accommodating, and adjusting itself to an environment that it needs to sustain itself as a viable living community. In this case, this living organism is American Christianity, at once European and American. He contends that American denominations are mutations of an organism transplanted into a strange new environment. Our churches are an organism compromised by a religious environment hostile to national churches, a social environment characterized by capitalist impulses toward individual achievement, a moral environment sedimented in New England Puritanism, and a political environment that favors civic republicanism to constrain and limit government's control over and intervention into the public exercise of religion.

For HRN, the compromise of the churches to American social change was inevitable. Yet, he also holds that compromise could not or ought not to ultimately define the "Essence of Christianity." He says:

> The fact that compromise is inevitable does not make it less an evil. The fault of every concession, of course, is that it is made too soon, before the ultimate resistance "to the blood" has been offered. Even where resistance seems to have gone to the uttermost, the loyal man remembers that it might have been begun earlier, that it might have been continued a little longer, and that any compromise of the absolute good remains an evil.[8]

HRN's remarks are located at the historical juncture in the United States when American theological liberalism and its social gospel were muted by social decay, urban crisis, pervasive lynching, a world at war, and the dawning of the Great Depression. By 1929, while resisting an increasing conservatism mobilizing itself throughout American Christianity in regimes of fundamentalism, Pentecostalism, apocalypticism, and a burgeoning so-called neo-orthodoxy, each challenging mainstream political and theological liberalism, HRN kept his eyes turned toward urban crisis and American racism, the public, and its problems. Still, even here, one glimpses early intonations of the theological position that would latter mark him a "neo-orthodox" theologian, contrary to his own self-description. For him, any compromise of the churches to social change is a denial of the radical transcendence or sovereignty of God over all of culture and public life and of a Christ who transforms culture toward the purposes of God.[9] HRN later called this vision of radical transcendence "Radical Monotheism" (1943).

> For radical monotheism the value-center is neither closed society nor the principle of such a society but the principle of being itself; its reference is to no one reality among the many but to One beyond all the many, whence all the many derive their being, and by participation in which they exist. As faith, it is reliance on the source of all being for the significance of the self and all that exists. It is the assurance that because I am, I am valued, and because you are, you are beloved, and because whatever is has being, therefore it is worthy of love. It is the confidence that whatever is, is good, because it exists as one thing among the many which all have their origin and their being in the One—the principle of being which is also the principle of value. In him we live and move and have our being not only as existent but as worthy of existence and worthy in existence.[10]

Radical monotheism operates as a conceptual giant of American public theology within HRN's enduring wrestling with Christ and culture, on the one hand, and American Christianity and our pluralistic society, on the other.

When HRN offered his powerful critique of American Christianity in 1929, he had nothing other in mind, perhaps to a fault, than American Protestant churches. But he presupposed something then that I cannot today—that there is an "essence" which ultimately defines Christianity. Like Friedrich Schleiermacher, Ludwig Feuerbach, Albrecht Ritschl, and the early Ernst Troeltsch before him, he believed that Christianity was determined ultimately by a moral essence and that the churches are objective, external forms, incarnations of the eternal, radically transcendent essence establishing a high religion and a high morality that underwrite the content of a progressive liberal consensus and an American public theology. Christian religion may be empirical, but its religious and moral essence is world transcending and world transforming. American denominations manifest religious and moral failure. The churches are a betrayal of the essence of Christianity. He says:

Denominationalism in the Christian church is . . . an unacknowl-edged hypocrisy. It is a compromise made far too lightly, between Christianity and the world. . . . It represents the accommodation of Christianity to the caste-system of human society. It carries over into the organization of the Christian principle of brotherhood the pride and prejudices, the privilege and prestige, as well as the humiliations and abashments, the injustices and inequalities of that special order of high and low wherein men find the satisfaction of their craving for vainglory. The division of the churches closely follows the division of men into castes of national, racial, and economic groups. It draws the color line in the church of God; it fosters the misunderstandings, the self-exaltations, the hatreds of jingoistic nationalism by continu-ing in the body of Christ the spurious differences of provincial loy-alties; it seats the rich and poor apart at the table of the Lord, where the fortunate may enjoy the bounty they have provided while the others feed upon crusts their poverty affords.[11]

The strength of HRN's criticisms is based on his belief in a religious and moral essence of Christianity. His is a progressive theological lib-eralism. His faith, that is, his trust and loyalty, is to the fraternity of all, the unity of the church, and the primacy of love. Together, this triadic unity marks the essence of Christianity and an American public theol-ogy under the presence, guardianship, and trust of the conceptual giant of radical monotheism.

HRN saw the fragility and fragmentation of American Christian-ity as a consequence of the churches' alliances with malicious forms of racism, violence, injustice, and the greed of civil institutions such as education, law, and public service. He grasps these alliances as *sin*, indeed, the sin of compromise. American churches are "emblems of the victory of the world over the church, of the secularization of Christianity, of the church's sanction of that divisiveness which the church's gospel condemns,"[12] he says. American Christianity is neither a light in darkness nor a city set on a hill nor a prophetic institution guiding the nation toward the kingdom, reign, sovereignty of God under which all people are valued for their humanity and not for their instrumental use. HRN finds little moral difference between the ethics of the American churches and those centers of power and privi-lege that defined American civil institutions in the age of Jim Crow.

And the separation of white mainline churches from the black church in America is, for him, the paramount symbol of the sin of compromise, the compromise of American Christianity to white supremacy. He argues this tragic point.

> The sole source of this [racial] denominationalism is social; it demonstrates clearly the invasion of the church of Christ by the principle of caste. And the caste sense is, as always, primarily present in the economically and culturally superior group, and secondarily, by reaction, in the economically and culturally inferior society. Negroes have apparently taken the initiative in forming separate churches, but the responsibility lies with their former masters in the North and South.[13]

HRN interprets the rise of the black church in America as a tragic story. On the one hand, it signals the moral failure of the churches to promote the Christian ethics of unity, fraternity, and love, on the one hand. And on the other, the black churches are symbols of black self-realization, a prophetic response to the sin of compromise as blacks sought "to escape the danger of having their legitimate self-respect constantly wounded by the superior pride of their fellow Christians."[14] HRN concludes that "the color line has been drawn so incisively by the church itself that its proclamation of the gospel of the brotherhood of Jew and Greek, of bond and free, of white and black has sometimes the sad sound of irony, and sometimes falls upon the ear as unconscious hypocrisy—but sometimes there is in it the bitter cry of repentance."[15]

As prophetic as these utterances are, HRN was exercising what he would later call "reflective criticism." Reflective criticism is

> that method of self-examination in which one who participates in the faith and work of the church, in its order and life, seeks to bring into his own and his companions' full awareness the principles of individual and communal believing and doing, to analyze the consistency and inconsistency, the origins and consequences of such principles. Such self-examination, I believe, is part of the work of metanoia we continually carry on in the church in the hope of purification, clarification, and integration, or holiness.[16]

The practice of reflective criticism, or immanent criticism, excites HRN's Christian prophetic social witness, calling the churches to repentance and urging the churches to faithfully embrace the "Essence of Christianity." "The road to unity is the road of repentance," he says. And "it demands a resolute turning away from all those loyalties to the lesser values of the self, the denomination, and the nation, which deny the inclusiveness of divine love. It requires that Christians learn to look upon their separate establishments and exclusive creeds with contrition rather than with pride."[17] Radical monotheism (the Nimrod of HRN's public theology) stands in as a theological giant, championing the healing of the wounds that divide and directing the reconciliation of a nation morally defined by classism and racism. It offers a high religion and a high morality; it is a conceptual giant guarding the essence of Christianity in its full triunity: the fraternity of all, the unity of the church, and the ultimate determinacy of love.

The Fracturing of Public Theology

An awful lot has changed since *The Social Sources of Denominationalism* and HRN's powerful critique of American Christianity and American culture under the giant of radical monotheism, insisting on the sovereignty of God over all of culture. Our times are in need of an American public theology that is capable of criticizing our public culture driven by economic globalism through multinational corporate expansionism, war and violence, ecological threat of our nonbeing, pervasive poverty, and fear and trembling as we press through the quagmire of our economic downturning while maintaining lifestyles that assure us that all is well. We are in need of public theologies—theological, conceptual, and symbolic giants—that connect and integrate the spirituality of religious people, their participation in institutional religions, and their democratic citizenship.

To be sure, the last quarter of the twentieth century and the beginning of the twenty-first century have witnessed real *publicity* of religion in public life through television, spiritual-empowerment books, DVDs, and the Internet. Pat Robertson, Franklin Graham, Jesse Jackson,

Al Sharpton, Louis Farrakhan, T. D. Jakes, Joyce Meyer, Paul and Jan Crouch, Juanita Bynum, Creflo and Taffy Dollar, Ron Parsons, Benny Hinn, and many, many others are household names. For better or worse, they are our contemporary producers and makers of the sacred. They are gospel regulators and the voices of Christian witness to the world and nation. And each is expected to comment on America's ills. Marginal to the contemporary sources of *publicity* are the American intellectual classes, including the academically educated theologian. Contributing to this contemporary obscurity is the loss of traditional organs that once advanced American public theology.

Gone are the days when the public read debates among American theologians on whether God exists, as they did in 1930s. Gone are the days when a priest would debate an atheist before thousands over the radio. That priest was Father Frederick Coppleston, and the atheist was Bertrand Russell. Gone are the days when the American reading public was exposed to a world of theological disagreement over U.S. involvement in the Manchurian invasion and two brothers squared off in a series of essays in the *Christian Century* that would seal their names on the history of American public theology. They were Reinhold and H. Richard Niebuhr. We are not likely to witness a group of theologians evoke national debate as when *Time* magazine plastered the "Death of God" on its cover in 1960.

American public theology has lost its comfortable sites of the public lectures, weekly church and community journals and papers, political coalitions formed around issues such as labor and race. And it seems misplaced in the fast, snapshot world of mass telecommunications and tabloid presses. We are not likely to see academic theologians on late-night television or talk shows. Outside the world of text and press, academic theologians hardly seem significant to the hectic, frazzled worlds of telecommunication and entertainment journalism. Theology seems publicly irrelevant, falling outside of the most pervasive realms of public communication, the mass media.

Not only has the loss of traditional sites for the propagation of American public theology been a contributing factor to its marginalization, but also the longstanding liberal consensus on which it nourished itself between the 1930s and the 1960s has also collapsed with the decline of the ecumenical movement in the United States. The consensus between political and theological liberals formed around war (WWII and the cold war), labor, and race relations positioned many American academic theologians in public places. From within a wide circle of affiliations, they offered moral and spiritual critiques of the evils and necessity of war. They actively joined with labor workers, defending their causes of fair wages, adequate living conditions, and job security. They gave their intellectual gifts of religious and social criticisms toward eradicating malicious forms of racism and legitimating cross-cultural and cross-denominational support for civil rights.

The liberal consensus crashed as academic theologians divided over Vietnam, with the growth of radical, leftist political agendas in Latin America and other third-world geopolitical spheres, and as liberal democracy itself came under the suspicion of emergent right-wing conservatism in the mainline churches. These social factors further fragmented a liberal consensus among theologians, church leaders, and the laity. The vitality of American public theology from 1960s to the 1990s dissipated with the fragmentation of its liberal coalitions. High religion gave way to popular religion. Academic public theologians yield to church theologians and parachurch ministries as the public voice of theology on the issues of our times, from poverty and wealth, education and government, to family values and sexuality. In the wake of its public marginalization, how can America's academic theologians position themselves between the church and society?

This state of affairs for American public theology has not gone unarticulated by the Stanford theologian Van A. Harvey. Although criticizing the marginalization of theology in American intellectual life, as I have written elsewhere, Harvey's judgment is equally applicable to the marginalization of theology in American public life.[18] He targets the increased professionalization and specialization of theology in America's divinity schools and seminaries as the culprits that have rendered academic theology practically irrelevant for the critique of our public life. Conceiving their projects in technical and academic terms, rather than appealing to laity, theologians confine themselves to their own circle of other academics. Moreover, many seminary and divinity students who are not headed for careers in the academy find much of academic theology irrelevant and unpractical, as do many members of the clergy. Because of the daily demands of church life and pastoral care, many clergypersons are not likely to turn to much of contemporary academic theology for help or consolation, not even for continuing education.[19] Even among other faculties of the American academy, theology is suspect as a critical discourse in academic exchange.

Harvey lays the blame on academic theologians themselves, being moved intellectually by every narcissistic turn and fad infiltrating higher learning. "It could be argued that . . . Protestant theology has been characterized by narcissism and faddism that have virtually destroyed it as a serious intellectual discipline and deprived it of any respect in might thus claim," says Harvey.[20] To many, theology suffers from a proliferation of constructive theologies that ultimately render the discipline absurd, without a defining subject or content. Harvey says that academic theology has undermined its own relevance as "the slightest breezes that have stirred the trees of the groves of academe" have shaped it. What can be made for a discipline's integrity that fragments between a "theology of the death of God," a "theology of play," a "theology of hope," a "theology of liberation," a "theology of polytheism," a "theology of deconstruction," and even redundantly, a "theology of God,"[21] says Harvey.

Harvey's criticism is, of course, satirical yet stinging. Nevertheless, he makes a salient point about the state of academic theology and its significance in the formation of a twenty-first-century public theology in our postmodern absence of theological conceptual giants. From the 1970s to the present, it seems that political and theological liberals have suffered a crisis of political and religious irrelevance. A critic at a recent consultation that I attended offered an important charge, namely that we progressive liberal theologians suffer a public-relations problem. The title of the conference itself, ironically, makes his point: "Rekindling Theological Imagination: Transforming Thought for Progressive Action."

For many, the ethical mandates of the social gospel have been well spent and the leftist agenda of Christian liberation theologians have fallen quiet as many of the poor, for whom they speak, would rather have access to and be satisfied with the material goods of our capitalistic, market-driven culture as signs of God's preferential option for the poor than to make solidarity with the poor a universal identity of God's favor.

Here, it seems that economic advantages appear to be better bait for attracting the poor and marginalized throughout the world with God's favor than preaching the message of God's solidarity with them.

Our postmodern climate of theological formation seems to have followed the wave of narcissism, overwhelming our religious and moral resources. HRN's talk of sin appears captive to the prosperity gospel; talk of repentance seems displaced by talk of self-help; talk of righteousness appears muted by talk of "spirituality"; talk of active, passionate care for the poor, sick, dying, and the destitute seems pacified by talk of "How much shall I make this check out for?"; and talk about responsibility toward the sojourner within our gates or of our being a refuge for the dispossessed appears compromised by border markers saying all are welcomed except your dark and your destitute. So much of our contemporary state of theology turns to acts of redescription, either making "Christian identity formation" the primary concern of the church in the world or theologians getting bogged down into the quagmire of irreconcilable theologies of difference.

The market of American theology appears captive to U.S. rabid individualism and consumerism driven by market forces turning theology into commodities among which we may shop: black theology, womanist theology, Latino/a theology, disabilities theologies, queer theology, or GLBTIQ theology. There stands before us the possibility of an emergent D.L. or down-low theology (the theology of straight men who sleep with men). Black cultural critic Michael Eric Dyson urges black churches to develop a "theology of homoeroticism," an "Afriqueer-merican" theology,[22] and a possibility for a hip-hop theology.

As a critical intervention into the public and its problems, created by the operations of state power, on the one hand, and the fulfillment of democratic citizenship, on the other, American public theology seems lost for conceptual giants to mediate our competing claims. We seem lost for a distinctive discursive barring. For after deconstructing traditional interpretations of God, creation, the ordering of human relations, Christ, and the place of the church in the world, many students, pastors, religious seekers, and social leaders find our contemporary theologies practically and publicly bankrupt. Having deconstructed its Western theological canon, many inside and outside the academy also find academic theologians producing little that is preachable or teachable within local churches and community forums. And lamenting all of this is Van Harvey:

> Our common life is poorer because of [the] loss of public theology. Not only have we lost the languages of moral and communal discourse, . . . but we have lost the sense of what [Reinhold Niebuhr] called a "High Religion" and what it might contribute to public life. One does not have to be a Christian to regret this loss or to utter the lament, "Oh Reinhold Niebuhr, where are you now that we need you?"[23]

Turning toward the Local

Our conflicts are magnified, and our democratic practices are taxed. Our democratic practices are indeed fragile and our common good uncertain as the voices of popular American religiosity have overshadowed any serious analysis of our democratic plight and longings. The tragedy of September 11, 2001, changed, perhaps forever, the taken-for-granted assurance of a secure America. And this loss has suppressed the ability of many citizens to entertain the possibility of error in our political judgments; we dare not engage in forms of reflective criticism, immanent criticism, which critique the norms of our democratic experiment as a nation. "Never Again!" or "9/11!" echoes "Remember the Alamo!" Our conflicts have hardened, and so have our national responses to them. The languages of evil, terror, or "God hates fags" have replaced the theological languages of a generous pluralism intonated in Rauschenbusch's "Social Gospel," Reinhold Niebuhr's "Impossible Possibility," Paul Tillich's "Protestant Principle," Richard Niebuhr's "Radical Monotheism," and Martin Luther King Jr.'s "Beloved Community and World House."

To insist on the reclamation of these religious languages, symbols, and beliefs in our postmodern moment is to be ruled by nostalgia, nostalgia expressed in Harvey's lament for Reinhold Niebuhr. But what are we to lament? It is an American public theology absent of conceptual giants refereeing the particularisms and parochialisms of local faiths and moralities, the operations of state power determining the goods and ends of ordinary citizens, and the extension of state power throughout the globe. Lamented are the languages of public theology, religious languages doing for us the work of prophetic criticism of both American Christianity and our democratic culture. In our postmodern moment, with its absence of powerful conceptual giants, we want an American public theology that can mediate seemingly interminable local conflicts between distinct publics and direct them toward creative conflicts that, although challenging, continue to nurture our democratic longings.

A new Christendom? Or a benign relativism of distinct publics? Neither will do; neither will contribute to the flourishing of our common life. Our interests are so wide, our desires for individual fulfillment so deep, and our democratic longings are too great to be content with such totalizing options. While Harvey and other academic theologians may lament the fallen conceptual giants of a past American public theology, I insist that we can afford neither the time nor efforts given to such laments. Rather, we must turn elsewhere in search of *The Voice* of American public theology for our twenty-first-century needs.

The postmodern points us there, to the local. Is it possible that perhaps there, in the local and its local publics and faiths, if we look hard enough for traces, something of the community of care and commitment to the poor that once located Rauschenbusch's *Theology of the Social Gospel* will be found embodied? Perhaps HRN's critique of the sin of compromise may be found in local formations of citizens bound by a single mission of mercy to those who fall outside of the nation's care. They did not only mourn the social devastation of New Orleans's poorest communities but also organized themselves into powerful regimes of support and care. Their ministries of care and action inscribe on their bodies an American public theology that immanently put to shame many megachurch leaders and preachers of prosperity who fled the devastation, never returning, and shamed our national government into repentance.

Weak might be the triumphalism of "the kingdom of God" and the uncompromising devotion to a "radical monotheism" that checks every competing loyalty of citizens to their distinct publics by appealing to a cause and loyalty greater than our existing parochialisms. But is it possible that the nearness of God's sovereign love and God's new social order may be vibrantly embodied in the democratic practices and activism of the faithful ordinary who make sanctuaries of homes and advocate for the needs of America's homeless, hungry, and economically empty? Limp may be our evocation of the "Beloved Community" preached by Martin Luther King Jr. But may it not be immanently realized in the concerns and activism of the faithful ordinary for those millions of young muted voices incarcerated in U.S. prisons, undereducated in U.S. schools, and overdetermined by the never-ending and never-winning U.S. wars of drugs and crime? With one or three strikes, their incarcerations bring an end to their prospects for democratic citizenship.

A new Christendom or the banality of relativism staking warring publics will not satisfy our need for a twenty-first-century public theology. So we must turn to the local, faithful ordinaries to mine their creative conflicts for resources of our democratic longings. Vincent Harding has devoted his career to preserving their Christian activism. He says:

> Advancing democracy, healing the nation, developing humane institutions—whatever we call it—is a grand and costly vocation. Some have paid the cost with their lives, on behalf of us all, but the cost continues. For what is also obvious by now is that the fulfillment of democracy is a continuing task, one that each generation must actively take up, coming to grips with the harsh enemies of apathy and ignorance, cynicism and immobilizing fear.[24]

The postmodern may have turned us irrevocably toward the local (distinct publics), but perhaps that is its contribution to the future of American public theology in the absence of giants. The local constitutes the site of our creative conflicts when the ordinary democratic practices of citizens are affirmed and resistance toward totalizing the distinct interests of distinct publics are interrupted with visions of our common life that are wider, deeper, enlarging, and empowering of our democratic longings. Perhaps in such localities of the faithful ordinaries, traces of the "Great Hope" of democratic fulfillment, the "Impossible Possibility" of increasing love between not only individuals but also communities of people, and the celebration of "Beloved Community" may be embodied just enough to keep hope directed toward creative conflict and our democratic longings in the absent speeches and voices of the giants of American public theology in our postmodern moment.

Chapter 14

Walking on the Rimbones of Nothingness

Embodied Scholarship for Those of Us Way Down Under the Sun

Emilie M. Townes

*John strode across infinity where God sat upon his throne and looked off
towards immensity and burning worlds dropped from his teeth. The sky
beneath John's tread crackled and flashed eternal lightning and thunder rolled
without ceasing in his wake.*

*Way off he heard crying, weeping, weeping and wailing—wailing like the
last cry of Hope when she fled the earth. Where was the voice? He strained
his eye to see. None walked across the rimbones of nothingness with him,
but the wailing wailed on.*[1]

THIS PASSAGE, FROM *JONAH'S Gourd Vine*, the first novel by anthropologist,
folklorist, and novelist of the Harlem Renaissance Zora Neale Hurston,
was written in 1934 in three to four months. The book is based loosely

Earlier versions of this address are in *Criterion* 46, no. 3 (Fall 2008/Winter 2009):
16–23, 34, titled "The Dancing Mind," and in *The Journal of the American Academy
of Religion* 77, no. 11 (2009): 1–15. Parts of this essay are adapted from a lecture I
gave for the Association of Theological Schools titled "Crafting Research That Contributes to Theological Education," 2007 Lilly Conference on Theological Research,
Pittsburgh, February 23, 2007.

215

on her parents' lives and told through the stories of John Pearson, a minister in the small black Florida town of Eatonville; his wife, Lucy Potts; and other women in the town. Hurston uses the biblical passage of Jonah 4:6-11 for the novel's title as she depicts Pearson as the gourd vine; weaknesses and destructive tendencies are the worm that destroys the vine.

Hurston's work has been incalculable in helping scholars recognize the importance of folklore in theological and ethical reflection. In her essay "Conversions and Visions," Hurston, the sociocultural anthropologist, seeks to recover the role of vision in black religion—noting that it almost always accompanies conversion and always accompanies the call to preach.[2] She then explains that along with traditional conversion vision there are variations such that "the imagination of one may carry him to the last judgment and the rimbones of nothing, the vision of another may hobble him at washing collard greens. However, in each case there is an unwillingness to believe—to accept the great good fortune too quickly. So, God is asked for proof."[3] Then, in classic Hurston fashion, she details the lengths to which folk will go to avoid the salvation that is found in conversion—fruitlessly.

Hurston uses the phrase "rimbones of nothing" again in her classic *Their Eyes Were Watching God.* After the death of her husband, the tyrannical Joseph Starks, the main character, Janie, is enjoying her freedom and though not oblivious to the new suitors who come calling, Hurston writes, "All that they said and did was refracted by her inattention and shot off toward the rimbones of nothing."[4]

It is clear from how Hurston uses the phrase that rimbone china is not what she has in mind. Hurston points us elsewhere: to that space beyond Mircea Eliade's *axis mundi* (the center of the world) or Arnold van Gennep's liminality (the transitional ritual space in initiation between sacred and pollution).[5] This eschatological space of nothingness is not the egolessness of Eastern philosophies or Jean-Paul Sartre's stubborn attempt to vindicate the fundamental freedom of the human being against determinism.[6]

Hurston points us to that space in which creation itself enters our lives in ways too deep for words and only sounds and images roil our souls; it challenges our vision and our scholarship. To walk across the rimbones of nothingness is to know that there is more there than what we can account for by the precision of our analysis or the depth of our intuition. Walking across the rimbones of nothingness as scholars of religion means we take all that we have learned, all that we hope to say, research, and teach, and place it in a space of the ultimate unknown, where the immensity of our world drops from our scholarly teeth into global creation in which we recognize that our scholarship, which is our form of conversion vision, can be put to good use in the fiercely mundane as well as in the fastidiously erudite.

Not unlike Toni Morrison's image of the dancing mind, in which we meet each other in the "dance of an open mind when it engages another equally open one—an activity that occurs most naturally, most often in the reading/writing world we live in,"[7] walking across the rimbones of nothingness encourages us to tease out the possibilities and the realities; our dreams, hopes, and nightmares; and the mundane and the humorous in the academy, the classroom, and religious gatherings of our various communities. Conversion visions of the sort we do are demanding and yet can be playful. However, they must always be done with precision, rigor, and humility.

Seeking Truth and Truth Telling

W. E. B. Du Bois, one of the exemplary thinkers of the twentieth century, offers an important admonition to the work of scholars of theology and religion. Writing just one year after the publication of *Jonah's Gourd Vine*, Du Bois states:

> One is astonished in the study of history at the recurrence of the idea that evil must be forgotten, distorted, skimmed over. We must not remember that Daniel Webster got drunk and only remember that he was a splendid constitutional lawyer. We must forget that George Washington was a slave owner, or that Thomas Jefferson had mulatto children, or that Alexander Hamilton had Negro blood, and simply remember the things we regard as creditable and inspiring. The difficulty, of course, with this philosophy is that history loses its value as an incentive and example; it paints perfect men and noble nations, but it does not tell the truth.[8]

These are sobering words for me as a social ethicist who uses social history as part of my methodology. When I first read this insight from Du Bois, I found it echoed within me as much as his more famous insight, "The problem of the Twentieth Century is the problem of the color-line."[9] I have felt the impact of his words time and again as our studied, selective amnesia or willful oblivion has painted a perfectly simplistic picture of a complex, fascinating, dynamic, and peculiarly American society with restlessly changing cultures and demographics.

We are encouraged to remember the good or dwell on the bad to the exclusion of the other. This is bad history because it does not tell the truth of the living and breathing that goes on between these two poles of the human drama. It should caution scholars in religious and theological studies of various sorts to be circumspect about our research, writing, and teaching when we veer too far one way or the other without considering what lies in between. Because, like history that paints perfect men and women and noble nations through selective methodologies, our scholarship can lose its value and vision as incentive and example.

Most scholars would agree that an imperative for our scholarship is that it be rigorous, relentless, and responsible to the issues of the day while pushing our understanding of what is before us in our modern/postmodern worlds. Additionally, our scholarship should *also* help map out strategies for creating a more just and free society and world. Shake dancing with despots in the name of scholarly exchange is tricky business. With a history (and a present) that includes such vulgar spectacles as auction blocks and lynchings and pedestals, it is ludicrous for any of us to believe for one second that there is any possibility that our work as scholars and teachers is done in value-free, neutral space or spaces.

Moreover, living in a shadow box does not recognize the richness of black (or other cultures because it resorts to collapsing black realities into postmodern minstrel shows. It freeze-frames black life without recognizing our humanity or the rhythms and cadences of our living. Sadly, many of these brutalized and brutalizing images have been internalized in black communities and in the individual lives of black women and children and men and in our religious communities. Far too many of us skip rope with paralyzing demons in a dailyness that slips into an endless spiral of horizontal violence. Calling others and ourselves into *human*

behavior is exhausting. However, I believe this is what embodied scholarship can and must address. This scholarship is invested and accountable to everyday people and not only to scholarly enclaves. Seeking truth
and truth telling are key.

A strong influence that taught me the importance of working to
incorporate truth telling in my scholarship and the potency of wisdom
in my teaching are the old black folks of my grandmother's generation
who helped raise me.

and i can still hear them now

those older black women of my grandmother's generation

miss waddell
miss rosie
ms. montez
ms. hemphill
cousin willie mae

as they visited with each other (it was never called gossip)

in their kitchens
front yards
beauty shops
porches (stoops were a city thing in southern pines, nc)
sunday school classes
church socials

i can still here them now

the older black men of my grandmother's generation

mr. waddell
mr. press
bad bill
mr. hemphill
monkey joe

as that sat and discussed (it was never called gossip—that was what the
women did)

in the barber shop
under the tree of knowledge outside the barber shop
out in the front yard or side yard tinkering with their cars

after church
during the church socials

yes, i can still hear them

and you know, the only person i thought was older than these folks was god

and because they were old

i was taught they had wisdom

or should have

and they knew things that i thought i could never know because i couldn't
believe that i'd ever be as old as they were

because they were special

they had something that sustained them in a tightly drawn color-lined
southern and west southern pines

divided by u.s. route 1

and money

and power

and privilege

from the white folks they worked for in their kitchens, yards,
driving their cars, buying their groceries, tending to their dogs and
horses, and carrying their golf clubs

they wore a white starched shirt, best hat wearing crew on sunday morning

and i simply loved being in their presence

sitting quietly and saying nothing so that they would forget i was
there (or did they)

and do grown folks talk about life and living and losing and loving

they did not live a life tinted by rose colored glasses

instead, they turned to the joy they found in the lord

and the strength they found at the altar to put their children through
college

if that's where they wanted to go

and love all the children in that small community

    because that's what grown folks are supposed to do

and in that love they taught us more than our abc's and our plus ones and times tables

    they taught us what it meant to be wise by their actions and not just their words

    they even told us what to watch for to tell if what they were saying was true

        evil is as evil does

        stay out of corners

        keep your legs together

        a hawk always circles his prey

and if one of them exhibited the negative side of the wisdom they shared

    we knew it and even failure (or humanness) became an occasion to learn what it meant to love the lord with all you heart, mind, soul, and body

yes, i still hear them

    ummph . . . ummph . . . ummph

    lord, jesus

    say amen, somebody

    have mercy

    sucking of teeth

    low whistle

and i see them

    proud black people who knew when to bend and not break

    going to their jobs

    making a way out of no way

    succeeding

    failing

    being human all the time

but the wisdom and giving of it never left

> because they believed with every ounce of their being that they had to pass good things on to the next generation
>
> and the one thing they had that no amount of the ku klux klan, paddy rollers, or sheriff departments could take away—even with fire houses and lynching trees
>
>> was what they knew about life and how to survive it and even thrive
>>
>> they had what ethicist peter paris calls practical wisdom[10]

so these exemplars of practical wisdom help me keep the time beat

> remind me of, or teach all of us about where we've come from
>
> so that we are not tempted to make decisions in thin air
>
>> but instead lean into the thick isness of our lives
>>
>>> the agonies and the ecstasies
>>
>> to find our bearings for the journey

this wisdom, this way of truth-telling, is not showy, but it is steady

> it helps folk know how and more importantly what to look for in living
>
> it brings the past in the present and the present into the future
>
>> so that we remember we are a people in time and of time
>>
>> and nothing we do puts us outside of time

and this is important because we can never get away from the history that brought us here

> even if we do not know it

and it is dangerous to be in a position where we cannot remember what we never knew[11]

Scholarship and Practical Wisdom

To walk across the rimbones of nothingness means that we may need to tarry a bit before we attempt to be rational, critical, analytical, precise, and rigorous in our scholarship and teaching. I know that in my own scholarship, I more often than not crash and burn if I fail to think through first: Why am I doing this? In fact, why do any of us do the scholarship we do? Teach the classes that we teach?

Here I am talking about more than, we do the scholarship we do because we are interested in it, or care about it, or are passionate about it, or we think it is necessary. These are more than appropriate personal scholarly benchmarks for our work, and they should and must be a part of what we do when we engage in trying to understand, defend, debunk, question, cajole, illuminate in our research and writing. I am focusing more on what, for me, is the important first step of rimbone walking: Why the research in the first place? Because I believe that what should drive our research in large measure is that we are exploring traditions that have driven people to incredible heights of valor and despicable degrees of cravenness. In other words, the research we do is not a free-floating, solitary intellectual quest. It is profoundly tethered to people's lives—the fullness and the incompleteness of them.

I use the image of tethering intentionally because I do not want to suggest that our work is *circumscribed* by the traditions we explore or not but, rather, that we are consciously and perhaps at times unconsciously responding to the drama of history lived in creation and we cannot or we should not proceed as if we are engaged in ideas as if people are not related to them. Another way to say this is that I don't believe that scholarship is or should be an objective enterprise.

Here, I am not equating objective with rigorous. They aren't the same thing at all, and I always argue for deep-walking, rigorous scholarship. What I am arguing against is the kind of disinterested research tack that doesn't figure in that our work is going to have a profound impact on someone's life in some way and somehow. I worry when we think that we are *only* dealing with ideas and concepts as if they have no heart and soul behind them. If they matter to us, they will matter to others.

We should do our work with passion and precision and realize that we should not aspire to be the dipsticks for intellectual hubris. I am well aware that I am arguing against some of the foundational assumptions in my training and my readers, where the scientific-research model and its attendant view of reality give us a solid grasp of disciplinary content and methodologies. I appreciate actually exploring ideas with gusto and trusting the trail in which my research leads me rather than trying to steer it into the lanes I'd rather travel. However, this training did not teach me how to be scholar *and* teacher in the schools where I have been on the faculty. It did not prepare me for the calls in the wide variety of communities that ask me (and you) to help them think through the issues they face and to translate my public lectures into the everydayness of their lives to develop survival strategies and to encourage them to trust the integrity of their own insights.

Our academic training hopes that we are smart enough to fit our disciplinary work to "contexts as different as the religious studies department of a major university or the ministry concerns of a small Roman Catholic diocesan seminary."[12] This is a tall order, and working our way through this is one of those vocational or professional challenges that we may not speak of often or choose to suffer through on our own and in silence unwisely.

We are called to be scholars in a society of bone-deep communities seeking humanity in the midst of injustices and hatreds. Our scholarship should not reify media-driven images of black living that trick all of us into believing and/or living into grotesque stereotypes of black life. It should not sanction death-dealing images of success that trick us into thinking our accomplishments are ours alone. It must not serve as salve for mind-numbing bromides of racism, sexism, classism, heterosexism, homophobia, and militarism that include fear tactics, terrorist acts, bullying, lying, avoiding, fronting, and simply not giving a damn about anything but amassing power, getting your way, and piling up legacies. Walking across the rimbones of nothingness does not lead to nowhere; visions seldom do, but it does take work and attentiveness to decipher them at times.

Therefore, it is vital that our scholarship bear the marks of practical wisdom for this generation and beyond. (It has been a source of ongoing bemusement for me that when I first drafted this essay, I realized that I was now as old as those old black folk I carry in my ear and eye.) In what ways, then, do we determine the options for good moral behavior? What have we stored in our methodological toolkits that helps us dig deep into the chaos and order of our worlds to hear and see what is there? What criteria do we use to choose the best option for good moral acts in light of all that we've discerned? What do we keep stored away at our desks or offices or classrooms that never sees the light of day in our public lectures or writings or preaching because some dawnings are best left private or personal or strategic? What standards of values of virtues do we use to evaluate our decisions to do so? What markers do we have in our work that tell us it's time to stop thinking about it, rewriting it, rethinking it, reediting it, recalling it, and make a declarative statement? Timing is key, and there is such a thing as too soon or too late.

From Concepts to Tools

To walk across the rimbones of nothingness to answer these questions and more means that the challenges become integrity, consistency, and stubbornness—not only objectivity as the sole marker of scholarly brilliance. These do not displace objectivity. No, they become part of our methodological toolkit as well *and* are as valued as the call for objectivity, because there is much to be said for holding ourselves accountable, which is, I think, ultimately what the call for objectivity in the religious disciplines is about. We just forget that a serious *and* capricious God has a hand in creation, and our intellectual musings often forget God's laughing side. This makes too much of what we do humorless and inept.

When recognizing these things, we can do relevant scholarship, excellent teaching, learning, *and* activism with dancing minds that point to that vital triumvirate of love, justice, and hope. We are then moving from *concepts* in hermeneutical, historical, pastoral, theoethical discourses to *tools* that demystify and deconstruct, that help build and enlighten.

Part of what is involved in crafting scholarship that will contribute to the academy and the lives of people beyond the library or our studies or our offices or classrooms is that we must think in more expansive ways than our disciplinary homes have often trained us to think, with our intellect focused primarily on our scholarly navels. This is tricky business because in doing so, we may also be challenging the holy of holies in many disciplines and reconfiguring the standards of excellence in them.

But challenge them we must as we use our scholarship to recognize, explore, and critique the various cultural traditions found in our communities. For example, for African American communities, it is to recognize that our community is not a Greek chorus, the Harlem Gospel or Love Fellowship choirs, or the Dixie Hummingbirds but a cacophony of birth and death and the rich textures of living that go on in between and remember we have to pass this on with conviction and vigor. It is not enough to store up knowledge if we do not share it; in fact, it's sinful to do so. We must explore how the traditional wisdom that comes from the beauty shop and the tree of knowledge outside the barber shop have not lost their insights as we tease through the prison industrial complex, HIV/AIDS, levees breaking, welfare reform, clergy sexual and professional misconduct, politicians who turn lying into a high art form as folks not only slip through the cracks but are also impaled on the sharp spikes of empire building and Christian triumphalism dressed up in the drag show of compassionate conservatism, turning the rally cry of "Yes we can" to the tough question of "How?" and the working to make that *how* real. Folk know this stuff in their bones, and not to intricately integrate them into our intellectual musings is not only foolish, but it is also bad scholarship.

It is vital that we develop the fine art of careful listening so that we can gather the information we need. Patience and silence are sometimes very good things in theoethical reflection, and in making use of them, we must be ready to not like what we hear, see, feel, taste, and smell when we do listen and learn from what is happening. An open mind is a key value to hold in scholarship that walks across the rimbones of nothingness. Coupled with this is avoiding the temptation to close our observations, our analysis, our critique, our conversations off too quickly. We must learn the difference between gradualism and good moral discernment each day. We must ask creation to speak to our hearts, minds, and souls to bring new life and encouragement in the face of despair and annihilation. We do these things because the preservation of our communities is our telos on this side of the Jordan. Never in the lives of those of us in the African Diaspora has this been more important. For although we may have hope with the election of Barack Obama as president, we are sobered by the rise of hate crimes that has followed in its wake. We watch our own begin to walk away from the moral values that kept us sane, whole, and holified people from slavery to Jim and Jane Crow to segregation to desegregation to diversity to multiculturalism to whatever we want to call what we're doing now. With practical wisdom, we learn the importance of the steady and persistent rimbone walking of the everydayness of faithfulness.

Conclusion

Hurston challenges us to stride across infinity, to look at the immensity of the sometimes literally burning worlds in which others and we live. To do, no, to be committed to scholarship that is rigorous, accessible, and can be used as tools for insight, knowledge, and wisdom to build a more just world within worlds—this is truly a conversion vision.

One from which we begin to take the first steps away from Du Bois's damning judgment that his study of history reveals "the recurrence of the idea that evil must be forgotten, distorted, skimmed over"[13] and my musings on what this can mean for all of our disciplines. It is to move toward intellectually walking into a new future that is more vibrant, more humane, more alive with possibilities that engage others and ourselves.

Yes, I can still hear them—those old black folk who raised me, loved me, and taught me to dare to step out into infinity where God sits upon God's throne looking off toward immensity as burning worlds drop from God's teeth. They taught an outright colored stubbornness that refuses to stop until the work we do as scholars and teachers lives in a hope that has not fled the earth and is made manifest for all of us who live here, way down under the sun.

Chapter 15

Still on the Journey

Moral Witness, Imagination,
and Improvisation in Public Life

Barbara A. Holmes

For nothing is fixed, forever and forever and forever, it is not fixed; the earth is always shifting, the light is always changing, the sea does not cease to grind down rock. Generations do not cease to be born, and we are responsible to them because we are the only witnesses they have. The sea rises, the light fails, lovers cling to each other, and children cling to us. The moment we cease to hold each other, the moment we break faith with one another, the sea engulfs us and the light goes out.—James Baldwin, "Nothing Personal"[1]

IN THIS POST–CIVIL RIGHTS, post-9/11, post-Katrina world, there are no maps or GPS systems to guide us or our institutions toward moral flourishing. Yet, we know that the period of waiting is over, and we are on the move again. The responsibility is to honor and learn from the past, and simultaneously to reclaim a theology of public life that invites the emergence of the beloved community. Given where we are on the journey, neither tinkering nor angst will do. The Obama-Nation and the generations that precede and follow must completely reform absolutely everything. The scholarship of many African American ethicists, such as that of Peter Paris, inspires the interplay of moral witness, imagination, and improvisation as means toward that end. Until change comes, the moral imperative is to speak truth to power, to imagine outcomes that cannot come into view in any other way, and to reshape public life creatively.

"Generations Do Not Cease to Be Born"

James Baldwin offers a view of reality that we avoid at all costs. We are not here to stay; others will follow us. He says that everything is shifting, nothing is fixed. The implication is that the life journey may be exhilarating, but it is also perilous. We have no time to congratulate one another on victories won during the twentieth century, because the ground is moving underneath our feet. What a blow to our careful mythologies about permanence! The truth of the matter is that we are on a journey, that was already underway when we arrived. We take the world as it is and shape it as we go. As we change the life space, it changes us.

Bernice Johnson Reagon, founder of the singing group Sweet Honey in the Rock, spoke about the life journey at a 2007 speaking engagement. She said, "Why would you travel on a road that someone else built? It will take you where they want you to go. Instead walk to the edge of a cliff and leap."[2] Her suggestion that we leap into the unknown is not a call to end it all; instead, we are urged to dive into possibilities, to explore and invent, and to see the world differently with every glance.

I am convinced that it is possible to change our world, to lay down our weapons, and to institute a politics of care and concern. Public life can be restored through creative acts of moral witness, imagination, and improvisation. The hope is that we can reorient the life of the community toward one another in ways that will allow us to embrace a "cosmological spirituality" that invites remembrance and innovation.[3]

Becoming Moral Witnesses

Today everything is accessible all of the time. Fifty years ago, the world was viewed through the lens of limited and local day-to-day experiences. Public life changed when television was invented. Television was in its infancy during the 1950s, when a naive nation gathered around black-and-white sets to watch a program called *Truth or Consequences*. The premise of the game was that you had to tell the truth before "Bertha the Buzzer" sounded, or you faced the consequences.

The questions were "straight lines" that had jokes for answers. No amount of study would allow the contestant to avoid the inevitable. The consequences ranged from silly stunts and embarrassing tasks to reunions with long-lost loved ones. Like others across the nation, my parents sat transfixed and delighted as they watched snippets of human life that ranged from the ridiculous to the sublime. The television set became the center of family entertainment and a lens that allowed a passive and private view of the world.

For the first time in the human era, we could observe the world from the privacy of our homes. The nation saw what it wanted to see, and it saw what it didn't want to see. The "glass darkly" entertained and then lulled unsuspecting viewers. It was not long before programming shifted from game shows to reality. War-torn bodies in one war or another were displayed during the evening meal. Viewers sitting on their sofas folding clothes or reading the paper were horrified as Jack Ruby shot Lee Harvey Oswald right before their eyes.

We saw the tears stream down Martin Luther King Jr.'s face as he prepared himself for sacrifice and death. We watched Princess Diana wed and John Kennedy Jr. and his father die. We watched Representative Barbara Jordan speak truths that many knew. She was not the first to accuse the Nixon presidency of moral failure, but it was the incongruity of the messenger's embodiment as a black woman and the shock of her rhetorical genius that kicked the final supports out from under a crumbling administration.[4] When these events unfolded, we didn't gather in public spaces to talk about them; others talked for us. We watched as commentators explained what we thought, but through it all, we were witnesses.

"We Are the Only Witnesses They Have"

James Baldwin is right. There will be those who follow us, and we are the only witnesses that they have about our times, our failures, and our successes. The task is to leave clues as to the jazz of community formation and the surprising potential of public dialogue. We must mark memory trails that point to the glitches and unlikely moments of inspiration as we offer insights into the multidimensional and layered aspects of reality.

Our generation must point to a cosmology that is not fixed, a collective consciousness rich with the repositories of lives well led. And always we pass on reassurances that instability and change offer the opportunity for imaginative improvisations. The task is to shake off our fatigue from the "culture wars" and become moral witnesses.

Witnessing is usually a pastiche of hope, history, and prophecy. We think that we know what witnesses are supposed to do because the legal system is available to all of us through the media. When Judge Judy of television fame barks "Step up" with a no-nonsense stare, we know that it is time for the witness to testify, but what does it mean to be a moral witness in twenty-first-century public life? In a legal context, witnesses have the duty to report with veracity what they see, and despite the great potential for error, we base life-and-death decisions on their testimony.

Attorney and law professor Barry Scheck has spent the last few years of his life unraveling the tangle of mistakes that result from eyewitness testimony. Those errors result in the incarceration and sometimes execution of innocent people. In response to the intrinsic anomalies of our "justice system," Scheck cofounded the Innocence Project, a national litigation and public policy organization dedicated to the exoneration of wrongfully convicted persons. With regard to "eyewitnesses," the Innocence Project Web site offers this insight:

> Eyewitness misidentification is the single greatest cause of wrongful convictions nationwide, playing a role in more than 75% of convictions overturned through DNA testing.
>
> While eyewitness testimony can be persuasive evidence before a judge or jury, 30 years of strong social science research has proven that eyewitness identification is often unreliable. Research shows that the human mind is not like a tape recorder; we neither record events exactly as we see them, nor recall them like a tape that has been rewound. Instead, witness memory is like any other evidence at a crime scene; it must be preserved carefully and retrieved methodically, or it can be contaminated.[5]

"Contamination" is an unusual word to use to describe a process that was not "pure" at the outset. The problem with witnessing has less to do with the function of memory or the recording capabilities of the human brain than it does with the fact that we are a storytelling people. Any African griot worth her salt knows that something is always added to history, to observation, to witnessing, and then there is always the trickster element. Nothing is fixed; even the most foundational elements of faith allow room for improvisation. How else would we be able to appropriate the ancient as viable truth for the present?

In faith contexts, we have eyewitness reports of divine comings and goings. A witness watches the prophet Elijah taken up in the heavens; observers report the risen Christ suddenly appearing in a locked room. Although the witnesses will record their truths, those testimonies settle nothing. Testimonies with regard to the truth of a spiritual matter cannot survive the vicissitudes of time unless those attestations are offered as a break in the ordinary that invites creative interpretation.

For these reasons and many more, I believe that the moral witness of a generation can be preserved as faithfully in art as it is in memory and history. The holocausts against the Jewish, American Indian, Palestinian, and African diasporan people, to name a few, are so shocking to the moral fiber of the human community that artists become the best moral witnesses. What other medium can hold such horrors? A good example is found in the testimony of Pablo Picasso's *Guernica*. This painting, commissioned for the Spanish Pavilion of the 1937 World's Fair, continues to speak through the ages about the perils of imperialism and war. It commemorates the Nazi bombing of a Basque village in northern Spain on April 27, 1937. According to sources, 1,600 people civilians died. It was a massacre of outrageous proportions on a civilian population.[6]

The moral witness of the painting *Guernica* is irrefutable. On the day that Colin Powell went to the United Nations to lie us into a "shock-and-awe" bombing that would kill Iraqi civilians in catastrophic numbers, a press conference was held in the room where *Guernica* is prominently displayed. On this occasion, the painting was blocked by flags and covered with a blue curtain.

Obviously some were concerned that Picasso's anti-war masterwork would not make a very good backdrop for speeches and press conferences advocating the bombing and invasion of Iraq. As the US talks about its "shock and awe" strategy (the potential launching of over 800 Cruise Missiles against Baghdad in two days), and its willingness to use "bunker busting nuclear bombs" against Iraq. . . . Picasso's work is a chilling reminder of what such military operations would mean for civilian populations. On Feb. 5th, 2003, US Secretary of State Colin Powell spoke before the United Nations to make his case for a US attack on Iraq. Picasso's mural was completely covered up and the flags of Security Council member nations were placed before the censored artwork. As Maureen Dowd, writing for the New York Times, wrote, "Mr. Powell can't very well seduce the world into bombing Iraq surrounded on camera by shrieking and mutilated women, men, children, bulls and horses."[7]

The images of *Guernica* so amplified the cries of the innocent in one era that they pierced the thin veil of national hubris and preemptive murderous intent some sixty-six years later. If we don't act as moral witnesses regarding the matters that confront us in our lifetimes, the rocks will cry out and the paintings will testify.

Imagining the Reformation of Public Life

If we conceive of the imagination as a power or capacity we all possess at least in nascent form, then analogous to a virtue such as patience, it becomes strengthened through practice.[8]

The reform of public life as we know it is no longer a pipe dream or a utopian focus of discussion. The consequences of years of rampant unregulated capitalism, the dominance of Eurocentric economic policies that tout competition, maximize dichotomies, and grind the poor to powder eventually led to the 2008 collapse of the worldwide economy. Because we are in the midst of the mayhem, there are no vantage points for objective analysis. From the midst of cultural and financial chaos comes an unspoken agreement that change is necessary and that bold acts of civic reconstruction will arise from the collective imagination of the people.

There is a distinct difference between dreaming and imagination. Dreaming gained credibility as a rhetorical device when Martin Luther King Jr. spoke of the future using dream language. However, his prophetic vision, once articulated, moved from the realm of private dreams to collective imagination. This is a crucial transition, because, as noted phenomenologist Alfred Schutz acknowledges, "We cannot dream together." When we dream, there is a complete relaxation of the attention to life. Dreaming is in essence a complete turning away. But a prophetic dream remembered and publicly articulated can prod the imaginations of the people.

While the death of the dreamer did not kill the dream, it left an awakened populace uncertain as to the path forward. The most natural response after the loss of a leader is to draw up plans to fulfill the dream. It is always easier to create blueprints than to engage in the more laborious process of collective imagining. Taking what is known and what is expected, one can devise a fairly decent plan of action, but that plan will not exceed the boundaries of accepted knowledge. It takes imagination to transcend the possible and catapult communities toward outcomes that lie just beyond the limits of human reason.

Imagining the Impossible

Imagination is often a last resort in public life because we don't trust our own inherent creativity. We fear that we will reap the bizarre if imagination is allowed a place at the table of civic reconstruction. Nothing could be further from the truth. Imagination necessarily carries within it a kernel of the ordinary, as intellectual ballast. Like a hot-air balloon tied to the ground, human imagination can be limited to what the human mind can conceive. This is problematic, because often the resolutions to age-old civic problems require more.

A good example of the limits of human imagination can be found in the election of Barack Obama as president of the United States. His emergence came without warning. There was nothing in the history of the last half of the twentieth century, nothing in the testimony of its witnesses, that could have forecast the event. Change is an odd thing. We expect warnings before change comes because we see so many examples in nature. Before an earthquake decimates a city, the ground rumbles and heaves. Before a marriage dissolves, the atmosphere in the relationship changes, hope becomes scarce, and self-preservation becomes a priority.

Although I am delighted that political events unfolded as they did, election outcomes don't defer the responsibility to imagine a future together. Presidents must be pragmatists; we can imagine more. Ultimately, we are not called to produce outcomes, because imagination is an act of faithfulness that makes room for the possible. We imagine a future with full knowledge that at any moment the in-breaking of God's grace may take us by surprise, transcend the known, and invite the regenerative brooding of the Holy Spirit.

Improvisation in Public Life

> Improvisation comprises unpredictable variations on a theme. It brings novelty to bear on the familiar, not for the sake of destroying the latter, but for the purpose of heightening the individuality and uniqueness of the agent and his or her creative ability. . . . All creative activities are commensurate with this art of improvisation. Moral formation and political leadership are not exceptions.[9]

In Memphis, there is an improvisational group that performs the angst of its audiences. It is not unlike the "psychodrama" of the 1960s, but with the rhythm and openness of the twenty-first century. I watched in amazement as the facilitator began with a simple phrase. She looked at the audience and said, "What's going on?" and we were off and running. As a guarded northeasterner, I expected silence, and instead I watched unpredictable issues emerge in the darkened theater that ranged from the care of feral or domesticated cats to sibling rivalry, deeply harbored moral dilemmas, and racial discomforts.

The disclosures were so profoundly intimate that I found myself looking around the room, wondering what would have happened if the questions had not been asked. Would all of this anxiety have remained in a subliminal state of potential implosion? The relief in the room as the evening drew to a close was palpable. Each improvisation exaggerated but pinpointed the source of the pain—the overlooked dysfunction. The truth was on display and the consequence was healing. No buzzers, no stunts, just truth unfolding as a molting but potentially beautiful butterfly. Participants and observers left the building stunned by the social potential of improvisation.

On that night, I witnessed public dialogue as performance. Improvisation creates opportunities for laughter, community formation, and sharing, even while we continue the work of justice. We cannot bridge the gaps between us in the ordinary ways, but performing our possibilities may inspire us to unveil a shared future. If everything must change from the way we "do" church to how we educate children, we will have to experiment. In the West, there seems to be a fear of being wrong, of making mistakes of not being able to set forth a flawless blueprint of the future.

I contend that mistakes made in a creative microcosm may be the only way out of broken systems. We will have to try one thing or another and talk about the benefits and detriments. Do girls/boys learn better in same-sex classrooms? Have we learned the wisdom of indigenous people in the Americas with regard to the rituals, which seem to help teens traverse the perilous pathways to adulthood? Is the church/pew standoff permanent, or can a lay priesthood of believers and a new urban, contemplative activism lead the church out of its malaise and inspire relevancy? Do deeply held religious beliefs contribute to deeply held inclinations toward misogyny, homophobia, racial and gender bias? How do we connect the gifts of the academia with the needs of the community? And finally, can an American society be restructured to work as well for the "have-nots" and the "almost-haves" as it has for the "haves"?

I don't have the answers because we are still on the journey. I want public life to be filled with debate and ingenuity. I want to imagine an escape from the clutches of corporate marauders, who also need to be redeemed for the community. We bless and invite "enemies" because we have been the enemies of God, and because belovedness is not limited to the innocent. As Cornel West notes, "You can learn to love your crooked neighbor with your own crooked heart because you're connected to a power and grace greater than your ego."[10] The road is ahead, the challenges continue to arise, and we are still on the journey!

Conclusion: Toward a Single Garment of Destiny

Imagine a political system responsive to the people and respectful of global neighbors, a health system that is comprehensive in scope and not profit driven, an educational system shaped by innovation, improvisation, and practicality. Imagine a seminary education that grounds its curriculum in partnerships with wide-ranging communities. Imagine a politically and spiritually mature populace, engaged in every form of public dialogue, and the translation of that dialogue into collective moral witness.

We have not been invited to build permanent habitations on this journey. Our engagement with the powers is intense and transitory. Sometimes the questions we are being asked to resolve in public life have jokes for answers or no answer at all. When we demand responses, we get parables and psalms, metaphors and prophecies. It seems clear to me that we are being invited to use similar tools: art, dialogue, witnessing as griots, imagination, and improvisation to inspire the changes that will bless future generations.

For Reflection and Study

Key Ideas

- American public theology
- cosmic community
- creative acts of moral witness, imagination, and improvisation
- ecowomanism
- embodied scholarship
- faithful ordinaries
- New Christendom
- post-Christian

Resources for Further Study

Anderson, Victor. *Creative Exchange: A Constructive Theology of African American Religious Experience*. Minneapolis: Fortress Press, 2008.

Floyd-Thomas, Stacey M., ed. *Deeper Shades of Purple: Womanism in Religion and Society*. New York: New York University Press, 2006.

Harris, Melanie L. *Gifts of Virtue, Alice Walker, and Womanist Ethics*. New York: Palgrave MacMillan, 2010.

Holmes, Barbara A. *Race and the Cosmos: An Invitation to View the World Differently*. Harrisburg: Trinity Press International, 2002.

———. *Liberation and the Cosmos: Conversations with the Elders*. Minneapolis: Fortress Press, 2008.

Thinking Critically and Constructively

1. Watch the movie *Avatar*. Does the movie awaken your moral imagination? If yes, in what ways? Are there themes in the movie that resonate with ideas in these essays?
2. What is your moral vision for the twenty-first century? What metaphors for a just moral community come to mind?

Afterword

Marcia Y. Riggs and James Samuel Logan

THE INSPIRATION AND SOMETIMES source for these essays is the scholarship of Princeton Seminary's emeritus professor of Christian social ethics Dr. Peter J. Paris. The important leadership of Dr. Paris as president of the American Academy of Religion, the Society of Christian Ethics, and the Society for the Study of Black Religion is matched by his contributions to the field of Christian social ethics. His scholarship teaches students and scholars. He teaches students that doing ethical reflection requires that we understand history and traditions in order to better understand and analyze our present realities. He teaches scholars that excellent scholarship contributes substantively to its author's academic discipline and enlarges a people's vision of the world that they inhabit. We are reminded by Dr. Paris that God's creation is a moral community that is local and global, human and nonhuman, and we are called to "do justice, love mercy, and walk humbly with our God."

A significant part of Dr. Paris's scholarship has focused upon African Americans and Africans. From his analysis of black leaders in church and society and the social teaching of the black churches to his exposition of the moral discourse and spirituality of African American and African peoples, Dr. Paris demonstrates the way in which social ethics must be grounded in particular human experiences and communities as it addresses issues affecting all of society. His scholarship pushes individuals and groups to struggle through the unavoidable trials and tribulations of human association on the basis of a moral vision of hope. This moral vision of hope invites us to be mutually vulnerable (acknowledging real human differences and disagreements) as we strive to be accountable and covenant with one another to seek our common good. As Cornel West notes,

> Peter Paris is one of the greatest Christian ethicists of our time. His scholarly corpus is magisterial. His teaching career at Vanderbilt and Princeton Theological Seminary is legendary. His church activism is exemplary. And his deep sense of humanity—of love and service to others—pervades his very being. The grand legacy of Peter Paris is deep and wide.

We dedicate this volume to Dr. Peter J. Paris.

Notes

INTRODUCTION

1. This term is borrowed from C. Eric Lincoln, *Race, Religion, and the Continuing American Dilemma* (New York: Hill & Wang, 1984, 1998). In 1944, Gunnar Myrdal, a Swedish social scientist, did research that exposed the way in which there is a deep contradiction between America's democratic ideals and its treatment of African Americans, what he termed the American Dilemma. Lincoln exposes the ways in which the American Dilemma continued in the late twentieth century.

2. The term is borrowed from W. E. B. Du Bois, *The Souls of Black Folk* (1903), in *W. E. B. Du Bois: Writings* (New York: Literary Classics of the United States, 1986). *Souls* was a collection of essays by Du Bois in which he described "the cruelties of racism and celebrates the strength and pride of black Americans."

CHAPTER 1: MAPS OF MEANING

1. See the following article for an interesting critique of African Diaspora formulations that fail to include Africa and Asia: Tiffany Ruby Patterson and Robin D. G. Kelley, "Unfinished Migrations: Reflections on the African Diaspora and the Making of the Modern World," *African Studies Review* 43, no. 1, special issue on the Diaspora (April 2000): 11–45.

2. Peter Paris, *The Spirituality of African Peoples: The Search for a Common Moral Discourse* (Minneapolis: Fortress Press, 1995), 33.

3. Ibid., 131.

4. Members of the organization African Americans for Humanism (a component of the Council for Secular Humanism) and other international humanist organizations argue the counterpoint to Paris's assertion, that non-divinity-based thinking and orientation have a long history in Africa and the African Diaspora. African humanist groups would include: Action for Humanism in Nigeria and the Uganda Humanist Association. Readers may find the following Web sites useful for basic information: http://www.iheu.org/ and http://www.secularhumanism.org/, accessed May 16, 2011. In terms of non-divinity-based thinking in the Diaspora, see, for example, Anthony Pinn, *By These Hands: A Documentary History of Humanism* (New York: New York University Press, 2003).

5. Paris, *Spirituality of African Peoples*, 12.

6. See Toni Morrison, "The Site of Memory," in Russell Ferguson et al., eds., *Out There: Marginalization and Contemporary Cultures* (Cambridge: MIT Press, 1990), 299–305.

7. Paris's reliance on John Mbiti's framing of African religion certainly lends truth to this claim in that Mbiti has been critiqued often for what appears an effort to rationalize African religious sensibilities by arguing for their similarity to Christian structures and understandings. See John Mbiti's *African Religion and Philosophy* (New York: Doubleday, 1970). For critiques of Mbiti's framing of African religion, see Benjamin C. Ray, *African Religions—Symbol, Ritual, and Community* (Englewood Cliffs, N.J.: Prentice Hall, 1976). Additional perspective can be gained through attention to Jacob K. Olupona and Sulayman S. Nyang, eds., *Religious Plurality in Africa: Essays in Honour of John S. Mbiti* (Berlin: De Gruyter, 1995).

8. Paris, *Spirituality of African Peoples*, 20.

9. Paul Gilroy, *The Black Atlantic: Modernity and Double Consciousness* (Cambridge: Harvard University Press, 1993), 15.

10. Ibid., 40.

11. Michelle Wallace, "Modernism, Postmodernism and the Problem of the Visual in Afro-American Culture," in *Out There*, ed. Ferguson et al., 40. Wallace speaks about the manner in which the "Black Aesthetic" becomes a geography of connection between Africa and the Diaspora. Paris, as has been noted, makes use of "African spirituality" to mark this shared geography.

12. Michael A. Gomez, "Introduction," in Michael A. Gomez, ed., *Diasporic Africa: A Reader* (New York: New York University Press, 2006), 4.

13. Gomez's introduction noted in note 12, for example, suggests this type of thinking on religion.

14. This discussion is connected to an earlier effort to think through the nature and meaning of the African Diaspora as religiously significant and formative. See Anthony B. Pinn, "Introduction," in Anthony B. Pinn, ed., *Black Religion and Aesthetics: Religious Thought and Life in African and the African Diaspora* (New York: Palgrave Macmillan, 2009). However, whereas Paris uses "spirituality" as a theoretical framework, I turn to the notion of the "Black Labyrinth" to frame the complex and religious significance of the Diaspora.

15. Paris, *Spirituality of African Peoples*, 22.

16. Ibid.

17. Patterson and Kelley, "Unfinished Migrations," 20.

18. Donald Carter, "Preface," in Khalid Koser, ed., *New African Diaspora* (New York: Routledge, 2003), x.

19. Ibid., xiv–xv.

20. I find sociology of the body particularly helpful in my efforts to think through the nature and meaning of the body and embodiment. In particular I am indebted to texts such as Bryan Turner, *The Body and Society* (Oxford: Basil Blackwell, 1984); Chris Shilling, *The Body and Social Theory*, 2nd ed. (Thousand Oaks, Calif.: Sage, 2003); and Simon J. Williams and Gillian Bendelow, *The Lived Body: Sociological Themes, Embodied Issues* (New York: Routledge, 1998).

21. Paris, *Spirituality of African Peoples*, ix.

22. Ibid., 74.

23. Ibid., 16.

24. Linda B. Arthur, ed., *Religion, Dress, and the Body* (New York: Berg, 1999), 1.

25. Ibid., 6.

26. "Introduction," in Vicente Berdayes, Luigi Esposito, and John W. Murphy, eds., *The Body in Human Inquiry: Interdisciplinary Explorations of Embodiment* (Cresskill, N.J.: Hampton, 2004), 14.

CHAPTER 2: HOMECOMING IN THE HINTERLANDS

1. Reverend Mgbeke George Okore obtained her primary school education in the Church of Scotland Mission School from 1940 to 1946, she earned her domestic science teacher's training at Asaga-Ohafia Girls' School in 1947, and taught for three years in the Central and Ohafia Girls' School. After teaching in several Presbyterian schools from 1955 to 1959, Rev. Okore became the headmistress of Mary Slessor Memorial School, and later the principal of the Hugh Goldie Training Center in Arochukwu. She received her diploma in Christian education from Ewart College in Canada, and her bachelor of arts degree in religious studies from the University of Toronto in 1976.

2. Katie G. Cannon, "The Sign of Hope in Three Centuries of Despair: Women in the Black Church Community," in *Human Rights and the Global Mission of the Church*, Boston Theological Institute Annual Series, vol. 1 (1985): 44–50.

3. The significant history covering various aspects of the Presbyterian Church of Nigeria is recorded in E. A. Ayandele's *Missionary Impact on Modern Nigeria, 1842–1914*; F. K. Ekechi's *Missionary Enterprise and Rivalry in Igboland, 1857–1914*; Ogbu Kalu, ed., *A Century and a Half of Presbyterian Witness in Nigeria, 1846–1996*; Geoffrey Johnston's *Of God and Maxim Guns: Presbyterianism in Nigeria, 1846–1966*; Donald M. McFarlan, *Calabar: The Church of Scotland Mission, 1846–1946*; J. Ade Ajayi's *Africa in the Nineteenth Century until 1880s* and his *Christian Mission in Nigeria, 1841–1891*. Respectfully, I acknowledge my debt to these key texts.

4. C. P. Groves, *The Planting of Christianity in Africa*, vol. 2 (London: Lutterworth, 1954).

5. For a detailed ethnographical discussion of the overarching common cultural connections that unify as well as differentiate these three religious sites, see Rosalind I. J. Hackett, *Religion in Calabar: The Religious Life and History of a Nigerian Town* (New York: De Gruyter, 1989).

6. See "The Society for the Extinction of the Slave Trade and Civilization of Africa," in Sir Thomas Fowell Buxton, *The African Slave Trade and Its Remedy* (1839).

7. A. A. Okon, *The Church of Scotland and the Development of the British Influence in Southern Nigeria* (PhD thesis, University of London, 1973).

8. Hope Masterton Waddell, *Twenty-Nine Years in the West Indies and Central Africa: A Review of Missionary Work and Adventure, 1829–1858*, with a new introduction by G. I. Jones, 2nd ed. (London: Cass, 1970).

9. Katie G. Cannon, "Christian Imperialism and the Transatlantic Slave Trade," *Journal of Feminist Studies in Religion* 24, no. 1 (2008): 127–34. Aspects of this topic are discussed in *The African Slave Trade and Its Remedy*, the biography (1839) of Sir Thomas Fowell Buxton (1786–1845), a British philanthropist and politician who joined William Wilberforce and others in founding the British and Foreign Anti-Slavery Society.

10. Hackett, *Religion in Calabar*, 58 and 83n12. William H. Taylor, *Mission to Educate: A History of the Educational Work of the Scottish Presbyterian Mission in East Nigeria, 1846–1960* (Leiden: Brill, 1997).

11. Hackett, *Religion in Calabar*, 72.

12. Martin Luther King Jr., *Strength to Love* (Philadelphia: Fortress Press, 1981), 28.

13. Efiong U. Aye, *Presbyterianism in Nigeria* (Calabar: Cross River State-Wusen Press, 1987).

14. Due to our different points of departure, my definition of enculturation is very different from the way that many African religious scholars use the term *inculturation*, as celebration of the Africanization of Christianity. Instead, I argue for eradicating inherited traditions embedded in Christian cultures that deny bodily integrity, structurally suffocating the well-being of us all. My African colleagues, such as Laurenti Magesa in *Anatomy of Inculturation: Transforming the Church in Africa*, present the real-life consequences and substantive traditional trade-offs in the long history of evangelism, wherein the Christian faith is brought from one geographical location and inserted in different sociocultural and economic-political situations.

15. Jeanette Hardage, "The Legacy of Mary Slessor," *International Bulletin of Missionary Research* (October 2002): 178–81.

16. John S. Mbiti, *African Religions and Philosophy*, 2nd ed. (Portsmouth, N.H.: Heinemann, 1990), 24.

17. Quoted in Jeanette Hardage, *Mary Slessor—Everybody's Mother: The Era and Impact of a Victorian Missionary* (Eugene, Ore.: Wipf & Stock, 2008), 35. See also D. Amaury Talbot, *Women's Mysteries of a Primitive People: The Ibibios of Southern Nigeria* (London: Cassell, 1915), 23–26.

18. Laurenti Magesa, *African Religion: The Moral Traditions of Abundant Life* (Maryknoll, N.Y.: Orbis, 1997), 146–48.

19. Hardage, "The Legacy of Mary Slessor," 181.

20. Agwu Kalu, *Dr. Ibiam . . . the Challenge of His Life* (Aba: Presbyterian Church of Nigeria, 1988).

21. Presbyterian Church of Nigeria, http://www.recweb.org, accessed June 27, 2011; Toyin Falola, *The History of Nigeria* (Westport, Conn.: Greenwood, 1999).

22. This article received in 2001, "Akanu Ibiam, 1906 to 1995, Presbyterian Church of Nigeria," was researched and written by Rev. Dr. Emele Mba Uka, a Project Luke Fellow, professor of theology in the department of religion and philosophy at the Federal University of Calabar, Nigeria.

23. Ibid.

24. Ibid.

25. Adewale Ademoyega, *Why We Struck: The Story of the First Nigerian Coup* (Nigerian Publishers: Evans Brothers, 1981).

CHAPTER 3: WOMEN IN RASTAFARI

1. Phillip D. Curtin, *Two Jamaicas; The Role of Ideas in a Tropical Colony* (New York: Atheneum, 1970), 33–34.

2. Barry Chevannes, *Rastafari: Roots and Ideology* (New York: Syracuse University Press, 1995), 19. See also http://www.jamaica-guide.info/past.and.present/religion/creole/, accessed June 27, 2011.

3. Curtin, *Two Jamaicas*, 172–73.

4. Chevannes, *Rastafari*, 128.

5. Ibid., 126.

6. Maureen Rowe, "The Woman in Rastafari," *Caribbean Quarterly* (2000): 141.

7. Obiagele Lake, *Rastafari Women: Subordination in the Midst of Liberation Theology* (Durham: Carolina Academic Press, 1998), 95.

8. Velma Grant, "CH661: Theology of the Black Church Research Paper," Candler School of Theology, Pitts Theology Library, Emory University, Atlanta, 16–18.

9. Lake, *Rastafari Women*, 59.

10. Maureen Rowe, "Gender and Family Relations in Rastafari: A Personal Perspective," in *Chanting Down Babylon: The Rastifari Reader*, ed. Nathanial Samuel Murrell, William David Spencer, and Adrian Anthony McFarlane (Philadelphia: Temple University Press, 1998), 73.

CHAPTER 4: RELIGIONS PLURALISM IN AFRICA

1. See http://www.pluralism.org, accessed May 16, 2011.

2. Patrick J. Ryan, *Imale: Yoruba Participation in the Muslim Tradition: A Study of Clerical Piety* (Atlanta: Scholars, 1975), 146.

CHAPTER 5: THE AMERICAN CONSTITUTION

1. I have been on several panels at major national conferences where I have presented on this theme of "Blacks, the Bible, and the Constitution." Several conferences have been at the Interdenominational Theological Center. In the last few years I have struggled with such questions as, What does the Constitution mean to black Americans religiously and ethically? How has this document shaped their religious and moral beliefs? How has the Constitution informed blacks' sense of agency? I was born and reared in the period of American history when even those black people who could not read or write would frequently ask, "What does the Constitution say about black people's freedom?" We heard our teachers and preachers speak of the Constitution and the Bible, and sometimes it seemed like all in the same breath. Progressive black leaders have cited this document in every phase of black people's struggle in America. The language of the Constitution was invoked by conservative and liberal black preachers during the 1950s and '60s. See Joseph H. Jackson, *Unholy Shadows and Freedom's Holy Light* (Nashville: Townsend, 1967); Martin Luther King Jr., *Stride Toward Freedom* (New York: Harper & Row, 1958); and *The Autobiography of Malcolm X*, ed. Alex Haley (New York: Grove, 1965). Strangely, the age of the prosperity gospel in the black church has silenced the black preacher's prophetic voice on the themes of God, justice, the Bible, and the Constitution.

2. See Charles Mills's *The Racial Contract* (Ithaca: Cornell University Press, 1997). Mills's work is most valuable for viewing traditional social-contract theory in light of the phenomenon of race. Racial-contract theory is to some extent a meta-contract, which determines the bounds of personhood and parameters of inclusion and exclusion in all other contracts that come after it. It manifests itself both formally and informally. It is an agreement, originally among European men in the beginning of the modern period, to identify themselves as "white" and therefore fully human, and to identify all others, in particular the natives with whom they were beginning to come into contact, as "other": nonwhite and therefore not fully human. So race is not just a social construct, as others have argued, it is more especially a political construct, created to serve a particular political end, and the political purposes of a specific group. The contract allows some persons to treat other persons, as well as the lands they inhabit, as resources to be exploited. The enslavement of millions of Africans and the appropriation of the Americas from those who inhabited them are examples of racial contract at work in history (such as John Locke's claim that Native Americans did not own the land they lived on because they did not farm it). This contract is not hypothetical, as Thomas Hobbes describes the one argued for in his *Leviathan*. This is an actual contract or series of contracts, made by real men of history. It is found in such documents as papal bulls and Locke's writings on Native Americans, and acted

upon in such historical events as the voyages of discovery made by Europeans and the colonization of Africa, Asia, and the Americas. The racial contract makes possible and justifies some people, in virtue of their alleged superiority, exploiting the peoples, lands, and resources of other races. (This definition is adapted from Celeste Friend, "Social Contract Theory," in the *Internet Encyclopedia of Philosophy*, 4b, http://www .iep.Utm.edu/s/soc-cont.htm, accessed June 27, 2011.)

3. U.S. Constitution article I, section 2, clause 3, the "three-fifths of all Persons" standard for representation and direct taxes. See also U.S. Constitution article I, section 9, clause 1. Leon A. Higginbotham Jr. notes that the framers of the Constitution were subtle in that reference to slavery: "It is indeed ironic that the first time the word 'slavery' appeared in the United States Constitution was when the institution of slavery was abolished by ratification of the Thirteenth Amendment in December 1865. The founding fathers' refusal to use the word 'slavery' in the Constitution of 1787 reveals that they did not want to acknowledge to the world their legitimization of the precept of black inferiority." *Shades of Freedom: Racial Politics and Presumptions of the American Legal Process* (New York: Oxford University Press, 1996), 68.

4. See Benjamin Quarles, *Lincoln and the Negro* (New York: Da Capo, 1990).

5. I have chosen these typologies as heuristic ways of looking at how blacks have responded to the troubling paradox of the Constitution as a source of both oppression and liberation. The reader will note that the purpose of the typologies is to illuminate the nuances of the complexities of the argument regarding blacks and their constitutional rights.

6. "'Certificate of Freedom' Issued by a Brigade Commander in the 13th Army Corps Helena [Ark.] Feby 23' 1863 to Daniel Webster" in *Freedom: A Documentary History of Emancipation 1861–1867: Series I, vol. 1: The Destruction of Slavery*, ed. Ira Berlin, Barbara J. Fields, Thavolia Glymph, Joseph P. Reidy, and Leslie S. Rowland (Cambridge: Cambridge University Press, 1985), 300–301.

7. Frederick Douglass, "I Denounce the So-called Emancipation As a Stupendous Fraud," in *Lift Every Voice: African American Oratory 1787–1900*, ed. Philip S. Foner and Robert James Branham (Tuscaloosa: University of Alabama Press, 1998), 694. Reprinted from the *Washington National Republican*, April 17, 1888.

8. Ibid.

9. See Quarles, *Lincoln and the Negro*; see also *Assuring Freedom to the Free: A Century of Emancipation in the USA*, ed. Arnold M. Rose (Detroit: Wayne State University Press, 1964).

10. For a thorough account of Taney's decision and public responses to it in 1857, see *African American History in the Press 1851–1899: From the Coming of the Civil War to the Rise of Jim Crow as Reported and Illustrated in Selected Newspapers of the Time, vol. 1: 1851–1869*, ed. Marie Ellavich et al. (Detroit: Gale, 1996), 53–68; see also Peter Irons, *A People's History of the Supreme Court* (New York: Penguin, 1999), 155–90.

11. Higginbotham, *Shades of Freedom*, 74.

12. Henry Highland Garnet's sermon "Let the Monster Perish," in Foner and Branham, eds., *Lift Every Voice*, 435. Taken by this source from A Memorial Discourse by Rev. Henry Highland Garnet, Delivered in the Hall of the House of Representatives, Washington, D.C., on Sabbath, February 12, 1865.

13. See King, *Stride Toward Freedom*.

14. Henry Highland Garnet, "Speech by Henry Highland Garnet Delivered Before the National Convention of Colored Citizens, Buffalo, New York, 16 August 1843," in *Black Abolitionist Papers, vol. 3*, ed. C. Peter Ripley, Roy E. Finkenbine, Michael F. Hembree, and Donald Yacovone (Chapel Hill: University of North Carolina Press, 1991), 403.

15. Ibid.

16. See Louis R. Harlan, *Booker T. Washington: The Wizard of Tuskegee, 1901–1915* (New York: Oxford University Press, 1983).

17. W. E. B. Du Bois, *The Education of Black People: Ten Critiques, 1906–1960*, ed. Herbert Aptheker (Amherst: University of Massachusetts Press, 1973).

18. For a marvelous insight into blacks' attitudes as well as those of whites in the Union Army about fighting for their freedom during the Civil War see *Freedom: A Documentary History of Emancipation 1861–1867, Selected from the Holdings of the National Archives of the United States, Series II: The Black Military Experience*, ed. Ira Berlin, Joseph P. Reidy, and Leslie Rowland (Cambridge: Cambridge University Press, 1982).

19. Francis J. Grimke, *Thoughts and Meditations, vol. 3,* ed. Carter G. Woodson (Washington, D.C.: Associated Publishers, 1942), 145.

20. See Harlan, *Booker T. Washington*.

21. See W. E. B. Du Bois, "A Negro Nation Within a Nation, June 1935," in *The Seventh Son: The Thought and Writings of W. E. B. Du Bois, vol. 2*, ed. with an intro by Julius Lester (New York: Vintage, 1971), 399–416.

CHAPTER 6: THE CHALLENGE OF RACE

1. See Langston Hughes, *The Ways of White Folks* (New York: Knopf, 1933).

2. See *The Negro American: A Documentary History*, ed. Leslie H. Fishel Jr. and Benjamin Quarles (Glenview, Ill.: Scott, Foresman, 1967), 344.

3. See Reinhold Niebuhr, *Moral Man and Immoral Society: A Study in Ethics and Politics* (New York: Charles Scribner's Sons, 1932).

4. W. E. B. Du Bois, *The Souls of Black Folk* (Greenwich, Conn.: Fawcett, 1968 [1903]), 16–17.

5. *Malcolm X Speaks*, ed. George Breitman (New York: Grove, 1966), 8.

6. Elizabeth Sifton, *The Serenity Prayer: Faith and Politics in Times of Peace and War* (New York: Norton, 2003), 109.

7. Cited in Sydney E. Ahlstrom, *A Religious History of the American People* (New Haven: Yale University Press, 1972), 651.

8. Howard Zinn, *SNCC: The New Abolitionists* (Boston: Beacon, 1964).

9. Reinhold Niebuhr, cited in Sifton, *Serenity Prayer*, 213.

10. Cited in Charles Marsh, "The Beloved Community: An American Search," in *Religion, Race, and Justice in a Changing America*, ed. Gary Orfield and Holly J. Lebowitz (New York: Century Foundation Press, 1999), 56.

11. T. Thomas Fortune, cited in Philip Dray, *At the Hands of Persons Unknown: The Lynching of Black America* (New York: Modern Library, 2002), 58.

12. Ida B. Wells-Barnett, cited in ibid., 59–60.

13. See Rosemary Ruether, "Black Theology and Black Church," *Journal of Religious Thought* 26, no. 2, Summer Supplement (1969); and idem, "Is There A Black Theology? The Validity and Limits of a Racial Perspective," in her *Liberation Theology* (New York: Paulist, 1972); Paul Lehmann, "Black Theology and 'Christian' Theology";

Fred Herzog, "Theology at the Crossroads"; and Helmut Gollwitzer, "Why Black Theology," all in the *Union Seminary Quarterly Review* 31, no. 1 (Fall 1975).

14. Unpublished manuscript in my possession. See his book on Catholic theol-
ogy and race, *Hearing Past the Pain: Why White Catholic Theologians Need Black
Theology* (New York: Paulist, 2007); see also *Interpreting White Privilege: Catholic
Theologians Break the Silence*, ed. Laurie M. Cassidy and Alex Mikulich (Maryknoll,
N.Y.: Orbis, 2007).

CHAPTER 7: RACE, RELIGION, AND THE RACE FOR THE WHITE HOUSE

1. See Brian Ross, "Obama's Pastor: God Damn America, U.S. to blame for
9/11," march 13, 2008, http://abcnews.go.com/Politics/DemocraticDebate/story?id
=4664308&page=1, accessed May 18, 2011.

2. See http://www.npr.org/templates/story/story.php?storyId=88478467, accessed
May 18, 2011, for a transcript and audio of the speech.

3. For transcripts of this event, see http://www.huffingtonpost.com/2008/04/28
/jeremiah-wright-at-nation_n_98949.html   and   http://www.chicagotribune.com
/news/politics/chi-wrighttranscript-04282008,0,3113697.story, both accessed June
27, 2011.

4. For a discussion of the black church as "invisible institution" see Albert Raboteau, *Slave Religion: The "Invisible Institution" in the Antebellum South* (New York:
Oxford University Press, 1980).

5. See "Black Theology: Statement by the National Committee of Negro Churchmen, June 13, 1969," in *Black Theology: A Documentary History, 1966–1979*, ed.
Gayraud S. Wilmore and James H. Cone (Maryknoll, N.Y.: Orbis, 1979), 100–102,
for an early articulation of the meaning of black theology.

6. "Black Power: Statement by the National Committee of Negro Churchmen,
July 31, 1966," in ibid., 23–29.

7. You can read and listen to Stokely Carmichael's speech on Black Power at
http://www.americanrhetoric.com/speeches/stokelycarmichaelblackpower.html,
accessed May 18, 2011.

8. See The Malcolm X Project at Columbia University, http://www.columbia
.edu/cu/ccbh/mxp/, accessed May 18, 2011.

9. In 1787 in Philadelphia Richard Allen and others were members of the segregated section of St. George's Methodist Episcopal Church in Philadelphia. One
Sunday in church, Richard Allen was trying to make his way to the segregated section. But someone up front began to pray. In most churches, when someone begins to
pray, everyone, out of respect for the prayer, stops where he or she is. Allen stopped
when he heard the prayer begin. But he was physically interrupted in his prayer
when some men forcefully removed him. Unfortunately, Allen had stopped to pray
while being in the segregated white section. Out of this incident, Richard Allen went
on to found the African Methodist Episcopal Church (A.M.E.). Like their southern
brothers and sisters, these northerners built their own independent black church in
response to political, state-sponsored segregation.

10. Trinity United Church of Christ, http://www.tucc.org/, accessed May 18,
2011.

11. Ibid.

12. W. E. B. DuBois, "The Talented Tenth," September 1903, http://teaching
Americanhistory.org//library/index.asp?document=174, accessed May 18, 2011.

13. Barack Obama, *Dreams from My Father: A Story of Race and Inheritance* (New York: Random House, 1995); idem, *The Audacity of Hope: Thoughts on Reclaiming the American Dream* (New York: Vintage, 2006).

14. This refers to a forty-year study in which black men were infected with syphilis and never properly treated. See http://www.cdc.gov/tuskegee/timeline.htm, accessed May 18, 2011.

PART 2, FOR REFLECTION AND STUDY

1. See http://www.npr.org/templates/story/story.php?storyId=88478467 for a full transcript and audio recording of the speech, accessed May 23, 2011.

2. See Adrienne Christine Miles, "Is America Really Post-Racial? A Definition and Reassessment of Post-Racialism in the U.S.," March 14, 2008, for an article that surveys various definitions of postracialism in the United States, http://racism-politics .suite101.com/article.cfm/postracialism_in_america, accessed May 23, 2011.

3. See Ivan Kenneally, "Post-Racial Immigration Quandary," *Washington Times,* May 14, 2010, http://www.washingtontimes.com/news/2010/may/14/post-racial -immigration-quandary/, accessed May 23, 2011.

CHAPTER 8: "WHO IS THEIR GOD?"

1. Martin Luther King Jr., "Who is Their God?" *The Nation* 195, no. 11 (October 13, 1962): 210.

2. King himself struggled with definitions of the church, and he used the term "true *ekklesia*" to distinguish the body of Christ at its best from the traditional, institutional church. See Martin Luther King Jr., *Why We Can't Wait* (New York: New American Library, 1964), 92.

3. Martin Luther King Jr., "A Challenge to the Churches and Synagogues," in Mathew Ahmann, ed., *Race: Challenge to Religion* (Chicago: Regnery, 1963), 157; and Martin Luther King Jr., *Where Do We Go from Here: Chaos or Community?* (Boston: Beacon, 1968), 96.

4. Peter Paris's treatment of King as a representative of "the prophetic strand of the black Christian tradition" figured prominently in the conceptualization and organization of the content of this essay. See Peter J. Paris, "The Bible and the Black Churches," in Ernest R. Sandeen, ed., *The Bible and Social Reform* (Philadelphia: Fortress Press, 1982), 141–44. This essay also draws from Lewis V. Baldwin, "Revisioning the Church: Martin Luther King Jr. as a Model for Reflection," *Theology Today* 65, no. 1 (April 2008): 26–40; and Lewis V. Baldwin, *The Voice of Conscience: The Church in the Mind of Martin Luther King, Jr.* (New York: Oxford University Press, 2010).

5. C. Eric Lincoln, "The Black Church and a Decade of Change," Part II, *Tuesday at Home* (March 1976): 7; Jim Douglass, "The Crucifixion of Martin Luther King," *The Other Side* (September-October 1996): 42; and Lewis V. Baldwin et al., *The Legacy of Martin Luther King, Jr.: The Boundaries of Law, Politics, and Religion* (Notre Dame, Ind.: University of Notre Dame Press, 2002), 104–9.

6. Baldwin et al., *Legacy of Martin Luther King, Jr.,*104–6; and Stephen E. Berk, *A Time to Heal: John Perkins, Community Development, and Racial Reconciliation* (Grand Rapids: Baker, 1997), 150 and 195.

7. Perry D. Young, *God's Bullies: Native Reflections on Preachers and Politics* (New York: Holt, Rinehart and Winston, 1982), 310–12; and Flo Conway and Jim

Siegelman, *Holy Terror: The Fundamentalist War on America's Freedoms in Religion, Politics and Our Private Lives* (New York: Dell, 1984), 86.

8. Quoted in John J. Ansbro, *Martin Luther King, Jr.: Nonviolent Strategies and Tactics for Social Change* (Lanham, Md.: Madison, 2000), 315n115; and Richard J. Neuhaus and Michael Cromartie, *Piety & Politics: Evangelicals and Fundamentalists Confront the World* (Washington, D.C.: Ethics and Public Policy Center, 1987), 12, 89, and 310.

9. James D. Hunter, *Culture Wars: The Struggle to Define America* (New York: Basic Books, 1991), 17; and Neuhaus and Cromartie, eds., *Piety & Politics*, 89.

10. Daniel C. Maguire, *The New Subversives: Anti-Americanism of the Religious Right* (New York: Continuum, 1982), 40.

11. Ibid.

12. Ibid., 39–42; and Baldwin et al., *Legacy of Martin Luther King, Jr.*, 104–6.

13. Neela Banerjee, "More Black Clergy Embracing GOP Ideals, Creating Division," *The Tennessean*, March 6, 2005, 17A.

14. Baldwin, "Revisioning the Church," 33–35.

15. Anthony B. Pinn, *The Black Church in the Post-Civil Rights Era* (Maryknoll, N.Y.: Orbis, 2002), 135–39; Maynard Eaton, "Bishop T. D. Jakes Discusses Mega-Churches," *The Sacramento Observer*, September 22–28, 2005, C1; Adele M. Banks, "Black Megachurches: Serving the Soul of a Rising Middle Class," *San Antonio Express-News*, August 17, 1996, 1; Jasmyn Connick, "Pimpin' Ain't Easy: The New Face of Today's Black Church," *Jacksonville Free Press*, October 20–26, 2005, 4; and Luisa Kroll, "Megachurches, Megabusinesses," *Forbes*, September 9, 2003, 1.

16. Rick Warren, "Myths of the Modern Mega-Church" (event transcript, The Forum on Religion & Public Life, Key West, Florida, May 23, 2005), 31.

17. John Blake, "Pastors Choose Sides Over Direction of Black Church," *The Atlanta Journal-Constitution*, February 15, 2005, 1A.

18. Eaton, "Bishop T. D. Jakes Discusses Mega-Churches," C1; and Paula L. McGee, "Pastor or CEO? The New Black Church Leaders," *NBV: The National Baptist Voice* 5, no. 3 (Summer 2006): 64–65.

19. "Our Opinion: The Sin of False Profits—Bishop Eddie Long Shouldn't Count Himself Among the Needy That His Charity Was Created to Help," *The Atlanta Journal-Constitution*, August 30, 2005; John Blake, "Long Not Welcome by All at Seminary: Graduation Invite Provokes Protests," *The Atlanta Journal-Constitution*, May 5, 2006; and Darryl Fears, "King Funeral Site Reflects Changes in Black America," *Washington Post*, February 7, 2006, A1. In 2010 Bishop Long was accused by four young men of sexual coercion; a lawsuit was filed by the young men and was settled out of court in 2011; see http://www.ajc.com/news/judge-long-suit-close-921527.html, accessed June 27, 2011.

20. King, *Where Do We Go from Here?* 36; and Martin Luther King Jr., "Dives and Lazarus," unpublished version of sermon, Ebenezer Baptist Church, Atlanta, Georgia (March 10, 1963), The Library and Archives of the Martin Luther King Jr. Center for Nonviolent Social Change, Inc., Atlanta, Georgia, 8. King once said, "If I have any weaknesses, they are not in the area of coveting wealth. My wife knows this well; in fact, she feels that I overdo it." See James M. Washington, ed., *A Testament of Hope: The Essential Writings and Speeches of Martin Luther King, Jr.* (New York: HarperCollins, 1991), 371. Although King conceded that Jesus "never made a universal indictment against all wealth," he nevertheless believed that high moral

leadership, especially in the church, demands a different set of values and priorities from those of pimps and drug dealers, who exploit people for personal profit, and who ride around in fine cars, live in expensive homes, and delight in fine clothes and precious jewelry. See Martin Luther King Jr., "A Speech," unpublished version, St. Thomas AME Church, Birmingham, Alabama (February 15, 1968), King Center Library and Archives, 9; and King, *Where Do We Go from Here?* 36.

21. Martin Luther King Jr., "Transformed Non-Conformist," unpublished version of sermon, Ebenezer Baptist Church, Atlanta, Georgia (January 16, 1966), King Center Library and Archives, 4–5.

22. Martin Luther King Jr., *Strength to Love* (Philadelphia: Fortress Press, 1981 [1963]), 59.

23. Baldwin, "Revisioning the Church," 26–40.

24. King, *Strength to Love*, 30.

25. Clayborne Carson and Peter Holloran, eds., *A Knock at Midnight: Inspiration from the Great Sermons of Reverend Martin Luther King, Jr.* (New York: Warner, 1998), 176–77. King's attitude toward women and gays were quite liberal for his time, despite claims to the contrary. See Martin Luther King Jr., "The Crisis in the Modern Family," sermon in Clayborne Carson et al., eds., *The Papers of Martin Luther King, Jr., Volume 6: Advocate of the Social Gospel, September 1948–March 1963* (Berkeley: University of California Press, 2007), 212; and Devon W. Carbado and Donald Weise, eds., *Time on Two Crosses: The Collected Writings of Bayard Rustin* (San Francisco: Cleis, 2003), 285 and 292–93.

26. Martin Luther King, Jr., *Stride toward Freedom: The Montgomery Story* (New York: Harper & Row, 1958), 25; and Carson and Holloran, eds., *A Knock at Midnight*, 177.

27. The term "coalition" or "alliance of conscience" was used by King in reference to the voting rights campaign in Selma, Alabama, in 1965, during which he brought together Protestants, Catholics, Jews, and persons from virtually every socioeconomic status in a struggle to secure the right to the ballot for black people. See King, *Strength to Love*, 62; and Carson and Holloran, eds., *A Knock at Midnight*, 72–73.

28. King, *Why We Can't Wait*, 77; and Martin Luther King, Jr., *The Trumpet of Conscience* (San Francisco: Harper & Row, 1968), 69–70.

29. For this idea, I am indebted to Victor Anderson, "Farewell to Innocence: Can the Black Church Be a Moral Light in Its Contestations with Difference?" unpublished paper (2000), author's files, 1–2; and idem, "Project Dialogue: Response to James Davison Hunter's Musings on Multiculturalism and Speaking American," unpublished paper (1993), 1–3. Also see Baldwin, "Revisioning the Church," 36–37.

30. Jeff O. Carr, "Should We Kill the Preachers? How Negro Ministers Destroy the Legacy of Dr. King and Make a Mockery of Jesus the Christ," *The Third Eye* (January 2001): 9–14; "The Souls of Black Folk," *Savoy* (April–May, 2005): 72–73; and Eaton, "Bishop T. D. Jakes Discusses Mega-Churches," C1.

31. Martin Luther King Jr., "A Cry of Hate or a Cry for Help?" unpublished version of statement (August 1965), King Center Library and Archives, 4; and idem, "Revolution and Redemption," unpublished version of closing address, European Baptist Assembly, Amsterdam, Holland (August 16 ,1964), King Center Library and Archives, 9.

32. Lewis V. Baldwin, "The Perversion of Public Religion," *Orbis* 5, no. 7 (April 2006): 12; and John D. Elder, "Martin Luther King and American Civil Religion," *Harvard Divinity Bulletin*, New Series, 1, no. 3 (Spring, 1968): 1718.

33. Baldwin, "Revisioning the Church," 26–27.

34. King also turned his critique inward to keep himself true to his calling and purpose, for he knew that he stood under the judgment of the gospel he preached. By consistently embarking upon a painful self-critique and examination, he was much like the ancient Hebrew prophets. See Lewis V. Baldwin, *There Is a Balm in Gilead: The Cultural Roots of Martin Luther King Jr.* (Minneapolis: Fortress Press, 1991), 328–29; and Baldwin, "Revisioning the Church," 39.

35. King was a loving critic of the church, as evidenced by his reflections in his "Letter from the Birmingham City Jail" (1963). See King, *Why We Can't Wait*, 89–91.

36. Henry Bettenson and Chris Maunder, eds., *Documents of the Christian Church*, 3rd ed. (New York: Oxford University Press, 1999), 375.

37. Baldwin, "Revisioning the Church," 34–39.

38. This and other questions have arisen out of my reading of Donald E. Messer, *Calling the Church & Seminary into the Twenty-first Century* (Nashville: Abingdon, 1995), 15–125.

39. Lewis V. Baldwin, "To Be Maladjusted: A Critique of the Church Based on the Kingian Model of Prophetic Witness and Activism" (the 2009 Paul S. Stauffer Lectures in Ethics and Social Policy, Lexington Theological Seminary, Lexington, Kentucky, April 17, 2009), 43–44.

40. Martin Luther King Jr., "An Address," unpublished version, the 61st General Convention of the Episcopal Society for Cultural and Racial Unity, St. Louis, Missouri (October 12, 1964), King Center Library and Archives, 4; and idem, "Pharisee and Publican," unpublished version of sermon, Atlanta, Georgia (October 9, 1966), King Center Library and Archives, 2–3.

41. Carson and Holloran, eds., *A Knock at Midnight*, 72–73; and King, *Strength to Love*, 62.

42. King, *Strength to Love*, 25–35.

43. Ibid., 21–22; and King, *Why We Can't Wait*, 89–93.

44. Baldwin, "Revisioning the Church," 39–40.

45. Ibid., 40.

CHAPTER 9: ONWARD, CHRISTIAN SOLDIERS!

1. Michelle Goldberg, *Kingdom Coming: The Rise of Christian Nationalism* (New York: Norton, 2006), 6–7.

2. Mark Juergensmeyer, *Terror in the Mind of God : The Global Rise of Religious Violence*, Comparative Studies in Religion and Society 13, 3rd ed. (Berkeley: University of California Press, 2003), 28.

3. Randall H. Balmer, *Thy Kingdom Come: How the Religious Right Distorts the Faith and Threatens America* (New York: Basic, 2007), 64; Sara Diamond, *Spiritual Warfare: The Politics of the Christian Right* (Boston: South End, 1989), 138; Chris Hedges, *American Fascists: The Christian Right and the War on America* (New York: Free Press, 2006), 10.

4. Julie Ingersoll, "Mobilizing Evangelicals: Christian Reconstructionism and the Roots of the Religious Right," in *Evangelicals and Democracy in America*, ed. Steven Brint and Jean Reith Schroedel (New York: Russell Sage Foundation, 2009), 2:187.

5. Robert H. Krapohl and Charles H. Lippy, *The Evangelicals: A Historical, Thematic, and Biographical Guide* (Westport, Conn.: Greenwood, 1999), 83–85.

6. Balmer, *Thy Kingdom Come*, 65.

7. Susan Friend Harding, *The Book of Jerry Falwell: Fundamentalist Language and Politics* (Princeton: Princeton University Press, 2000). See chap. 5, "Cultural Exodus."

8. Ibid., 156.

9. See appendix A in Perry Deane Young, *God's Bullies: Native Reflections on Preachers and Politics* (New York: Holt, Rinehart and Winston, 1982).

10. Jerry Falwell, *Listen, America!* (New York: Doubleday, 1980), 6.

11. Falwell delivered this sermon at Thomas Road Baptist Church on Sunday night, March 21, 1965. It is printed in its entirety as appendix B in Young, *God's Bullies*, 311.

12. Harding, *The Book of Jerry Falwell*, 27.

13. For a sharp analysis of Jerry Falwell's theological and social ties to southern neo-Confederate political sensibilities, see Daniel K. Williams, "Jerry Falwell's Sunbelt Politics: The Regional Origins of the Moral Majority," *Journal of Policy History* 22, no. 2 (2010): 125–47.

14. This sermon is transcribed in Harding, *The Book of Jerry Falwell*, 157–61.

15. Falwell, *Listen, America!*, 151.

16. Ibid., 124.

17. Ibid., 185.

18. "Gay Tinky Winky Bad for Children," BBC News Entertainment, February 15, 1999, http://news.bbc.co.uk/2/hi/entertainment/276677.stm, accessed May 12, 2011.

19. "Falwell Apologizes to Gays, Feminists, Lesbians," CNN.com, September 14, 2001, http://archives.cnn.com/2001/US/09/14/Falwell.apology/index.html, accessed May 12, 2011.

20. Linda Kintz, *Between Jesus and the Market* (Durham: Duke University Press, 1997), 6.

21. Eddie L. Long, *Taking Over: Seizing Your City for God in the New Millennium* (Lake Mary, Fla.: Charisma House, 1999), 153.

22. Ibid., 57.

23. Ibid., 127.

24. Ibid., 19.

25. Bishop Eddie L. Long, *Stop the Silence March*, VHS video produced by B.E.L.L. Ministries, Atlanta, November 2004.

26. Bishop Eddie L. Long, *First the Natural Then the Spiritual*, VHS video produced by B.E.L.L. Ministries, Atlanta, March 2003.

27. On May 31, 2011, Bernice King announced that she is leaving New Birth Missionary Baptist Church to start her own ministry; see http://www.ajc.com/news/dekalb/bernice-king-confirms-shes-963106.html, accessed June 27, 2011.

28. Jonathan L. Walton, *Watch This! The Ethics and Aesthetics of Black Televangelism*, Religion, Race, and Ethnicity (New York: New York University Press, 2009), 188–89.

29. Adele Oltman, *Sacred Mission, Worldly Ambition: Black Christian Nationalism in the Age of Jim Crow* (Athens: University of Georgia Press, 2008), 17.

30. See chap. 3, "Standing on the Promises" in Walton, *Watch This!*.

31. Julius Bailey, *Around the Family Altar: Domesticity in the African Methodist Episcopal Church, 1865–1900*, The History of African-American Religions (Gainesville: University Press of Florida, 2005).

32. Evelyn Brooks Higginbotham, *Righteous Discontent: The Women's Movement in the Black Baptist Church, 1880–1920* (Cambridge: Harvard University Press, 1993), 187.

33. Scott Kurashige, *The Shifting Grounds of Race: Black and Japanese Americans in the Making of Multiethnic Los Angeles*, Politics and Society in Twentieth-Century America (Princeton: Princeton University Press, 2008), 133.

34. Ibid.

35. "Martin Luther King Jr. Annual Holiday Celebration," dir. Bishop Eddie L. Long, perf. Bishop Eddie L. Long, WAGA-Fox 5, 2002; http://www.myfoxatlanta.com, accessed June 27, 2011.

36. Albert J. Raboteau, *A Fire in the Bones: Reflections on African-American Religious History* (Boston: Beacon, 1995), 56.

37. Higginbotham, *Righteous Discontent*, 8.

38. Kurashige, *Shifting Grounds of Race*, 139.

39. Long, *Stop the Silence March*. In 2010 Bishop Long was accused by four young men of sexual coercion; a lawsuit was filed by the young men and was settled out of court in 2011; see http://www.ajc.com/news/judge-long-suit-close-921527.html, accessed June 27, 2011.

40. Robert Draper, "And He Shall Be Judged," *GQ* (May 2009), http://www.gq.com/news-politics/newsmakers/200905/donald-rumsfeld-administration-peers-detractors, accessed May 20, 2011.

41. Jesse McKinley and Laurie Goodstein, "Bans in 3 States on Gay Marriage," *New York Times*, November 6, 2008, http://www.nytimes.com/2008/11/06/us/politics/06marriage.html, accessed May 20, 2011.

42. Amanda Marcotte, "Is Sharron Angle a Christian Reconstructionist?," *Slate* August 18, 2010, http://www.slate.com/id/2264348/; Anjeanette Damon, "Sharron Angle's View Rooted in Biblical Law," *Las Vegas Sun*, August 6, 2010, http://www.lasvegassun.com/news/2010/aug/06/angles-view-rooted-biblical-law/; Sarah Posner, "Rand Paul: We Wouldn't Need Laws If Everyone Were Christian," *Religion Dispatches*, May 21, 2010, http://www.religiondispatches.org/dispatches/sarahposner/2654/rand_paul%3A_we_wouldn%E2%80%99t_need_laws_if_everyone_were_christian/, all accessed June 1, 2011.

CHAPTER 10: OVERCOMING CHRISTIANIZATION

1. Barbara Dianne Savage, *Your Spirits Walk Beside Us: The Politics of Black Religion* (Cambridge: Harvard University Press, 2008), 2, emphasis added.

2. Peter J. Paris, *The Social Teaching of the Black Churches* (Philadelphia: Fortress Press, 1985), 90–91.

3. Savage, *Your Spirits Walk Beside Us*, 279.

4. Ibid., 2, 203.

5. Paris, *Social Teaching of the Black Churches*, 10, 11.

6. Ibid. Womanist theologian Delores Williams makes a similar assertion in her identification of "the black church universal" as an entity that is separate and distinct from "black denominational churches." Williams identifies the former as the tradition of inclusion and affirmation, and the latter as sometimes being a space that

practices exclusion and suppression. See Delores S. Williams, *Sisters in the Wilderness: The Challenge of Womanist God-Talk* (Maryknoll, N.Y.: Orbis, 1993), 60.

7. Paris, *Social Teaching of the Black Churches*, 74.

8. Ibid., 92, 93.

9. Yolanda L. Watson and Sheila T. Gregory, *Daring to Educate: The Legacy of the Early Spelman College Presidents* (Sterling, Va.: Stylus, 2005).

10. Latta R. Thomas, *Biblical Faith and the Black American* (Valley Forge: Judson, 1976), 118.

11. Jacquelyn Hall, interview with Septima P. Clark, July 25, 1976, Southern Oral History Program, University of North Carolina at Chapel Hill, 9.

12. Ibid., 6, 8.

13. In 1956, because of her membership in the NAACP, Clark lost her more-than-thirty-year employment as a public school teacher. See ibid., 69. Also see Septima P. Clark, *Echo in my Soul* (New York: Dutton, 1962), 3, 111–18.

14. Septima Poinsette Clark, "Citizenship and the Gospel," *Journal of Black Studies* 10, no. 4 (June 1980), 465–66.

15. Clark wrote of her parents' teachings (1) about "being truthful, strengthening people's weaknesses, and seeing that there is something noble and fine in everybody"; (2) to avoid "sinful relationships"; and (3) to "share your service." See Clark's two autobiographies *Ready from Within: A First Person Narrative* (Trenton: Africa World, 1990), esp. 97–98; and *Echo in My Soul* (New York: Dutton, 1962), esp. 28–29.

16. For Clark's church and club participation see Rosetta Ross, *Witnessing and Testifying: Black Women, Religion, and Civil Rights* (Minneapolis: Fortress Press, 2003), 58–67. Titles of speeches, papers, and articles Clark wrote exemplify her use of and interpretation through Christian vocabulary. See, for example, "The Bible and the Ballot," Box I, Number 21, n.d.; "The Christian as Patriot," Box I, Number 25, n.d.; "What Religion Does," Box I, Number 76, n.d.; and "Why I Believe There Is a God," Box I, Number 77, n.d., all in the Septima Clark Papers, Special Collections, the College of Charleston Libraries, Charleston, South Carolina. Also see, Clark, "Citizenship and the Gospel."

17. Niccolo Machiavelli, "In What Way Princes Must Keep Faith," chap. 18 in *The Prince*, trans. Luigi Ricci (New York: Penguin NAL, 1952), 92–94.

18. Acacia Salati, "A Place at the Table," United Methodist News Service Commentary, February 18, 2009, http://www.umc.org/site/apps/nlnet/content3.aspx?c=lwL4KnN1LtH&b=1723955&ct=6770931, accessed May 12, 2011.

19. Diane Nash, "Inside the Sit-ins and Freedom Rides: Testimony of a Southern Student," in *The New Negro*, ed. Mathey H. Ahmann (Notre Dame, Ind.: Fides, 1961), see esp. 47–49.

20. This name derives from a distinction made between persons in the biblical story who left Egypt and wandered in the wilderness under the leadership of Moses and those who entered the promised land under the leadership of Joshua.

21. Greenberg Quinlan Rosner, "Young Evangelical Christians and the 2008 Election," *Religion and Ethics NewsWeekly*, September 29, 2008, http://www.greenbergresearch.com/index.php?ID=2251, accessed May 12, 2011.

22. "Brown v Monkey," *The Greene Room: Politics and Pop Culture Blog*, February 22, 2009, http://www.huffingtonpost.com/jehmu-greene/brown-v-monkey_b_169312.htm, accessed May 12, 2011.

23. Yolo Akili, presentation, overview of the Work of Men Stopping Violence, March 20, 2009, Atlanta.

24. See Trinity United Church of Christ's Web site, http://www.tucc.org, accessed May 12, 2011.

25. Barack Obama, *Dreams from My Father: A Story of Race and Inheritance* (New York: Random House, 1995), 429.

26. Savage, *Your Spirits Walk Beside Us*, 274, 279.

CHAPTER 11: A MORAL EPISTEMOLOGY OF GENDER VIOLENCE

1. Study of the secretary-general, *Ending Violence Against Women: From Words to Action* (New York: United Nations, 2006).

2. Kathleen O'Brien, "With Obama in the White House, Some Wonder if Black History Month Is Still Necessary," *The Star-Ledger*, February 6, 2009, 23.

3. See Dorothy Roberts, *Killing the Black Body: Race, Reproduction, and the Meaning of Liberty* (New York: Pantheon, 1997).

4. Peter J. Paris, *The Spirituality of African Peoples: The Search for Common Moral Discourse* (Minneapolis: Fortress Press, 1995).

5. Ibid., 161.

6. Sean Gardner, "NYPD Inaction Over a Missing Black Woman Found Dead Sparks a Historic Racial Bias Lawsuit," *Village Voice*, May 6, 2008, 6, http://www.village voice.com/content/printVersion/433849, accessed May 19, 2011.

7. Gardner, "NYPD Inaction"; Michael Brick, "Two Defendants, Two Juries and Horrors Spoken Twice," *New York Times*, February 18, 2006, B3, http://www.ny times.com/2006/02/18/nyregion/18murder.html, accessed May 19, 2011.

8. Gardner, "NYPD Inaction."

9. Ibid.; also see Michael Brick, "Witness Comes Back to Describe a Beating," *New York Times*, March 3, 2006, B4, http://www.nytimes.com/2006/03/03 /nyregion/03murder.html, accessed May 19, 2011.

10. Gardner, "NYPD Inaction."

11. Ibid.

12. Ibid.

13. Ibid.

14. Shaila K. Dewan, "Police Defend Differences in Searches for 2 Women," *New York Times*, May 14, 2003, B4, http://www.nytimes.com/2003/05/14/nyregion /police-defend-differences-in-searches-for-2-women.html, accessed May 19, 2011.

15. Gardner, "NYPD Inaction"; also see Tina Kelley, "New Yorker Is Missing after Walking Father's Dog," *New York Times*, March 5, 2003, B3, http://www.nytimes .com/2003/03/05/nyregion/new-yorker-is-missing-after-walking-father-s-dog.html, accessed May 19, 2011.

16. Gardner, "NYPD Inaction."

17. Dewan, "Police Defend Differences."

18. Gardner, "NYPD Inaction."

19. Ibid.

20. In 2008 the family won the right to sue police for racial bias in their handling of their daughter's case. Their lawsuit alleges that the NYPD has a "practice of not making a prompt investigation of missing-persons claims of African Americans, while making a prompt investigation for white individuals," Gardner, "NYPD Inaction." Also see Nancie L. Katz, "Mother of Slain Girl Wins OK to Sue Police for Bias

in Lack of Investigation," *Daily News*, April 3, 2008, 16, http://articles.nydailynews
.com/2008-04-03/local/17896013_1_abner-louima-case-honors-student-quick
-police-response; Michael Brick, "Awaiting Verdict, Victim's Family Feels '03 Killing Is Eclipsed Again," March 23, 2006, B1, http://www.nytimes.com/2006/03/23
/nyregion/23murder.html, both accessed May 19, 2011.

21. Dána-Ain Davis, *Battered Black Women and Welfare Reform: Between a Rock
and a Hard Place* (Albany: State University of New York Press, 2006), 67. In 1996
the Personal Responsibility and Work Opportunity Act was passed with bipartisan
support by a Republican Congress, led by Newt Gingrich and a Democrat president,
Bill Clinton, completely overhauling welfare.

22. See my more extensive discussion of punitive aspects of welfare reform in
Disruptive Christian Ethics: When Racism and Women's Lives Matter (Louisville:
Westminster John Knox, 2006).

23. Ibid.

24. Davis, *Battered Black Women and Welfare Reform*, 74.

25. Ibid.

26. Ibid.

27. Ibid., 50.

28. Davis offers critical analysis of implementation of the Family Violence
Option (FVO) that was added to New York state policy enforcing the 1996 Personal
Responsibility and Work Opportunity Reconciliation Act; ibid., 18, 83–85.

29. Ibid., 84.

30. Ibid., 85.

31. Venita Kelley, "'What Is It About the Walls?' A Summary Report of Afri-
can American Women's Experiences of Domestic Violence in Lincoln, Nebraska," in
María Ochoa and Barbara K. Ige, ed., *Shout Out: Women of Color Respond to Violence
Against Women*, (Emeryville, Calif.: Seal, 2007).

32. Ibid., 11.

33. Ibid.

34. Hillary Potter, *Battle Cries: Black Women and Intimate Partner Abuse* (New
York: New York University Press, 2008).

35. Ibid., 160.

36. Ibid., 161.

37. Ibid.

38. Kelley, "'What Is It About the Walls?" 20.

39. Paris, *Spirituality of African Peoples*, 161.

CHAPTER 12: AN ECOWOMANIST VISION

1. Peter J. Paris, *The Spirituality of African Peoples: The Search for a Common Moral
Discourse* (Minneapolis: Fortress Press, 1995).

2. Alice Walker, "Womanist," in *In Search of Our Mothers' Gardens: Womanist
Prose* (New York: Harcourt Brace Jovanovich, 1983).

3. Paris, *Spirituality of African Peoples*, 52.

4. Ibid., 51.

5. John S. Mbiti, *Introduction to African Religion* (London: Heinemann, 1992).

6. This list is compiled by Karla Simcikova's analysis of Alice Walker's ecowomanist identity and summarizes Walker's promotion of "coexistence on the planet,
based on the recognition of our connectedness to one another through our common

humanity." In addition to the values cited, Simcikova includes unity in diversity, equality, reciprocity, harmony, and peace in the world as other significant values gleaned from Walker's work. See Karla Simcikova, *To Live Fully, Here and Now: The Healing Vision In The Works of Alice Walker* (New York: Lexington, 2007), 5.

7. See Edward P. Antonio, "Ecology as Experience in African Indigenous Religions," in *Living Stones in the Household of God: The Legacy and Future of Black Theology*, ed. Linda Thomas (Minneapolis: Fortress Press, 2004), 146–57. Teresia Hinga, "Gikuyu Theology of Land and Environmental Justice," in *Women Healing Earth: Third World Women on Feminism, Ecology, and Religion*, ed. Rosemary Radford Ruether (Maryknoll, N.Y.: Orbis, 1996), 172–83; and Terence Ranger, "Women and Environment in African Religion," in *Social History and African Environments*, ed. William Beinhart and Joann McGregor (Athens: Ohio University Press, 2003), 72–86.

8. Peter Paris, *Virtues and Values: The African and African American Experience* (Minneapolis: Fortress Press, 2004), 2.

CHAPTER 13: AN AMERICAN PUBLIC THEOLOGY IN THE ABSENCE OF GIANTS

1. David Buttrick, *A Captive Voice: The Liberation of Preaching* (Louisville: Westminster John Knox, 1994), 113.

2. Ibid., 109–10.

3. John Milbank, *Theology and Social Theory: Beyond Secular Reason* (Oxford: Blackwell, 1993), 380.

4. Cornel West, *Democracy Matters: Winning the Fight Against Imperialism* (New York: Penguin, 2004), 2.

5. José Casanova, *Public Religions in the Modern World* (Chicago: University of Chicago Press, 1994), 4–5.

6. Ronald F. Thiemann, *Constructing a Public Theology: The Church in a Pluralistic Culture* (Louisville: Westminster John Knox, 1991), 173.

7. H. Richard Niebuhr, *The Social Sources of Denominationalism* (Cleveland: World, 1929), 3.

8. Ibid., 5.

9. H. Richard Niebuhr, *Christ and Culture* (New York: Harper & Row, 1951), 191.

10. H. Richard Niebuhr, *Radical Monotheism and Western Culture* (Louisville: Westminster John Knox, 1993 [1943]), 3.

11. Niebuhr, *Social Sources*, 6.

12. Ibid., 25.

13. Ibid., 259.

14. Ibid., 261.

15. Ibid., 263.

16. H. Richard Niebuhr, *Theology, History, and Culture* (New Haven: Yale University Press, 1996), 63.

17. Niebuhr, *Social Sources*, 283.

18. Van A. Harvey, "On the Intellectual Marginality of American Theology," in *Religion and Twentieth-Century American Intellectual Life*, ed. Michael J. Lacey (New York: Cambridge University Press, 2001), 71–85.

19. Ibid., 191.

20. Ibid., 173.

21. Ibid.

22. Michael Eric Dyson, *Race Rules: Navigating the Color Line* (Reading, Mass.: Addison-Wesley), 106.

23. Harvey, "On the Intellectual Marginality of American Theology," 192.

24. Vincent Harding, *Hope and History: Why We Must Share the Story of the Movement* (Maryknoll, N.Y.: Orbis, 1990), 53.

CHAPTER 14: WALKING ON THE RIMBONES OF NOTHINGNESS

1. Zora Neale Hurston, *Jonah's Gourd Vine: A Novel* (Philadelphia: Lippincott, 1934), 87.

2. Zora Neale Hurston, "Conversions and Visions," in *Negro: An Anthology*, ed. Nancy Cunard (London: Wishart & Co., 1934), 32–34.

3. Ibid., 32.

4. Zora Neale Hurston, *Their Eyes Were Watching God* (Philadelphia: Lippincott, 1937), 93. However, it is her use of "the rimbones of nothing" in *Jonah's Gourd Vine* that has echoed with me over the years since I first heard Katie Geneva Cannon's redaction of the phrase in the early 1990s for a conference theme: "Walking Across the Rimbones of Nothing."

5. See Mircea Eliade, *The Sacred and the Profane: The Nature of Religion*, trans. Willard R. Trask (New York: Harcourt Brace, 1961 [1959]) for a fuller discussion of Eliade's concept of the center; and Arnold van Gennep, *Rites of Passage*, trans. Monika B. Vizedom and Gabrielle L. Caffee (Chicago: University of Chicago Press, 1960) for a fuller discussion of van Gennep's use of liminality. Victor W. Turner expanded on van Gennep's early work in *The Ritual Process: Structure and Anti-Structure* (Chicago: Aldine, 1969).

6. Jean-Paul Sartre, *Being and Nothingness: An Essay on Phenomenology*, trans. Hazel E. Barnes (New York: Philosophical Library, 1956).

7. Toni Morrison, *The Dancing Mind* (New York: Knopf, 1996), 7–8.

8. W. E. B. Du Bois, "The Propaganda of History," in *Black Reconstruction in America: An Essay Toward the History of the Part Which Black Folk Played in the Attempt to Reconstruct Democracy in America* (New York: Russell & Russell, 1966), 722.

9. W. E. B. Du Bois, *The Souls of Black Folk: Authoritative Text, Contexts, Criticism*, ed. Henry Louis Gates Jr. and Terri Hume Oliver (New York: Norton, 1999), 5.

10. Peter J. Paris, *The Spirituality of African Peoples: The Search for a Common Moral Discourse* (Minneapolis: Fortress Press, 1994), 144–46.

11. Katie Geneva Cannon, "Remembering What We Never Knew," *Journal of Women and Religion* 16 (1998): 167–77.

12. E-mail exchange with William R. Myers, Director of Leadership Education, The Association of Theological Schools in the United States and Canada, Fall 2006.

13. Du Bois, "The Propaganda of History," 722.

CHAPTER 15: STILL ON THE JOURNEY

1. James Baldwin, *The Price of the Ticket: Collected Non-Fiction, 1948–85* (London: Michael Joseph, 1985), 393.

2. Lecture by Bernice Johnson Reagon, Theology and Arts plenary, Memphis Theological Seminary, Rhodes College, July 2007.

3. Ibid., 135.

4. Barbara A. Holmes, *A Private Woman in Public Spaces: Barbara Jordan's Speeches on Ethics, Public Religion, and Law* (Harrisburg: Trinity Press International, 2000), 47.

5. Innocence Project Web site, January 2, 2009, http://www.innocenceproject.org/understand/Eyewitness-Misidentification.php, accessed May 16, 2011.

6. Mark Vallen, "Pablo Picasso's 'Guernica' Censored at U.N.," February 5, 2003, Art for a Change Web site, http://www.art-for-a-change.com/News/guernica.htm, accessed May 16, 2011. See also *The Sidney Morning Herald*, "Shroud Over Guernica," Laurie Brereton's speech to federal Parliament on February 5, 2003, on war with Iraq, http://www.smh.com.au/articles/2003/02/05/1044318661158.html, accessed May 16, 2011.

7. Vallen, "Pablo Picasso's 'Guernica' Censored at U.N."

8. Sandra M. Levy, *Imagination and the Journey of Faith* (Grand Rapids: Eerdmans, 2008), 115.

9. Peter J. Paris, *The Spirituality of African Peoples: The Search for a Common Moral Discourse* (Minneapolis: Fortress Press, 1995), 146.

10. Cornel West, *Hope on a Tightrope: Words and Wisdom* (New York: Smiley, 2008), 78.

Index

Wright, Richard, 88
Wright, Reverend Jeremiah A.,
    99–101, 113–19, 169
Wuthnow, Robert, 197

Yahweh/God, 106, 114–15
Yoruba, 31, 53–58

Zion, 40, 42, 46, 49